GOING HOME

GOING HOME

THE RUNRIG STORY
TOM MORTON

MAINSTREAM
PUBLISHING

EDINBURGH AND LONDON

In memory of Euphemia Jones Adam MacCalman

First published in Great Britain 1991 by
MAINSTREAM PUBLISHING COMPANY (EDINBURGH) LTD
7 Albany Street
Edinburgh EH1 3UG

ISBN 1 85158 411 0 (cloth)
ISBN 1 85158 412 9 (paper)

A catalogue record for this book is available from the British Library

Designed by WIDE ART, Edinburgh
Phototypeset by Intype, London
Printed in Great Britain by Butler & Tanner Ltd, Frome

CONTENTS

ACKNOWLEDGMENTS

Additional research by Iain D. Macdonald and John Williamson. Tracy, Anne and Maureen transcribed. Susan managed to avoid giving birth during the first stage of this book's confinement, and John Magnus MacCalman kept quiet for the price of a *Thunderbirds* video. *The Scotsman* gave me a holiday, during which Matheson's Bakery in Cromarty supplied fresh rolls every morning (except Wednesdays). The Phoenix Bar, Inverness, and the Royal Hotel, Cromarty, provided relaxation and recuperation, while Academy Computers donated a free plastic floppy-disc holder. James Patrick arrived, eventually.

Thanks to Clive at The Record Shop, Lerwick, Blackfriars Music, and Greentrax, Edinburgh, and Mike in Aberdeen, the discography was finally assembled. The *West Highland Free Press* gave permission (gratefully received) for some appropriation of words during a conversation which followed Kingussie's victory in the Camanachd Cup final. I think. Torcuil Crichton conducted some inquiries. David Ross encouraged. Special appreciation to the medical hypnotist who removed the nicotine stains from my fingers once and for all – and, of course, to Marlene, Chris and Runrig for unstinting and friendly help. Not to mention access to embarrassing photographs. Without Bill Campbell at Mainstream it would never have happened. Without Penny Clarke at Mainstream it would have happened even more incoherently.

This book would not have been possible without the enthusiastic co-operation of all those who agreed to be interviewed by Iain, John and myself. Grateful thanks are offered, in the hope that the views expressed remain fairly represented between these covers.

Runrig have worked with many photographers over the years, and nearly all the pictures in this book are from the band's own copyright archive or from members' personal albums.

Particular credit must go to Dave Harrold, Malcolm Haywood, Sean Hudson, Andy Donald, Angus Smith, Bob Hutcheson, Derek Smith, Blair Urquhart, Douglas Mackinnon, Sam Maynard, Gus Wylie, John Paul, Harry Henriksen, Douglas Hogg and Cailean Maclean. Other pictures stem from the personal archives of myself and Iain D. Macdonald.

Thanks must go to BBC Scotland and Grampian TV. Other sources include the *Daily Record*, *The Scotsman*, the *Stornoway Gazette* and the *Oban Times*, the *West Highland Free Press* and Chrysalis Records. Special thanks to ace *Free Press* cartoonist, Chris Tyler.

If any copyrights have inadvertently been infringed, sincerest apologies. Grovelling apologies to the woman who replied to the *Free Press* advert about memorabilia and whose letter was mislaid. It won't happen again.

TOM MORTON
Cromarty, August 1991

FOREWORD

Hearthammer: Runrig, and the Memory of my Father

My father died 11 years ago, and I loved him very much.
He was a joiner, from South Uist, and some of my most beautiful
memories are of him simply providing for us: planing, sawing and hammering. Wood shavings in the sunshine and the hairs on his forearms. His eyes.
The geography of his face.

The landscape of our being.

Walking between Tarscabhaig and Ord on the Isle of Skye a few months
ago, I heard – on a still Tuesday afternoon – the distant sound of a hammer
on wood. And I remembered him with great power.

I wrote this poem for him that night:

THE SOUND OF A HAMMER

A complete lifetime has almost destroyed me,
but I hear the sound of a hammer
telling me that you loved me so, so much

Daddy

this sound on wood is your beautiful brow
sweating
and the house we stayed in, the hut, alive with children
hammering

this moment is complete silence
except the sound of hammer on wood
except the sound of hammer on wood
this moment is complete silence

and see, how the sweet shavings curled down from the sharp plane,
how the sweet shavings curled down from the sharp plane:

tonight the electric fire makes a soft, warm noise

but then, then there was the sound of a hammer on wood.

I believe that that's the same sound, the same silence, that Runrig are about: the silence of the landscape and the sound of the heart of Uist; the silence of the peat roads, the sound of the stones, the silence of the grass, the sound of our memories, the memories of our fathers, hearthammer, the memory of my father placing his huge, safe hands on our innocent heads. The miracle of innocence on a head of curls.

With the eyes of a child the wonder of it all. The years disappear like a ghost. Somewhere out of the sight of the night and the light of day. Now civilisation groans and the newsreel cries. Like a drowning man, his life in front of his eyes. But the need to keep control. The need to bare the soul at the edge of the world. At the edge of the world. At the edge of the world.

For a Gael, these are particularly powerful words: centuries of shame have left us embarrassed about being ourselves. Our landscape was bare, our fathers uneducated, our language useless. At least, that's what the newsreels, those inside our heads, told us. Looking towards the open skies waiting for the journey. Glasgow. Edinburgh. Inverness. Stirling. Stornoway. Aberdeen. Fort William. Dundee. London. Germany. Ireland. America. The big wheel. The big wheel. And the man from St Kilda went over the cliff on a winter's day. No wonder.

But the need to keep control. The need to bare the soul at the edge of the world.

This 'baring of the soul' has taken many forms: the Clearances and the Evangelical Revival of the 19th century bared many souls. Emigrant ships took us to Canada and beyond. Our fathers, and brothers, and uncles left for Auckland and Singapore and Leith with the Blue Star Line and the Ben Line and the New Zealand Shipping Company. Our mothers became domestic servants, or nurses, then bore seven children. We ourselves listened to Elvis Presley, learned Wordsworth and became students. Our sons and daughters sing *Loch Lomond* to a Gaelic drumbeat, and wonder.

I suppose they wonder: what was it all about? What was it like? What is it like? What will it be like? What did my father look like? What does that Gaelic word mean? Tell me something about Runrig, they ask me, and all I can tell is about myself. About my father. About my childhood. About each blade of grass I know.

Runrig's song *Siol Ghoraidh* tells that same story: it takes a powerful stand against the shame of the local simply by naming it. Here is a bold declaration that we can survive, that you, you are important. For in that song there is that wonderful naming of people in Gaelic by their *sloigh-neadh*: a hammer chant that declares what it is to be Angus, to be Donald, to be Ranald, to be Mary, to be Jean, to be human, to be a Gael.

It's really hard to put the sound of a hammer, the memory of your father and your own great love into words: Runrig turn it into an authentic music with that magnificent rolling sound that tells you that they, too, as children, lay on the top of Eabhal watching the grey-white, grey-white clouds, and wondered.

With the eyes of a child the wonder of it all. I used to search the stars at night and I felt so safe and small. Sweet sounds from a Mersey town and my nursery God. Lying under the covers. There was the first caress. There were the Labour years. There was the man who walked on the moon – something I never really believed. The Di Stefano twists the Charlton goals.

But I'm still here with the eyes of a child – the wonder never grows old.

The great Irish poet Seamus Heaney has a marvellous poem, *The Canton of Expectation*, in which he attempts to express how we all, as Gaels in a new world, feel:

> And next thing, suddenly, this change of mood.
> Books open in the newly-wired kitchens.
> Young heads that might have dozed a life away
> against the flanks of milking cows were busy
> paving and pencilling their first causeways
> across the prescribed texts. The paving stones
> of quadrangles came next and a grammar
> of imperatives, the new age of demands.
> They would banish the conditional for ever,
> this generation born impervious
> to the triumph in our cries of *de profundis*.
> Our faith in winning by enduring most
> they made anathema, intelligences
> brightened and unmannerly as crowbars.

Like myself, the Gaels in Runrig have surely experienced that and, like myself, they surely struggle to find the perfect balance within these conflicts: like the man from St Kilda we try and hold the edge as best we can, sometimes even with a personal *de profundis*. Like me they have opened their books in the newly-wired kitchens. Calum and Rory and Donnie and Malcolm – young heads that might have dozed a life away against the flanks of milking cows – were busy paving and pencilling their first causeways across the prescribed texts. Leaving this area, the paving stones of quadrangles came next and a grammar of imperatives, the new age of demands. What delights the heart, and is evident in the music, is that they have not made anathema the faith in winning by enduring most and have not, at least to my knowledge, become unmannerly as crowbars.

Heaney's poem finishes with a plea for the sound of a hammer that we all yearn for:

> I repeat the word 'stricken' to myself
> and stand bareheaded under the banked clouds
> edged more and more with brassy thunderlight.
> I yearn for hammerblows on clinkered planks,
> the uncompromised report of driven thole-pins,
> to know there is one among us who never swerved
> from all his instincts told him was right action,
> who stood his ground in the indicative,
> whose boat will lift when the cloudburst happens.

Angus Peter Campbell,
writer in residence at
the Gaelic college
Sabhal Mor Ostaig

Hearthammer, lads. Remember the heart hammer.

Runrig's music is something that, along with thousands of others, I'm proud to possess. By becoming international stars they have made the local universal and continue to give dignity to a scorned people and a scorned culture. That's no small thing. As long as they continue to yearn for hammerblows on clinkered planks, as long as they continue to stand their ground, we will continue to listen.

It's a privilege to pay tribute to men who can sing to my young daughter about my late father. All of us need and deserve that kind of song.

ANGUS PETER CAMPBELL
Isle of Skye, July 1991

CHAPTER ONE

THE BIG MUSIC

'Tune Into Fairtime Glasgow', it was called, 'Glasgow's own free festival for the unemployed'. In the summer of 1985 full-blown Thatcherism's glittering hardness held sway, but local authorities still had the resources to provide a little politicised fun. So Glasgow District Council ('Working to Try and Keep You Working') organised Fairtime, 'realising unemployment benefit cannot stretch to holiday entertainment' in an effort to 'instil some holiday spirit into what might otherwise be a gloomy summer'.

Glasgow was at that point awash with new pop and rock talent. Lloyd Cole had already swept back his fringe and captured an undergraduate moment with *Rattlesnakes* and Simple Minds had the glittering prizes within their grasp, but still waiting in the wings were the recently-signed Wet Wet Wet, Hue and Cry and Ricky Ross's Dr Love, soon to be rechristened Deacon Blue. But 'Tune Into Fairtime Glasgow' was not, alas, tuned into such activity. The programme of events included lost rock contenders like David Forbes, Zero Zero and Pure Glass, while Peter Morrison, Alistair MacDonald and Bill McCue were also in evidence.

Fair Monday, 15 July, dawned dull and bedraggled. I was, that morning, a hungover writer for the rock weekly *Melody Maker*, recovering from exposure the previous evening to a double bill comprising pre-acid house versions of the Soup Dragons and Primal Scream. But 'Tune Into Fairtime' beckoned. A free concert had been organised at the Queen's Park bandstand. The line-up was not compelling, but headlining was a group called Runrig.

I had been pestered to write about Runrig not, interestingly, by the band or their management but by two fans, photographer Mhairi Martin and soon-to-be film maker Douglas Mackinnon: 'They sell out everywhere they play . . . they're amazing . . . you must see them.' But memories of a stumblingly dated performance on a 1970s Gaelic TV show prevailed. They had beards, I pointed out, resting my case.

Nevertheless, I made my way through the drizzle to Queen's Park, chatted through Rolling Joe and the Jets to Paul and Willie from the PA company, and pondered the potential of Facade, Castlemilk's answer to Level 42.

Dusk began to fall, and the cold and wet began to tell on a sparse audience. Clyde Action's 'Fair Fun For Kids' packed up and went home. Then, as roadies larger, longer-haired and more beer-bellied than any I'd previously seen before trooped with nonchalant swagger on and off stage carrying rolls of gaffa tape, it began.

From the gathering gloom, strange shapes emerged, hundreds of them, huddling together for warmth beneath umbrellas and plastic bags. They kept coming. High up at the back of the stone amphitheatre surrounding the bandstand, Willie, Paul and I watched in amazement. It was my first sight of a Runrig audience. This, given the setting, was a particularly hardy one, willing to risk the Glasgow Fair rain and cold. But there were families, 30-something ex-hippies, leather-and-flat-top punks, the occasional Afghan coat, and many of the fashion-immune people not normally seen at gigs: rugby shirts were much in evidence, Fair Isle jumpers, Barbour jackets, even beards.

Runrig made their entrance, benefiting from the stage lights made irrelevant to the other bands by the drizzly daylight. It was a revelation. I can remember being first surprised by the power of that skirling guitar onslaught, then astonished by the soaring purity of Donnie's voice, this outlandish thing, transplanted from some Hebridean planet of kilts and choirs and purist Mod traditionalism into an alien electric world. There were beards and moustaches and dreadful dress senses on display, but it didn't matter.

Of course, I didn't have a clue what the Gaelic songs were about. But that didn't matter either, because by that time I was absorbed in the emotion and sound of the event. After all, you don't have to understand German to enjoy the last bit of Beethoven's Ninth, I reflected. A ridiculous comparison perhaps, but we were talking epiphanies here. Even the rain seemed less wet.

Dance Called America remains fresh in my memory; heard dozens of times since in many different locations, Queen's Park that Fair Monday is still its visual backdrop for me. The crowd, packed close into the front of the stage, were by this time quite literally steaming. Used to the self-absorbed solo swaying of ordinary concert-goers, the sight of the Runrig audience dancing in rings, hand in hand, unified, astonished me. Evaporating sweat rose in the air as Donnie introduced the song, and spoke of the savage contempt inherent in naming a dance for the gentry 'America', as the clans gathered in despair and departure, forced from their native land. That slow first verse has been retained by the band from those early performances, building the tension and sadness:

> . . . In the name of capital
> Establishment
> Improvers, it's a name
> The hidden truths, the hidden lies
> That once nailed you to the pain . . .

(© C. & R. Macdonald, Chrysalis Records, 1987)

Two heartbeats from Iain Bayne's drums, and that great rousing chorus swept up over the South Side of Glasgow, the soaking audience transported by its anthemic power.

I reviewed that performance, spouting favourable comparisons with

Springsteen ('Runrig's power and passion reverberate in the same way he relates to his American audience') and Big Country, then a name to be reckoned with. I described the crowd 'linking arms in solidarity which goes far deeper than any jingoistic nationalism', and ended by saying 'the band *is* the crowd, and the result is wholly uplifting'. It was the start of a long journalistic involvement with Runrig, which frequently reached heights of frothy-mouthed hyperbole calculated to provoke winces on re-reading. I met the band, interviewed them several times and concluded they were almost bizarre in their normality. I saw dozens of other major rock acts, but never witnessed that bonding between audience and performer so visible at Queen's Park and at every home Runrig gig I subsequently attended.

Gradually, I began to recognise the importance of Runrig, not just musically – as Big Country's elder, smarter, wiser brothers – and not just lyrically, although their evocation of Gaeldom's great historical struggles over land, culture and identity were enormously powerful. No, Runrig's unity with their audience, their position as a talisman providing a sign of hope, as heroes-but-our-very-own-heroes, made them unique. And, crucially, not just to native Gaelic speakers, but to West of Scotland Lowland chiels like myself. They revealed something about ourselves and our past which we wanted, needed to hear.

I acquired the records, some perennially wonderful, some best remembered rather than listened to frequently. But each gig hammered home the crucial fact about Runrig. Live, they are irresistible. And still improving. Since 1985, as their stature and confidence, particularly Donnie's, has grown with increasing success and financial security, their in-concert power has also developed, both in and outside of Scotland – and sometimes in fairly inauspicious surroundings.

In late 1989, Chrysalis backing them with major record company clout, Runrig were on a European tour, filled with all the enthusiasm of teenagers on a spree. I met them in Madrid, just after a hugely successful and occasionally riotous German leg. There were descriptions of 120 ebullient Queen's Own Highlanders taking over the stage at one club and being ordered back to base by their sergeant, who had commandeered Donnie's microphone. And the famous 'tell-those-pensioners-to-shut-up-there's-a-rock-band-trying-to-sleep' incident also occurred at one hotel on this tour, the first where record company cash had removed the constant tension of balancing accounts every 24 hours.

But Madrid was strange. A photo session with a local photographer most unimpressed by constant questions about the Spanish Civil War saw the band consenting to ridiculous poses atop a statue of Don Quixote and Sancho Panza. A previous photo session in London had involved the purchase, by the photographer, of matching leather jackets for all six band members, who consequently looked extremely threatening. Iain Bayne took off to find a pair of Spanish leather cowboy boots, while for the others, talk about the war and the siege of Madrid by Franco's forces led inevitably to the Cason de Buen Retiro, the less-publicised annex of the giant Prado museum which houses Picasso's masterful condemnation of the effects of

war, *Guernica*. In everyone walked, jackets squeaking, like Marlon
Brando's gang in *The Wild One*. The attendants looked askance, with
Calum almost ejected for taking flash photographs. Fulsome apologies from
a stricken percussionist, though, proved that this was no band of leather-
clad monsters. He was allowed to stay – and keep his camera.

The two trained artists in the band, Rory and Donnie, were understandably interested in the series of Picasso's preparatory sketches on display.
'Picasso's pretty overrated, you know,' said Donnie. 'Most of his early
cubist stuff was ripped off African sculpture.' Former pupils of Donnie
who remember his Art History lessons at Inverness Royal Academy and
Leith Academy may also recall such strong opinions. However, in the main
hall of the Retiro everyone was stunned by the sight of *Guernica* itself,
huge and virtually monochrome. 'It's very impressive,' murmured Donnie.

It was a good day, but the gig itself was, from the band's point of
view, a disaster. In a glitzy-but-tawdry city-centre night club, Runrig found
themselves guest band at the annual televised *Un Año De Rock* award
ceremony, a kind of Spanish *Brits Awards* in miniature. The audience,
mostly other bands and media celebrities, was as hyper-cool as it's possible
to be in central Spain. Dreadful local facsimiles of Blondie and Duran
Duran surfaced; Runrig themselves collected an award for Single of the
Year on behalf of Madonna, who, unsurprisingly, 'couldn't quite make it'.
The gold-plated plastic statuette was inscribed 'For *Like a Player*'. The
misprint caused much hilarity from its substitute recipients.

But the laughing stopped when the band went on stage. A small and

Hanging tough in Madrid

unreliable PA system, poor lights and an audience so wrapped up in its own posing that actually watching the band was a sign of unhipness all contributed to a sense of doom. This was not the traditional Runrig happy hunting ground. They were stripped of all the protection they normally enjoy. There was a small crowd, almost entirely apathetic. There was no 'show' as such, no massive production with lighting script and thunder-flashes. It was just the band, the songs, the voice and the playing.

We'll be back: at the Santiago de Bernabeu Stadium, Madrid

It was stunningly good. Sensing the apathy, Runrig went all out to win over the audience, conquering in some songs a double language barrier. There was a genuine edge in the performance, a ferocity rarely necessary in the community celebration which is a Scottish concert. And the photographs of the event show the anxiety, even the sweat. The percussive swirl of *Cnoc Na Feille* made a few of the Spanish recordbiz bigwigs pause between slurps of Cordoniu and San Miguel, and by the time a panting band finished their short set, there was genuine enthusiasm in the applause. No encore, though.

The pedigree of winning over hostile village-hall hop audiences had stood Runrig in good stead that night. But afterwards, all was not sweetness and light backstage, although the appearance of a bottle of whisky did lighten the atmosphere, even in this nowadays most moderate of bands.

'That's the first time we haven't had an encore in six years,' said Rory, wryly. 'Paris was bad, but we stole one there anyway.' The redoubtable Marlene, manager extraordinaire, sat smoking in a corner, while a procession of Spanish record company executives gathered round at her feet. This was after *Searchlight*; the band were fresh from seeing *The Cutter and the Clan* go gold; they were the biggest indigenous act in Scotland. Yet here they were, shorn of their main strength, that totally committed audience, and still with not just the urge to win over an uninterested audience, but the ammunition to make it happen. Almost.

One man totally besotted after that peculiar performance was Bruno, the Chrysalis representative in Spain. Next day he nursed the band from radio interview to television appearance, and it became clear that the paralytic poseurs of the previous night had, in fact, taken on board the impressiveness of that storming performance. Enthusiasm was the order of the moment.

Bruno proved to be made of sterling stuff as, after the day's work, he arranged a trip to the Estadio Santiago Bernabeu, home of Real Madrid FC and scene that night of a clash with none other than arch-rivals Atletico Madrid. For Runrig, football is, in the Shankly sense, something slightly beyond mere life or death. Their footballing allegiances run deep, particularly Donnie's attachment to Aberdeen and Peter's to Dunfermline. Indeed, the Munro collection of memorabilia includes one of Willie Miller's shirts, 'bloodstained and still unwashed', according to its second owner.

But Bernabeu is a long way from Pittodrie. The huge stadium resounded with cheering, vibrating with innumerable flags. Comfort in stand and terracing being of the essence, fans from both teams mixed freely and without hassle. Beer, coffee and incredibly delicious pastries were for sale.

No mutton pies, no Bovril . . . and no trouble. Then Calum spotted something.

'There's a Union Jack,' he said. 'Over there behind the Atletico goal.'

Bruno nodded his head. 'Yes,' he said. 'That' is the flag of Ultrassur, the Ultra South gang. They are fascist, right-wing Real supporters.'

There was a shocked silence from the Runrig contingent as the idea of the British flag as an international insignia of fascist thuggery was absorbed.

Real went two goals up late in the second half, and in the excitement the band's good humour returned. 'That's the first time we've really had the time to see anything of a city on this tour,' said Peter. 'It's a cliché, but it really is a case of arriving at the hotel, sound-checking, eating, playing the gig, going back to the hotel and leaving next day.'

Leaving the ground, though, Rory was in sparkling form. 'You know, I'll be 40 next birthday, and it doesn't matter. The music scene has changed so much, it's now possible to be a credible musician and not be a teenager.'

Donnie's confidence was undampened by the pouring rain as a taxi was earnestly sought. 'We'll be back to Madrid,' he smiled, wetly. 'Next time we'll be playing at Bernabeu.' I wondered what he was referring to but Peter's reply was instantaneous.

'Who needs music in stadiums,' he said, 'when we have football?'

Football and music. The two pursuits where large crowds of people can become unified in salutation of their heroes, can assume an identity because of them. In pop and rock music, however, the allegiance of the fan to the band usually involves some form of exclusivity: a form of dress, a lifestyle, an age-range, even a class. But Runrig's appeal crosses all such barriers.

Short of the Skye Gathering Hall, the Inverness Ice Centre has to be counted as Runrig's home venue. The four 1990 Christmas shows there brought to an end a year without an LP release but with the band riding a huge tidal wave of success. The *City of Lights* video had by that stage sold 50,000 copies, with more sales piling up towards Christmas, the *Capture the Heart* EP had been a Scottish success and had just broken into the UK top 50 singles chart, and live shows had become no-holds-barred affairs with big production budgets. In Scotland at least, Runrig were top of the heap. The top Scottish touring attraction? At this point Deacon Blue could sell out two nights in a row in the Scottish Exhibition and Conference Centre's main hall – some 16,000 people – and pack them in at places like Dundee's Caird Hall, the Edinburgh Playhouse and the Aberdeen Exhibition Centre. But not every year, and not with the same cost effectiveness as Runrig, a band living off live performances in Scotland since 1982. The 1990 tour saw 30,000 tickets sold and every venue packed out every night. It was Runrig's biggest-ever Scottish outing, and to attend any of the shows was to see a band reaching undreamt of peaks.

From the Monday to the Thursday before Christmas, Invernessians could, had they a mind to, have spotted Malcolm Jones jogging each night from the Station Hotel to the Ice Centre, small knapsack on his back. 'I'm just off to work,' he said on the evening I literally bumped into him during a pre-Christmas inspection of various hostelries. Those shows were special, and the band worked hard to make them so. They brimmed with confidence at the end of a tour, facing a committed, knowledgeable, not to say rabidly enthusiastic, audience.

As at Queen's Park more than five years previously, the crowd was a strange mixture. Entire families, including grandparents. Manchester hooded-sweatshirt hipsters in trainers worth more than the average croft. Heavy-duty biker types. Well-dressed couples on a very special night out (particularly if they'd had to pay black market prices for tickets). The young, the middle-aged, the very young. People of an age to be certain band members' grandchildren.

'RUN-RIG! . . . RUN-RIG!' came the chants. There was none of the self-conscious screaming found at other major rock gigs because the live chemistry between fans and band at a Runrig show is rarely about sex – although indefatigable would-be groupies do exist. Few of the crowd at the average Rangers game are there because they fancy the players. 'HERE WE GO, HERE WE GO, HERE WE GO . . .' No, Runrig are heroes, symbols of a collective success for the Gaels who once saw themselves as disenfranchised, disinherited, their culture bereft of connection with the 20th century and dying stubbornly on its feet. They want to see Runrig win because not only do the band articulate collective emotions, history and experience, but because Runrig's victory is everyone's.

Football clubs too have histories, some more savoury than others, with which fans can identify. But Runrig do not just stand for an ideology, or capitalise on the reverse side of the 'tartan Highlander' myth. Their songs ensure a more complex response. And for the non-Gael, the 'otherness' of Runrig, their language, their island roots . . . these things are of an experience they recognise, a land they've glimpsed from the distance or on holiday, a country which is still their own, a history they know they at least tenuously share. And all this talk about home, about the land, about great historical battles and about national identity . . . all this pricks at the heart and evokes the demand, 'I belong too – let me in.'

Comes the huge anthemic blast of *Alba* and the door is open. It's a party, tribal, with the moments of sadness, regret and comment such an event demands. The lovely *Ravenscraig* laments the passing of Scottish steel manufacture, and will be redundant itself after these shows are over; it will probably never be performed again.

Afterwards, David Ross of the *Glasgow Herald*, an original '70s fan, is impressed, not having seen the band for over a decade. 'Have you ever thought they're like the Corries?' It seems a very odd comparison, but there's a truth there. Like the bejerkined duo, Runrig's appeal is across the board, irrespective of age and touching sensitive areas of Scottish existence. Sentiment is a big part of both bands' perennial appeal.

But the Corries were never this loud, this visual, this exciting, this intelligent, this spirited or spiritual. At those Christmas shows, the huge Runrig canon of influences came together, aided by the best technology available. The result was supremely potent, transcending all the ''70s plod-rock' criticisms. Simply, the band were hot, very contemporary and utterly certain of themselves.

The Thursday concert was for charity, but each gig saw Scotland Against Nuclear Dumping given special permission to distribute leaflets and collect for their campaign. During the day, various band members quietly visited hospitals, hospices and schools on demand, courting no publicity, expecting no adulation – getting it anyway. After that night's show there was a mammoth party for friends, family and helpers, and then the band members disappeared south to their fiercely guarded private lives.

My experience of Runrig has been a lot shorter than many people's. I suffer the inadequacies of being essentially a Lowlander, fairly proud of my mixed heritage stemming from the Borders, Islay, Wales, Ireland and central Lanarkshire. Nevertheless, Runrig have touched me as they have many others. Even at my most cynical, I have gone to a Runrig gig determined to hate it and left uplifted, and that's about as much as you can say for any pop group. If, in fact, that's what they are.

So to business.

Runrig as heroes? Runrig as a toe-tappingly musical football team? Runrig as the renaissance of Gaelic culture? Runrig as red-hot rock band? Runrig as political touchstone? Runrig as religious evangelists? As a good band to go out and get drunk/off with somebody to? As a sentimental nostalgia trip out of sordid city life?

Best, I think, to find out who they are, where it all began, and how, first.

"If you ask me, all this Beatlemania stuff has gone to their heads!"

CHAPTER TWO

THE LONG
SUMMERS

The year was 1966, and the Skyevers were the biggest band west of Kyle.

To say the Skyevers were cool is an understatement of awesome proportions. They were the ace faces of Broadford and Portree, daring to wear drainpipes, winkle-pickers, Homburgs and chiffon scarves, fashion sensibilities gained from scouring the pages of *New Musical Express*, *Fab 208* and other magazines.

'I was really into mod fashion at that time. Tab-shirts and all that,' says Rory Macdonald, for it is, indeed, Runrig's bass player and joint chief of songwriting you can see, high-cheekboned and posing in those fading Skyevers photographs. 'We used to have to send away for the catalogues, like *Modern Man* and *Carnaby*. It was the only way we could get hold of the clothes.'

Being a mod in '60s Skye was not easy in a place where 'the club book' was often the only source of family apparel and the word 'mod' was understood to mean a festival of Gaelic traditional song and poetry. Obtaining such esoteric items as electric guitars was almost impossible, Rory found.

'You had to send away for them too, to Bell's Catalogue. In 1965 I was 16 and we were just going to start the Skyevers. I had just enough to afford a cheap electric guitar which cost 14 guineas at that time. To let you see how naive I was – it came, no amplifier of course. So I walked into the electrical shop in Portree and asked, "Do I need a plug for this?".'

Roderick Macdonald had arrived in the world, or rather Dornoch in Sutherland, in 1949. Four years later, a great deal happened all at once. The family moved to North Uist, from where Rory's father, Donald John, originated. Having joined the police after the war, a job as district welfare officer now tempted him back home. 'I was born almost as soon as their feet touched Uist,' says Malcolm Morrison Macdonald, alias Calum. But despite this family background – Mary Morrison was originally from the island of Scalpay – Rory cannot remember having a word of Gaelic at that stage: 'Not until I went to primary school at Lochmaddy.'

A ten-year period, remembered by both brothers as idyllic, went by on North Uist, then Donald John became a social worker on Skye and the family moved again, this time to Portree. There, connections destined to be crucial to the formation of Runrig were made.

'Donnie Munro was in my class at primary school and from then on right through,' Calum says. 'Rory by this time had his own friends and,

by 1965, his own band.'

'We played for three or four years in various forms, very similar in many ways to early Runrig,' his brother remembers. 'It was a ceilidh-type band, playing covers and Scottish country-dance music. Very like what we started doing with Runrig in terms of sound.'

Music was a major part of the Macdonald way of life, with Mary coming from a tradition of religious songwriting and Donald John an enthusiastic Gaelic singer. When Rory was seven, he was given an accordion by friends of the family.

'My father had fought in the war, and his best friend was killed beside him in a tank battle. Years later we went to that friend's home in Greenock to meet his parents. He had owned an accordion, and his parents gave it to me. The first melody I ever wrote was about him, and I called the tune after him – *Sandy MacIntyre*.'

A year later came the moment that, according to Rory, changed his whole musical outlook. He was staying at his grandparents' house in North Uist. 'On Friday nights Radio Luxembourg was playing all the Scottish requests, and everything had to stop so that we could listen to it. On Saturday nights it was Irish requests, and I was totally into all that – Jimmy Shand, Bridie Gallagher, the Gallowglass Ceilidh Band, Robert Wilson, all of them – and we would go up to the bedroom and have mock concerts. Then, one night, while playing around with the radio dial, I heard Frankie Vaughan singing *Tower of Strength* and I was totally hooked. That was the first pop-type record I ever heard, and that was the beginning of

Calum aged 10 –
complete with Beatles
wig – outside his
granny's house in
Scalpay, 1963

rock'n'roll for me.'

As the '60s arrived, the Mersey beat resounded over the Luxie airwaves to Portree, and as Rory progressed towards mod-dom, Calum was following in his musical footsteps. 'When I was 10, 11, 12, that was the most influential period of music I ever experienced. The Hollies, Dylan, the Searchers . . . but the Beatles were the main thing that mattered to me in life. I was totally obsessed by the whole pop thing at that time, more so, probably, than I ever have been since.'

The Skyevers filled an enormous gap in a Skye starved at that time of popular culture. 'We couldn't get to football matches or concerts,' Calum remembers, 'and there was no TV, so people like Jim Baxter or John Lennon had this air of being totally unobtainable. Films used to come round the village-hall circuit and, whenever an Elvis, Beatles, or James Bond film was showing, we had our own local Beatlemania with everyone crowding to see them.'

The Skyevers were not, perhaps, used to being screamed at. But immaculately dressed for the Friday night dances, they would pile out of their old Bedford van and give audiences a fair impression of current pop styles, both aural and visual. The fact that these denizens of cool, in their hipster jeans and Cuban heels, had to trot out the old accordion for endless sets of Scottish dance music bothered neither the band nor the audience. That was just the way it was.

The Skyevers inevitably 'progressed', but when Rory left Skye for a course in graphic art at Glasgow Art School in 1968 the band began to

A hard day's night,
Portree: Calum, 1963

An afternoon on the beach, Benbecula, 1968: (*left to right*) Rory, Alistair 'Wee Mac' Mackinnon and Bob Maclaine, with security staff Matthew Stewart and Hamish Maclean

falter. The Skyevers re-formed with different line-ups for the next two summers, and occasionally thereafter too. Calum, meantime, had become a musical snob.

'Big brother plays in a band, so you get a feather in your cap,' he laughs now. But big brother's influence continued throughout Calum's teenage years. 'When the progressive scene started, I just got right into that – Led Zeppelin, Captain Beefheart.' His brother intervenes: 'We were both into the same music, really.'

While Rory polished up his graphics skills in Glasgow, Calum, directly influenced by the possibilities for self-expression inherent in 'progressive' rock, began to write. 'Songs,' he says cautiously. 'More like poems,' his brother corrects him. Significantly, all in English, as by this time the Gaelic of the primary school playground had been deliberately abandoned. It was uncool, it was old fashioned, it was the province of ageing traditionalists who hated rock music. It was a case of 'hope I die before I get old (and remember how I used to speak Gaelic)'.

'By my mid- to late-teens I was starting to appreciate the landscape, getting into hill-climbing, but I was turning my back on things Gaelic.' Calum grimaces at the memory. 'Dad sang in Gaelic, so naturally that didn't enhance one's village cred. Gaelic music held no positive or exciting developments for young people at the time, and when it came to a choice between Alasdair Gillies singing *Puppet on a String* in Gaelic or The Beatles and *Sergeant Pepper* it had to be *Sergeant Pepper*.' Rory remembers a scene straight from a Scottish version of *Easy Rider*. 'It was my first year in Glasgow and I went to one of the Gaelic bars, the Park Bar on Argyle Street. I was refused admission because my hair was too long. So that was it – I never went back for years and turned completely away from Gaelic.'

In 1971 Rory arrived home in Portree as usual for the long summer break from college. He found his wee brother, having just left school, in the throes of perpetual songwriting – without an instrument. 'I had no real interest in learning to play an instrument,' says Calum, 'although Rory did

teach me a few guitar chords. I was quite content to bang out the rhythm on the back of a suitcase.'

The Skyevers having basically bitten the peat, Rory was able to provide some backing, and the results were recorded on a small tape-machine. Writing separately, setting the pattern for what was to come later, the two brothers would jam on each other's tunes, suggesting improvements and modifications here and there. It was a crucial summer, the one before Calum arrived in Glasgow to begin studying Physical Education at Jordanhill College. 'As time went on I began to realise that songwriting was becoming more and more important to me.' The summer over, Calum

Left:
Waiting for the Uist ferry at Uig in Skye: (*left to right*) Alan Sutherland, George Stoddart and Rory

Right:
Calum and Donnie in primary six, Portree Primary, 1964. Donnie is wearing glasses in the back row, and Calum is three along from him on the left

Victoria Park, Glasgow, 1971. Calum and Rory were sharing a flat in Balshagray Drive, at the start of their songwriting career

moved into Rory's bedsit in Balshagray Drive in Glasgow's West End, and things began to get serious.

Working on and off with David Williams, a musician Rory had played alongside in an abortive Glasgow band, songs began to emerge of, with hindsight, lasting quality. After Calum's first college term, he and Rory wrote *Going Home* about the experience of the end-of-term train journey north from Glasgow Queen Street to Mallaig. It was later to appear on the *Highland Connection* album, and remains a staple of live sets even today. *Blue Ribbons*, the basis of *Tear Down These Walls* from *Searchlight*, was also written during this period. Not that anyone was very interested. Tapes were sent to various producers and publishers, including local songwriter and manager of Thor Studios, Harry Barrie. He took the trouble to write a three-page critique of the tape submitted to him.

'I'm afraid at this time there's really nothing I can do for you,' he wrote. 'My reasons are, of course, the quality of the songs themselves. If I may be absolutely frank with you, your verses seem to be better than your choruses. It's quite strange really.' In addition, 'your lyrics are too concerned with imagery – why not try writing lyrics which are more down to earth? If you think of *Help Me Make It Through the Night . . .*' Harry did encourage Calum and Rory to 'keep writing': 'It's the only way to do it. Everyone is a potential hit songwriter. All you have to do is do it.'

'We were writing compulsively,' says Calum, 'but there was still the exciting prospect of actually playing live music, and that developed in a completely separate way to the songwriting.' At this stage Rory was playing in cover bands, and Calum was watching and tapping his feet in the wings.

Six songs were recorded for Murdo Ferguson's recording company, Gaelfon, including *Going Home*, with David Williams. The tape has vanished, although Rory thinks the original master still survives. Nothing came of it save experience, but significant influences were gathering thick and fast.

One was Fairport Convention. The band which pioneered the whole concept of folk-rock had an immense effect on the two Macdonalds. Rory in particular was impressed. 'That business of electrified jigs and reels was a real eye-opener. It influenced the whole of the first Runrig album.' But there was more. Calum identifies the exposure to Fairport, who utilised English and Irish folk roots, as preparing the way for his and Rory's rediscovery of their own Gaelic heritage. 'Fairport was when we started taking a real interest in traditional music.' Then came a moment which changed everything.

It's really Calum's story. 'It was one night in 1972, in Glasgow, and we were at a family wedding – my mother's second cousin. Angus Macleod from Scalpay was present – a really powerful singer, and a Mod gold medallist. He sang a couple of songs – I remember in particular *Far An Robh Mi'n Raoir* – and I was knocked out. He made a huge impression, and from then on I started taking a real interest in Gaelic song. I went home and wrote *Air An Traigh*, which is on *Play Gaelic*.'

Rory too found his anti-Gaelic stance wavering. 'Angus is one of the Gaelic singers who really sings from the heart with this tremendously powerful emotion. A lot of Gaelic singers are a bit restrained, a by-product of the National Mods – correctness of diction and singing the written musical notes.'

The Gaelic folk band called Na-h-Oganaich, featuring future *Dotaman* TV star Donnie Macleod and his sister Margaret, was then beginning to achieve popularity, and Calum thought of sending *Air An Traigh* to them. 'I didn't have the courage to let them hear it, though.'

A sense of their own history began to impinge on the Macdonalds' Glasgow existence. Calum: 'I started reading Scottish history, looking back at the things I'd rejected in my adolescence, asking questions like, Who am I? What am I doing here?' Rory admits he was badly informed. 'When we were at school we were never taught anything about our own background during history lessons. And perhaps even more inappropriately, during my Gaelic lessons it was mostly Celtic myths and legends and nothing of the more recent struggles.'

'That night at the wedding was so significant,' says Calum. 'It was being in Glasgow, the strangeness of it. One of my first impressions of Glasgow was being aware of a class system that I was not used to in Skye. In our street in Portree, the teacher, the doctor, the dustman and the tinker all lived side by side. I remember one of my first journeys in Glasgow, travelling from Milngavie and Bearsden through Maryhill to the city centre, and being struck by the extent to which people were segregated and it was all very strange. And the second thing which made an impression on me was that for the first time in my life I was not surrounded by the sea. After hearing Angus, the feeling of wanting to escape from it all, to get back to all those early influences, the Highland connection – that's when it all began to happen.'

Blair Douglas, a year younger than Calum, had left Skye with his family halfway through primary school, and settled in Glasgow. Calum and Rory, despite their initial unwillingness to join any expatriate Gaelic mafia, were delighted to join the Douglas family for Sunday night meals, as neither Macdonald was in any sense a culinary genius, or even good at opening tins. Blair, a talented accordionist, was at Glasgow University studying Scottish History.

'Nothing happened musically until we'd been going round there for a few months,' says Rory. 'In March 1973 Blair's mum Ina was the secretary of the Highland Society's North Uist and Bernera Association and one night she told us she needed a band for a function in a couple of weeks. Well, Blair knew I played the guitar, so we began to rehearse, just Scottish tunes. Calum was in all the practice sessions, and we realised we needed a drummer. So someone said, "What about Calum?"'

Calum, perpetually battering out rhythms on the arms of chairs and suitcases, seemed the obvious choice, had it not been for one small problem. 'I'd never played a drum kit, but I decided to go out and buy one.' Using the musician's friend – hire-purchase – one second-hand Ajax drum kit, yellow, with cymbals, was purchased from Alexander Biggar Ltd. of Sauchiehall Street. It cost £49, plus £11.20 in interest over two years –

OBAN GAELIC CHOIR

DANCE
TO
RUN RIG
in the
CORRAN HALLS
on
FRIDAY 19th OCTOBER
10 p.m. to 1 a.m.

TICKETS (Limited in number) ∴ £1.25

Available from An Comunn Gaidhealach Office, Corran Halls Booking Office, Esplanade Lounge Bar; Esplanade Post Office

with a deposit of £5.00 and 24 payments of £2.30.

'He came home one Saturday afternoon with this drum kit in a taxi,' says Rory. 'This bedsit we were in was part of a bigger house, and there was a TV lounge. Calum asked the landlord if he could rehearse his drums in the basement. He didn't even know how to set them up! I was sitting watching TV with this old man in his 70s and, halfway through a film, we heard this incredibly loud banging from underneath us. It was an unearthly racket, and the old man nearly jumped out of his skin, shouting, "What the hell was THAT?" There was complete uproar. The landlord told Calum to stop after five minutes, and that was the only time he played a kit until the dance.'

A final drumless practice at Blair's house saw a few eightsome reels, a *Gay Gordons* and a *Canadian Barn Dance* knocked together. And to general amazement, confident Calum volunteered to sing the sole 'pop' number of the set, Thin Lizzy's *Whisky in the Jar*. 'We were all,' deadpans Rory, 'very excited indeed,' although he himself was 'too embarrassed to sing'.

The question of a name remained. Suggestions such as 'Rockall' and 'The Jacobites' were rejected. 'Nothing seemed right,' said Calum, 'then, the weekend before the gig, Rory was poring over Blair's Scottish History notes and saw the phrase 'the run-rig system' and that was that. And not simply 'run-rig', but 'The Run-Rig Dance Band', or variations thereon, and so it would be for the next few years.

That first ceilidh date at the Kelvin Hall did, in fact, go well, according to Calum. Though for ex-mod Rory, the sartorial strictures were hard to bear. 'We had purple shirts, black trousers and bow ties, which Blair's mum and sister had organised for us. The bow ties didn't last beyond the

A very early practice. Blair and Calum outside Blair's parents' house, Braes, Skye

first number. Blair was a very accomplished player, and the response was very encouraging.' Afterwards, the excitement was lasting. 'We decided to carry on.'

Calum was quickly on the telephone, booking the Waternish Hall in Skye for six Friday nights over the summer. In the event, the first Runrig gig on Skye saw Calum and Blair performing as a duo, with Calum still the vocalist.

'It was tremendously exciting,' Calum grins in recollection. 'People came from all over the island – there were about 120 people there – but thank goodness it wasn't recorded by anyone. It was still mostly Scottish stuff, though. We did *Whisky in the Jar* and things like *Red River Rock* and *Popcorn*. As far as Blair was concerned, that was pop music. He was a purist, totally committed to Scottish music – he had a Carpenters album, I think! The band opened a door to new musical possibilities for him.'

Rory was gritting his teeth over his commercial art in Glasgow, longing for the holidays, when suddenly it all became too much for him. He gave up his job and headed north – 'It was all I wanted to do.'

The remaining nights at Waternish were quickly cancelled as offers came in thick and fast from all over Skye. Rory arrived, guitar at the ready, and that first Runrig summer began in earnest. Guitar, drums, accordion and vocals – the simple line-up seemed to appeal. Dates at the Skye Gathering Hall and a series of Saturday nights for the Portree British Legion – on 50 per cent of the door takings. More rock songs began creeping into the set, and their first appearance in the outer isles – at Balavanich gym – saw such gems as *Johnnie B Goode*, *Memphis* and other Chuck Berry numbers being featured.

It was an incredible time in Skye, that summer of 1973. Spring the previous year had seen the faltering beginnings of the *West Highland Free Press*, with Brian Wilson, Jim Innes and Jim Wilkie. The radical, youthful staff of the paper were natural soulmates for the band.

'I used to end up in the house with Rory whenever I would go up to Portree to deliver the paper,' says former editor and delivery driver Brian Wilson, now Labour MP for Cunninghame North and his party's Scottish spokesman on rural affairs. 'I knew them better socially than I did through seeing them as a band. But they were always great fun – they became the main dance band on Skye quite early on – just Blair, Rory and Calum at that time.'

Jim Wilkie of the *Free Press* was then promoting concert tours in an effort to raise money for the paper, and the summer of 1973 saw one such trip by the Corries taking in Stornoway. 'The Run-Rig Dance Band' went too.

'Calum was working as a road labourer during the day,' says Rory, 'and he'd be so tired after band nights he'd be sleeping in cranes, culverts, lorries, wherever. He'd be coming back on the ferry from Uist, then changing straight into his working clothes and off to the site.'

The trip to Uist gave the band their first press coverage, naturally enough in the *Free Press* ('Anything they wanted publicised was publicised,' says

Brian.) A story on 3 August 1973 described how three Portree boys were about to 'broaden their horizons' by going to play in Uist. Next week there was an advert for 'The Run-Rig Dance Band' at Kyleakin Badminton Club, admission 40p. But one lasting lesson was quickly learnt, says Calum. 'We realised that we would make more money booking ourselves into halls and promoting ourselves, rather than simply taking a fee.'

Another student was home in Skye that long summer, a refugee from Gray's School of Art in Aberdeen where he was studying painting and drawing. Like most of the youthful inhabitants of the island, Donnie Munro would, on a Friday night, look for the place where the action was.

'It was very funny. I came home from art school during the summer, and summer was always such a period of great expectations; going home with everybody being there, and life revolving around that. One night somebody said there was a dance on at the local village hall, and a band called Run-Rig was playing. I said, "Oh, who is it?" They said it was Rory Macdonald and I remembered the Skyevers who were totally unreal, the original Skye pop group. "Oh yes," I said, and that was fine. Then they said Blair Douglas, whom I knew. He was a year below me in primary school before he went to live in Glasgow, and I'd heard he'd become an accordion player. So again, that was fine, and I said, "So who else?" And someone said Calum Macdonald and I went, "CALUM MACDONALD! Calum was in my class at school," I said, "and I've never heard him sing a note or play an instrument or do anything musical whatsoever, ever! What the hell is *he* doing there!" Somebody said, "Och, he plays the drums." So I went up to listen to them, and it was just a brilliant time. I walked in, and they were playing Scottish country dance tunes, but I'd never heard them played that way before. They were really rough, but they had a kind of energy I'd never come across. Rory's guitar style didn't have thousands of chords. It was very basic chords, a very basic rhythm. There was electric guitar. electric accordion and drums, and Calum's style of playing . . . as far as technique was concerned, there was just nothing. But the funniest thing of all was that Calum was *singing* – actually playing and singing at the same time – I think it was *Whisky in the Jar* or something. So Calum started singing – oh, it was absolutely hellish. I can remember thinking just how bad it was, and I left the dance that night totally bemused at Calum doing anything, and this in particular. But I'd enjoyed the night.'

Like everyone else born in Skye before 1966, Donald Munro first saw the light of day in Uig, at the island's one hospital – now a youth hostel. Brought up 'between Portree and my grandparents' croft', he decided early on that art was to be his future. 'At maybe 12, I knew I wanted to go to art college and I aimed everything at that, minimising my efforts on every-thing except what I needed to do to get there.'

He arrived in Aberdeen in 1970 for his first term at Gray's School of Art, newly 17 and desperately homesick. For four years he specialised in drawing and painting, but the long summers kept calling him back. 'It was such a huge relief getting back to Skye. It's funny looking back on it now, because Aberdeen is not what anyone would call a huge city.'

Folk Club, Portree High School, 1966: (*left to right*) Iain Macrae, Donnie (on tambourine), Anne Maclean, Alex Welford and Skyever George Stoddart

That summer of 1973 saw Donnie ripe for some musical diversion. From a very early age he had been encouraged to sing. 'My mother used to sing, and rightly or wrongly the people round about me seemed to think I sang reasonably well. It was traditional Gaelic singing, but not heavy stuff – children's songs, pub stuff.'

Exposed as a child to the whole Gaelic Mod experience (as opposed to the Skyevers mod experience) he hadn't liked it much, although 'in fairness it did stimulate an interest at that point. One of my earliest memories of paying homage to rock and roll was of an eight-mile trek along with my elder brother from our grandparents' croft in Treaslane to Portree so that we could join in with the screaming in the Drill Hall as Presley swayed his way through *Kid Galahad*. It was preceded by some very old *Pathé News* footage which for some reason was still doing the rounds of the Highlands and Islands Film Guild. Funny little men playing football in extremely baggy shorts.'

By the third year at school, Donnie had discovered Simon and Garfunkel and, with a friend called Iain Macrae, was covering some of their greatest hits around various Portree classrooms. 'We sang harmonies really well. It was through working with Iain that I really got into harmony. Now, I tend to want harmonies where it's not strictly necessary, but that's just my own taste.'

Listening to records was a problem, however – not for Donnie the obsessive adolescent fandom of the Macdonald brothers. 'I didn't really

A star is born. Donnie at a wedding in the Royal Hotel, Portree, accompanied by Iain Macdonald (Cordovox)

listen to a lot of bands on record, and the simple reason back then was that my parents didn't have any sort of record equipment or hi-fi. Except in an odd sense. I remember really vividly finding one of those old wind-up gramophones that must have belonged to my grandparents, and a pile of old 78s . . . but I was into being a participant rather than collecting records like Calum. I was never a fan as such, but I enjoyed working with the Simon and Garfunkel material around that time, and I enjoyed access to contemporary pop and rock with radio and TV. On the heavier side, I liked listening to Jack Bruce and Cream.'

Two of the cartoons Donnie drew for the *Free Press*

But by the time 1973 came along, Donnie was strumming chords effectively enough and was prone to delivering the odd Corries number when sufficiently encouraged or suitably lubricated, or both. The strict teetotalism

of today was at that point still a long way off. However, one vaguely remembered night, somewhere in Skye towards the end of a summer which must have been glorious – although no one now recalls what the weather was like – the Munro tonsils were exercised in public, and history was made. Well, almost.

'It was at one of the dances the band were playing that summer, and the standard procedure was that there had to be an interval. I don't know why or how it came about, but I found myself playing on stage in the interval on my own with a guitar, facing the crowd at the dance, for the first time without Iain. The crowd were about inebriated enough to enjoy it. The first song I sang was Status Quo's *Down the Dustpipe*, with the line "I got a ten-dollar bill in my jeans . . ." '

So Donnie sang at a Runrig gig, without being a member of the band, and his unique voice was noted. Later, there were murmurings about him maybe, just possibly, joining. 'I'm still unclear as to whether or not they approached me, or I approached them. But it was left hanging, anyway.'

By that time, the magic summer was drawing to an end and reality, in the shape of colleges and work, was impinging ever more urgently. Having given up his design job in Glasgow, Rory decided to stay in Skye, free-lancing, mostly for the nascent Clan Donald Centre, while both he and Donnie also helped out on the *Free Press*, Rory with layouts and Donnie with a series of cartoons, *Munro's View*. Donnie then went back to complete his Honours DA at Aberdeen while Calum and Blair went back to Glasgow student life.

It had been a summer of realising possibilities, of dreams starting to assume solid shapes. The songwriting ambitions of Calum and Rory had taken a back seat to the adrenalin rush of playing live, of moving people about a dance floor. Key personnel were assuming their places, crucial contacts such as that with the *Free Press* established. And Runrig had begun, a band anchored in a community; conceived in Glasgow perhaps, but nurtured in the warm glow of a Skye summer.

Munroe's **View of The Skye Gathering Balls**

"I say, would you care to adjourn to the toilets for a quick quaff at the half-bottle".

Robert
Macdonald

The *Play Gaelic* sessions

CHAPTER THREE

WILD AT HEART

It was their last college year, and with Rory freelancing in Skye, Calum and Blair formed a loose, informal Glasgow band with friends, Donnie 'Large' Macdonald and Noel Eadie. Playing dances for the Highland Societies and Glasgow University Ossianic Society brought in cash and contacts, laying the groundwork for Runrig's future student following in central Scotland.

David Williams was still writing, and Calum worked with him on a few demos. Another informal musical outlet was The Norsemen, also featuring Donnie Large and another friend, Clem Mackenzie. But the summer beckoned, and this time confidence in Runrig's pulling power bred organisation.

'We booked a full summer dance programme in Skye,' says Rory, 'and this time we decided mostly to promote ourselves. So instead of playing for Ness Bowling Club we would go and hire a hall ourselves, get two mates at the door and print our own posters – we made more money that way.'

First, though, there was the little matter of a singer to be settled. No longer could the dulcet tones of Calum be coped with as the main vocal sound of Runrig, and the younger Macdonald brother was happy to agree.

'Donnie was the obvious choice,' says the first Runrig singer. 'We knew him from school and as part of the folk duo he had with Iain Macrae. So we approached him over a pint in the Royal Hotel in Portree.'

'He broadened the band,' his brother adds. 'He was singing all the time, singing those Corries songs, and he'd done a couple of supports.'

Agreeing with alacrity, Donnie became part of what he now calls 'a sort of totally good time'. Rory agrees. 'It was fun. Just a big social thing.'

'I didn't differentiate in any sense between performing at those dances and going to them as a punter,' says Donnie, 'because we were usually all in the same condition anyway. You know, it was all sort of merriment flowing on and off the stage, enormous carry-outs. It was part of a situation where it was all fun, part of what was going on at the dances, not serious at all. Serious in the enjoyment, but not serious in anything else.'

Jim Wilkie, by then playing and singing with soon-to-be members of the almost successful Glasgow soul band Cado Belle, remembers one of those 1974 dates with the critical eyes and ears of the professional musician. 'I'd arranged a six-week Highland tour – it was me, Colin Tully, Gavin Hodgson, who now works with Robert Palmer, Jim Yule, who went to New Celeste, Davy Roy and Charlie Johnstone. We were called Dog Eat Dog

Photographer Calum
captures Rory, Blair
and Donnie, with
Donald Mackinnon,
1974. Donald, the
band's first driver, free-
wheeled everywhere to
conserve the red diesel
on which the van ran

Mark Two. When our Portree date was announced, we were approached
to see if this group called Runrig could support us. Someone had told me
they had an outstanding accordionist.

'We had a PA and sound engineer – very unusual for the West Highlands
at that time. We arrived, and Runrig were sound-checking. My first
impression of the accordionist was that he was dead clumsy. I now regard
Blair as genuinely outstanding, so I presume he was just hamming it up.
Donnie's vocal sound struck me as very rounded – my background was in
black music, and I liked a coarser style of voice.

'I now think both Donnie and Rory have added something very original
to the whole dimension of Scottish music just by being true to their own
tradition. At that time I thought it was far too rounded, although rhythmi-
cally they seemed quite comfortable with Calum. It wasn't too bad, but I
just thought "no chance".'

For Runrig this particular gig was not a major success, according to Jim.
'That night we were waiting in the dressing-room and, within five minutes
of Runrig going on stage, the sound engineer burst in to say, "There's
someone threatening to smash up the mixing desk if you guys don't get
on." Then in walks someone who shall remain nameless because he still
lives in Portree, and he's demanding that we get on stage or there'll be
trouble because he didn't come here to see Runrig. They were playing kind
of Eagles stuff, Sutherland Brothers and so on . . . country-rock. Anyway,
we calmed him down, went on stage and played, and I think we paid
Runrig £15.'

Despite such setbacks, Runrig's fame was spreading. The summer of
1974 saw gigs in such far-flung outposts as Mallaig, Benbecula, Plockton
and Corran Halls in Oban where Brian Wilson saw them play, advised by

compère Billy Ford to turn up in time and to get themselves bow ties and jackets instead of appearing in open-necked shirts.

Fragments of a diary Calum kept during that summer survive and give a real flavour of those wild and crazy days. 22 June, and sometime song-writing partner David Williams was coming up to Skye for the crack.

> Met David on Byres Road . . . then got packed for Skye and made for somewhere en route where we could watch the World Cup match versus Yugoslavia. Seldom seen Skye look better. I feel optimistic about this summer.

The 27th saw the first gig of the summer in Portree, and an appearance by the legendary character known as 'Donald the Hall'.

> First summer engagement for the school youth wing end-of-term dance [at the Skye Gathering Hall]. Crack was good, band played well but a few things need polishing up. Then, just as we're about to get paid, Donald the Hall enters with perfect timing. 'Oh,' he says, 'there will be £10 off the bill you see, the buggers ripped the cistern off the wall – we've not got a drop of water in the house, and the plumbers won't be here until morning.' With that he clattered Irene Macleod [who was organising the dance] round the shoulders and staggered off with his broom.

'That was our first experience with Donald, a redoubtable character,' says Calum now. 'There were to be many more.'

Runrig are garbage . . . or were treated as such for transportation purposes. Macfarlane's rubbish van, 1974

Rehearsing *Proud Mary* at Ardgay Hall, 1974

Facial hair begins to
make its debut on the
Runrig chins

28 June: Rory got things organised for the dance in Kyle. A great success
– hired Donald John Sconser's van – took Lumbago down with us to
help Tubby at the door. He was in an extreme state of merriment before
we left Portree, as was Munro. Big sing-song on the way down. Donnie
did his Corries bit at half-time. After the dance we all searched for food
and slept in the hall. We all had sleeping-bags, but Lumbago had to sleep
in his three-piece suit, going demented for lack of food.

29 June: At first light straight to the Cedars restaurant. Lumbago had
four rounds of cheese and tomato sandwiches before the biggest plate of
bacon, sausage and eggs, black pudding and the like you ever saw in
your life. Got back to Portree at 12.30 p.m., and Donnie went straight
to work at the Portree Hotel.

On 3 July it was back to the Skye Gathering Hall, where all the band's
gear was stored.

Word has it that Donald the Hall was in good form by midday. Dubbans
Shaw – who with the bandaged head is still recovering from his fall last
Friday – came up to see him at nine o'clock with one on the hip. Then
he forced him to go down for a lager to the Rosedale, where they bumped
into a very rich Australian who originated from Uist and kept buying
them drinks. Donald said that he was loaded and they did not want to
take advantage of him by refusing rounds. He blamed the whole experience on 'that bugger Shaw'.

Transport was always a problem, although by this time such stalwart roadies as Buffy Macsween had become involved. Mallaig was the destination:

> Pouring rain all day. Couldn't find DJ Sconser so hired a 1300 estate from Macrae's. Virtually impossible to pack, especially in the Skye monsoon. Cut my hand, ripped a speaker, all the gear completely soaked. Buffy arrived at the house at 6 p.m. on the dot, the car anchors to a halt in a cloud of dust and gravel, pink shirt exposing a forest of chest hair, rubbing his hands and raring to go. He set off first with the estate and the gear. We left a bit too much later in Rory's Hillman Imp. The usual complications set in.
>
> Firstly we had to turn back for the money box, then we had to really rush for the ferry. But the Imp does not take kindly to rushing. Rory had to keep blowing into the petrol tank to keep it ticking over. Made it to the ferry as the ropes were cast, but they came back for us. Good weather in the south – pulled a big crowd. Big session afterwards, slept on the boat, wakened at seven with breakfast.

Donald the Hall

Summer jobs were the order of the day, with Donnie a barman in the Portree Hotel and Calum reaching the giddy heights of waste disposal executive, or bin-man.

> *22 July*: Try to get as much of my bin rounds done today as I'm off to Uist tomorrow. Working flat out, as much as the van will allow. Stuck for a van for Uist so I manage to get MacFarlane's to risk taking the rubbish lorry over. David Williams suffering from culture shock. Up at the Lachais Mhor [the dump] cleaning out the van as best as possible and then getting the gear packed.

Next day, the odyssey to Benbecula began.

> Got up at 7.30, prayed the van would start. Off we went for Uist, played on the ferry, then the van conked out on the ramp coming off. A real problem. There were no brakes at all, and we slipped into the railings at Alda's shop. Apart from the driver's seat and one passenger the rest sat on kitchen chairs in the back. Rory fell backwards as we took off. Benbecula, and David protesting greatly about the military presence. Playing football on the beach, then setting up. Blair had one of his box breakdowns. The rest of us went off to Creagory for a pint and a carry-out. Band went down a storm – 250 people, and the best we have ever played. Crack was excellent. Rory in usual clumsy form. Back at the bed-and-breakfast about five in the morning, sitting sharing out the takings, we were asking Rory why he was so accident prone. With that he replied, 'I don't know', stood up and banged his head on the top of the door post.

It was midday before anyone stirred, and inevitably there was a game of football on the beach to wipe out memories of the previous night's excesses. Then 'off to Creagory for a slap-up four courser', and the same again – another 250 people, more craziness, and £40 profit from two nights in Benbecula.

> *25 July*: Drove to Lochmaddy at five in the morning and watched the dawning. Magnificent sight of sun rising over Langash moor – Laldy comes off the night watchman shift at six, Callain starts work, Captain Iain hovering around. They start loading the cars. The rest get some kind of sleep on the ferry, but I have to wait. Van behaves on way to the boat, so I can go upstairs to join the others. Once we reached Uig the fun and games really started with the van – not entirely unexpected. When I started it up, a ferryman took the blocks away and it slid backwards into a big Rover behind. The bloke was English and a right prat – no humour at all. He kicked up merry hell and was going straight to the police. I managed to calm him down, saying we could go to the garage in Uig, get an estimate for the damage and I would pay him cash there and then.
>
> Now the garage in Uig knew me and my van very well – lots of dealings – so he gave me a wink and told the Rover man it would cost £5. I duly paid him and left. I was then told privately that the job would be at least £40 or £50, so one up for the home side. Uist trip a great success.

These were days of lager, whisky and, especially if you were a rubbish-man, not necessarily coming up smelling of roses.

> *2 August*: West side run – home early as it's Friday. Sammy Dooda gave me a hand clearing my van at the dump, he was shovelling like a man possessed. He'd been boozing with Donnie during the day, but then it's his 21st today. Had the worker session at the Caley at five, then after tea Donnie came round. Had to rescue him from the toilet seat. He had a bottle with him so celebrating extended to the van, the King's Arms and then everyone got involved. I remember my drums falling to bits and rolling away across the stage . . .

The diary entries became shorter and more cryptic as the summer veered hectically towards a close.

> *22 August*: Games day and the Games dance. Blair so relaxed he falls backwards and is pinned to the ground by the weight of his accordion. SOS to Peter Macsween.

> *23 August*: To Wick and Bonar Bridge, staying in Altnagar Lodge Hotel. Donald came upstairs with his weekend case – a brown paper bag tied with string. Horse play in hotel.

25 August: Home via Shin Falls and Invergordon and other strange places we shouldn't have been to. Pints and darts in Kintail, then a sing-song. Stopped off in Marine and King's Arms. Broke into the Gathering Hall to put the gear back.

On 28 August the band played Ardgay under the misprinted name 'The Running', the last time Blair was to perform with Runrig for almost four years. Calum's diary then hints at exceedingly nefarious goings-on involving the Society Ball associated with the Skye Gathering, attended by the upper classes in ill-mannered droves.

4 September: After tea the usual onslaught at the 'Balls' crowd – dustbins on cars, air out of tyres, tomatoes – not constructive enough.

A trip back to Glasgow to tie up loose ends there brought a chance to meet Murdo Ferguson of Gaelfon again, with whom there was now talk of recording a single.

21 September: Got up in Newton Mearns, at David's house; into Glasgow to the strains of *Layla*. Met Murdo, discussed plans. Meeting Brian Wilson in the Park Bar at 1.30 p.m., back up to Glencoe and home. There ends the summer. It's been a good one and points to a lot of what's to come. New job, Edinburgh for a change and a possible record coming out. Who knows?

Half-time during a football match on the beach at Luskentyre, Harris

All roads led to Edinburgh. Rory moved back from Skye, Calum and Donnie began working as house parents in a children's home, and the music continued, though without Blair. 'It just got difficult, working with Blair. It was a dodgy period, very strained,' says Rory, cautiously.

Runrig almost died a death there and then as Rory, Calum and Donnie began investigating new directions – 'a pop related band, not dance,' says Rory. 'We were looking for names and everything, but it didn't happen.' The Gaelfon recordings did, although no single resulted, and Donnie remembers the episode with amusement and some incredulity.

'Murdo was from Stornoway, and we recorded at his studio with this friend of Calum and Rory's from Glasgow, David Williams. I'd love to know where that tape is now because we never finished the recording. I'll always remember Murdo because there was one point when we wanted to overdub some things. We were totally raw and new to any recording technology, and so was he I'm sure. Anyway, he kept phoning us up and telling us "the double-tracking machine has broken down – I'm waiting for a new one"!'

Indeed, Rory thinks that that Gaelfon multi-track could be somewhere in Stornoway. Previous Gaelfon recordings by himself and Calum were, he says mysteriously, 'stolen out of Buffy Macsween's car' by person or persons unknown.

Gaelic songwriting was still something of a self-indulgent gleam in the

Macdonald brothers' eyes in 1974, although things changed the next year, encouraged by Blair's replacement, accordion player Robert MacDonald. 'Robert played with us for the first time back in Skye at Christmas 1974,' says Donnie. 'He'd been at school with us – in fact, I'd played with him at school, my guitar along with his accordion. He joined the band very much as a hobby – he just loved music, wasn't terribly serious about it – he just liked it.'

Robert enjoyed a wry sense of humour and general good crack, and his personality could manifest itself in a very self-effacing way – a mixture of Highland humility and lack of self-belief. The band's first TV appearance was a one-take live performance in front of a studio audience, and it was the setting for a classic from Bob. Just as the very nervous and shaky-kneed quartet were walking down the corridor from the dressing-room to the studio floor at the BBC in Glasgow, he uttered the immortal line, 'Listen, lads, I think we're kidding ourselves on here'. And a stickler for the snare-drum precision of Scottish dance music, he would often glare at an over-enthusiastic Calum during gigs and shout 'Snare! SNARE!'

Other characters came and went, all reinforcing the move towards Gaelic. Campbell Gunn, now a reporter with the *Sunday Post*, was then playing with the Gaelic group Na Siaraich, and met up with the Macdonalds and Donnie in Edinburgh. 'Oh, several times in the Thistle Hotel and West End Hotel,' he says. 'We'd sometimes have jams together. I even remember one night in the West End with Runrig, myself, Dick Gaughan, the Fureys and Davie Arthur. That was some night.' Becoming something of an honorary band member, Campbell began going out to Calum and Rory's house in Dalkeith. 'I soon got to know folk. We'd often end a jam session with a game of football.'

'We spent quite a bit of time with Campbell, playing at weddings and things with him,' says Rory, 'because at this point Donnie had slightly lost interest, having fallen in love. But we knew it wouldn't be a long-term thing.'

The summer of 1975 came and went, with Robert firmly ensconced as box player and Rory making the shift, on and off, from guitar to bass. The scale and geographical spread of concerts increased, but apart from holidays, including Easter and Christmas back in Skye, the live appearances were not that widespread on the mainland. There were one or two glorious exceptions, though, as Donnie remembers.

'One of the first places we played was called Kelly's Cavern, up in some terrace in Edinburgh. The woman there wasn't very sure about taking us on, this being Edinburgh and us being from the Highlands. Anyway, one of the things was she had a stripper on at the place – I remember her name was Cuddly Kim from those horrible yellow adverts around the door – a girl all decked out in flowers called Cuddly Kim. So we were a bit of a change – she was taking a bit of a chance. Anyway, all our friends came along, including a friend called John Lockhart, who arrived in complete formal Highland dress, walked up to the microphone and said, "Ladies and Gentlemen, I give you Runrig." It was a really, really weird situation, but it turned into quite a party. Presumably the woman was quite happy, beause our friends did quite a lot of drinking. And we never met Cuddly Kim.'

In October 1975 the first major breakthrough for Calum and Rory's songwriting came – in the form of second place in a BBC Gaelic song contest. But it was a controversial business. 'We wanted to perform the song ourselves,' says Calum, 'but the BBC said no way.'

Campbell Gunn went with Calum and Rory to watch the performance of the final six songs in the contest. *Sguaban Arbhair*, written on the M8 motorway between Glasgow and Edinburgh and eventually to surface on *Play Gaelic*, was, they found, to be performed by none other than Mary Sandeman, the well-known traditional Gaelic singer. 'The version she was given was completely rearranged from the original into a very traditional verse-chorus-verse-chorus thing,' says Campbell. 'It came second, but Calum just sat throughout it with his head in his hands.'

The ensuing row with producer Neil Fraser led to two things. One was an eventual invitation to come back and do some television work for the BBC using all-Gaelic material, the other was the beginning of the reputation Runrig have acquired in some media circles for being distinctly bolshy perfectionists. Neil Fraser is now head of Radio Scotland and remembers the incident with amusement. No grudges are held.

1976 dawned, and the first rumblings of punk began to reverberate up from the ICA and 100 Club in London towards Scotland. Runrig, having settled into their holiday performance mode, were by this time veterans of the Highland dance scene and largely unaffected. As in those summers of 1974 and 1975, the good times rolled along.

A typical set list of the day included some unlikely choices – John Denver's *Annie's Song*, several Jim Croce covers, *Banks of the Ohio*, *Swing Low Sweet Chariot*, *Fire and Rain* and *Sloop John B* – not to mention virtually the complete works of Creedence Clearwater Revival. Off-stage, though, it was a different story. Having made the breakthrough, such as it was, with the BBC via Gaelic songs, Calum and Rory churned out more and more material in their native language, fuelled by their constantly burgeoning desire to reflect their own heritage.

Their flat in Dalkeith became a songwriting sweatshop. The acquisition of a tape-recorder brought the chance to produce reasonable home demos, and Campbell Gunn remembers their first one well: seven tracks with Rory singing on one, Donnie on three and Campbell himself on three. But what to do with it? A copy was sent to the Corries' own record label in Edinburgh, who never replied. Campbell: 'Rory phoned up to find out what had happened and they just said the tape was ready for collection. When he pressed them about why they didn't like it, he was simply told that the drumming wasn't good enough.'

So thoughts turned towards Lismor Records in Glasgow, traditional home of music tartanry. Campbell was not happy about this, though. 'I'd had some dealings with them before, but I was apprehensive about approaching Lismor again because I'd had a contractual dispute with them.'

In the end, it was Rory who took the tape to Lismor, and Campbell found: 'They were quite excited by it. It was the kind of thing they had been looking for, and they agreed to do an album.' It was as simple as that. Recording was set for May 1977, but Campbell decided to pull out. 'I thoroughly enjoyed all that time but really I was never a member of the band.'

The Lismor deal was a major breakthrough, but there were immediate hassles. Used to recording simple accordion and drum backings for the tourist market, the production demands Runrig immediately started making were a surprise to Lismor's Peter Hamilton. 'They didn't have a clue what we were on about,' says Rory. 'I wanted to use Chris Harley as producer. I knew him from Skye and he was related to one of the Skyevers.' Donnie's version is slightly different. 'We knew he was a kind of pop person. As far as Skye was concerned he was the closest thing there was to a famous music industry person.' Rory shrugs. 'But that all fell through and we went to Black Gold studios in Kirkintilloch.'

There Ken Andrew and Ian McCredie, both former members of the bubblegum pop group Middle of the Road – as in *Chirpy Chirpy Cheep Cheep* – were studio owners and in-house producers. Tough negotiations with Peter Hamilton over the album's budget ('They were used to recording pipe bands in six hours, and thought offering us six days was generous') saw Calum's combative spirit prevail. 'We got 12 days – their longest-ever recording session,' he said, and Rory added, 'We had to fight like hell – but we got it.' And so, in May, recording began.

From the start, Donnie loved it. 'I was doing my teacher training at Moray House, so I was going back and forth from Edinburgh to the studios, and I mean it was just brilliant. It was a time when I really loved my situation, working with these songs, because it was such a gift for someone to say I could make a record. Just to illustrate my lack of ambition, if you like, I always remember saying to my parents about *Play Gaelic* that it was great I had been able to do this because some day as an old man I'd be able to say to my grandchildren, "This is a record I made once."'

Enjoyable it may have been, but it also took great chunks out of the time which should have been spent studying. '*Play Gaelic* got me a pass in Psychology. I'd better not name the member of staff, but I had a Psychology assignment I was supposed to do in Creativity and I had missed so many lectures and tutorials that I had basically done no work whatsoever. I was overdue with it, so in the end I put three of the songs from *Play Gaelic* on a cassette and wrote a little note explaining why I'd been absent so often, and how I'd failed to do the work. I was given an "A" pass.'

Other encouragements arrived. One of Calum's songs, *Tillidh Mi*, won through to the final of the Celtavision contest at the Pan-Celtic Festival in Killarney. It didn't win, but the band had a wonderful time, and made one very important contact. Gaelic broadcaster Martin Macdonald was there, freelancing for the BBC. 'I'd known Robert from Portree, in fact, I was distantly related to him and knew the Macdonald brothers' parents, but that was the first time I came across them as a band,' he says. 'I can

A wedding at the Royal Hotel, Ullapool. Securely seated, the band exhort guests on to the floor for an eightsome reel

remember interviewing them, and neither Calum nor Rory, nor Donnie were happy about being interviewed in Gaelic. Robert wanted them to, though, and in the end they did it. Gaelic was really Robert's first language. The rest of them were fluent enough, but they didn't have the confidence in front of a tape-recorder.' That meeting was to prove crucial in the near future.

Summer arrived, and for the first time Runrig set out for Skye with something in their minds other than having a good time and making a little pin money. The songs which would appear the following April on *Play Gaelic* – its release delayed so that marketing could coincide with the tourist season – were crying out for live performance. So Runrig returned to their old stamping ground, to their home audience, and quickly discovered the meaning of the biblical phrase 'a prophet without honour in his own land'.

A set list from that summer survives to this day, with gaffa tape still attached and the first chords of each song written carefully in green ink. You can tell it's Rory's as each song also carries the reminder 'bass' or 'lead'. A determination to get things right and a strong whiff of nervousness comes off that crumpled sheet of paper. It was the start of a new Runrig and elements still familiar today can be glimpsed. Apart from the songs off *Play Gaelic* like *Sguaban Arbhair*, the resonant *Cum 'Ur N'Aire* and all the rest, there's *Loch Lomond* – defended then, as now, as 'a very good song with lyrics that mean a great deal' – and, earliest of all, *Going Home*. Not to mention, of course, the Dylan cover *You Ain't Going Nowhere*, plus *Killiekrankie* and *The Flowers of the Forest*.

'The reaction was terrible,' grimaces Donnie, pained at the memory. 'Just awful. Everybody hated it. I mean in Skye, at that point in time, Runrig had become quite popular in their own limited way. People sort of looked on us as the kind of band they could go along and have a really good time to – you know, just dance and generally have a good time. Then, of course, they arrived at the dance and there we were performing songs they didn't know – that weren't in the charts, that weren't pop songs. They were actually songs in their own language and yet a lot of people were saying, "What on earth's happened? What's this all about?" That really was the reaction when we tried to do Gaelic songs.'

It was a shattering blow. The painful process of rediscovering their own heritage had taken Calum and Rory a long time. To bring it back home in the form of their own songs and have it thrown back in their faces was hard to take. 'Skye,' says Rory, shaking his head; 'the people just didn't appreciate what we were trying to do.' Donnie, who actually sang the songs, was more than disappointed. 'When you go to the toilet and somebody says to you, "What's happened to the band?", it's not the kind of thing you particularly want to hear.' Of course, the ceilidh stuff and the covers at the end of the night went down well enough, and it was still possible to rescue the evening. But on the mainland, reaction varied, too, and one wonders how many who proudly boast these days of being at a Runrig gig 'back then before they were big' and who can happily rhyme off chunks of *Alba* or *Siol Ghoraidh*, were in 1977 among the 'stop this crap and give us *Proud Mary*' brigade.

As for the band, their nerve shoogled a bit but held. There was to be no return to the wild and crazy days when anything went, and a half bottle, a few cigarettes and the crack was enough. From now on, things would get serious.

But not too serious. The 1977 gigs should not pass into history without a mention of 'Deek, the Flying Roadie', a PE teacher friend of the band who helped out at various venues on the West Coast with a half-time display of gymnastics, which caused enormous confusion in less-than-sober audiences. And there was the time Rory declared to a bed-and-breakfast host, 'I'm starving – I could eat a sheep', only to have an old black-faced ewe burst in on the astonished company seeking the source of such a cruel telepathic message. Of such moments are great memories made.

CHAPTER FOUR

PLAYING GAELIC

April 1978 finally saw the release of *Runrig Play Gaelic* on the Lismor subsidiary Neptune Records. As luck would have it, the BBC had started Radio Highland two years previously and were broadcasting a considerable number of programmes aimed straight at the Gaidhealtacht.

Iain MacDonald, now Radio Scotland's Highland Reporter, then just beginning his broadcasting career, remembers the arrival of *Play Gaelic* well. 'For a lot of people it just appeared out of nowhere. People knew Runrig as a sort of garage band, playing retreads of classic hits, chart stuff and rock stuff, and then this album appeared.'

This was before Radio Nan Gaidheal or Radio Nan Eilean appeared, so Radio Highland was effectively bilingual. 'They were looking for Gaelic music and, to be honest, Runrig were the only people in that market who were appealing to anything like a youth audience. That album got battered to death at Radio Highland. I remember there were three copies of it at one stage in the library and they were all unplayable, they had been played so much.'

Martin Macdonald was knocked sideways when he heard the LP. 'It was like the clouds opening. Nobody had expected it – I certainly hadn't.' The nearest Gaelic had come to pop music at this stage were appearances by the likes of the Eden Singers and the Macdonald Sisters on Fred MacAuley's *Se'Ur Beatha* BBC television programme, with Na-h-Oganaich covering the purist folk territory. 'Then Runrig burst on the scene, and they were Gaelic, you could feel they were Gaelic, but they were also pop, rock, for a much younger generation.'

Rory gauges the reaction cautiously. 'From the Gaelic establishment, it was generally encouraging.' 'Only Gaels listened to it,' says Calum. 'It was played on Gaelic radio, and it was seen as being totally new, totally revolutionary.' Some did not approve. Bill Kerracher, then head of Radio Highland, once referred to them scathingly as 'American music with Gaelic words'. A few older heads nodded wisely in agreement. Surely this was the devil's music.

'I find this stuff irresistible,' wrote Alistair Clark in his *Scotsman* column, 'but a staunch Gaelic purist might have another word for it.' Identifying 'occasional problems of intonation in the melding of electric guitar and voice', Alistair mildly criticised Calum and Rory for going 'too often for the soft option when something more colourful and abrasive is called for'. However, the album gave 'sure and sensitive examples of how Gaelic music can, as it were, lounge around in denims without losing either its

significance or its dignity'.

Under the headline 'Gaelic music: Looking beyond the tradition' in the *West Highland Free Press*, Aonghas Macneacail gave the album a rave review. 'We are in the realms of the thoroughly contemporary, the first Gaelic rock band,' he wrote. The words and tunes were 'an important addition to the corpus of modern Gaelic music. Whether or not Runrig are the band of the future, they are certainly the band of the present.' Ending with the immortal words, 'Rock on, Gaelic!', this was pretty much the kind of review you wanted in your local paper.

'The album was highly significant both for Runrig and for Gaelic,' says Iain MacDonald. 'It actually made people aware that you could – and it was very much seen as this – get away with playing late 20th-century music, doing it in Gaelic while drawing a lot of influence, musically speaking, from Gaelic teuchter music. And it got so much publicity from people like Radio Highland.'

However, according to Iain there was initially real resistance to the idea of *Play Gaelic* from the Gaelic establishment, 'although I suspect in the grand old spirit of "I told you so", you wouldn't find anybody to admit to that.

'But there was a lot of lip service to the effect of "Oh, it's good to see some young people making Gaelic music". Those people didn't expect it to last, didn't like it very much in real terms, and only gave it a nod because it was politically advisable. That way, Runrig became a political instrument at the time because they were the only young people doing their bit for the future of Gaelic – and they had more than just a good cause behind them. They had good music to back them up, and it was good news for the

Opposite:
Loading the gear on to the Barra ferry

Below:
Skye Gathering Hall, mid-'70s

denizens of the Gaelic movement.'

Jim Wilkie, very much the rock 'n' roll animal, didn't like it one bit. 'I still thought the sound was too rounded, but then it was a Gaelic album and I wasn't attuned to the Gaelic thing at all really. It was like Calum Kennedy meets the Shadows. In recording terms it was very outdated, but it did have quite a warm feel.'

Listening to the album today, especially now that it has been re-released by Lismor on a warts-and-all CD as *The First Legendary Recordings*, it's hard to see what all the fuss was about back in 1978. *Play Gaelic* doesn't sound like rock music at all, with its plaintive accordion, jangly acoustic guitar and truly Marvinesque electric guitar courtesy of Rory. It's nothing like as tough as Fairport Convention or Horslips, and the timid playing of traditional tunes as in *Ceol An Dannsa* couldn't have given Richard Thompson anything to worry about. This, after all, was 1978. Punk was then metamorphosing into new wave and Elvis Costello and literate power pop was about to burst upon the scene. *Play Gaelic* sounds incredibly dated, well out of the mainstream of popular music.

But then, Runrig *were* out of the mainstream and, tame as it might sound now, in the context of the Gaidhealtacht *Play Gaelic* was, as Martin Macdonald says, 'so completely and utterly different it was disturbing. One just asked – how could this have come out of Portree?' Iggy and the Stooges it wasn't, however.

Calum still loves the LP 'because of its feeling for the time', and while the production is primitive in the extreme, the playing basic and the harmonies occasionally wobbly, the material itself does carry a real emotive power. The overloud phased guitar on *Duisg Mo Run*, the opening track, can't disguise a typically memorable melody from Calum, reinforcing the student yearning for home of the lyrics. Robert only played on the dance medley, where the unimaginative production defuses the attractive image of 'Friday night and the lights are on in the village hall', although the choice of the

Sessions on the *Heb*

traditional *Criogal Cridhe*, with its historical context, is a significant pointer to future mining of this vein. It was Donnie's choice of song, and had been taught to him by his mother. It had also been a favourite of an early music teacher, Aileen Mackenzie, better known as 'Mrs La La'.

De Ni Mi is just a throwaway, but there are some moments where the future Runrig talent for touching the heart break the surface. And nowhere more so than on the closing track. *Cum 'Ur N'Aire*, subtitled 'this song probably sums up the whole point of the album', carries the germ of such stately anthems as *Dust* or *Hearts of Olden Glory*. 'Keep Aware' the title warns, and the song stems from the city/Skye dichotomy which was to give Runrig so much of their creative strength: the being apart and the longing to return – such a distinctively Highland emotion. Yet there is more than homesickness involved. Awareness of the fact that identity comes from one's native culture, from home, is the key.

> (Translation)
> The geese are rising from the machair
> The lambs are running and leaping
> At the back of the field
> But you are now lost in cities
> Never feel alone there
>
> The night lights are now around you
> Your moon is now of many types and colours
> But look at it with one eye only
> Because it can blind you
>
> Keep, keep your awareness
> On the west and on the place
> That raised you
> Remember, remember. Never forget
> That you left behind
> A culture that was special and of worth.

(© *C. & R. Macdonald, Isa Music, 1978*)

And despite the Shadowy guitar, the vocal harmonies come together on that song in a hypnotic, orchestral whole. It may not be rock 'n' roll, but the power is undeniable. As Martin Macdonald says, 'Calum was young then, and his writing was that of a young man. But he is an excellent writer.'

With the album out, Runrig now had something to build on in terms of nationwide marketing. Donnie was teaching at Inverness Royal Academy, Calum was starting his second year of teaching PE in Lasswade, Midlothian, and Rory was freelancing as a graphic designer in Edinburgh, but all were hungry for musical advancement. Not so Robert, whose allegiance to the band had always been worn lightly as far as a career was concerned.

'We wanted to go full-time,' says Calum, 'but Robert wasn't into it.' On the one hand, there was encouragement to go for it – the LP, well received

The new line-up: Blair
rejoins, 1978

The pipes, the pipes . . .
Malcolm blows up a
storm, somewhat pre-
Runrig

and selling in reasonable numbers – on the other, gigs were still hitting opposition. 'There was a lot of that,' says Iain MacDonald. 'There were a lot of very lukewarm receptions, especially on the mainland where they'd played before basically as a covers band. But that's the thing about Runrig. They plugged away; they converted people. They got better at the same time and they had to, musically, but over a period of time they overcame that resistance. And if you were a young Gael, then you were listening to rock 'n' roll music in your own language for the first time, and to be honest, that was fairly wonderful.'

Following the bad experiences with disaffected Sgiathanaichs, 'We were sneaking the Gaelic songs into the set,' Donnie admits, 'but sort of watered them down. We still played Scottish dance music and if there was a waltz we would maybe put a song in for it. Funnily enough, I think the Gaelic songs were better accepted outside of the Highlands. City audiences accepted them, mainly because they were mostly island students at university and perhaps they found it more accessible, getting back to their language because they were away from their own background.'

Meanwhile the band had enlisted two replacements for Robert. June 1978 saw Blair rejoining the band, by this time with a far more developed rock sensibility, courtesy of Jim Wilkie and friends in the The Electric Ceilidh Band with whom he'd been playing. And then there was Malcolm Elwyn Jones.

'My first impression of Malcolm,' says Jim, 'was that he was the kid with the long hair who would come and stand at the front of the stage at every dance The Electric Ceilidh Band played in 1977. He would just stand there every night with his arms folded, watching Neil play the guitar.' Neil Campbell was then recognised as *the* hot Highland guitarist – and a man famed for reacting to *Play Gaelic* with scathing laughter when he came to visit the band's flat one night and was given an earful.

Malcolm had seen Runrig play many times. Younger than the others in the band, he was born in 1959 in Inverness ('I don't remember much about it!'), and brought up in Skye from the age of five. 'I was 11 when I took up the bagpipes, and round about the same time I started getting interested in pop music. There was an old acoustic guitar in our attic at home, and gradually I began to knock a few simple chords out of it. I would have been about 15 at the time. By this time I'd been at the pipes for some four years.'

Like Calum and Rory, Malcolm was a serious music buff, collecting records by mail order, and into rock, blues and the more esoteric aspects of piping. 'At that stage I was obsessive about listening to music but not so serious about playing the guitar – it was simply fun getting together with a friend and trying to outdo each other with ragged approximations of Led Zeppelin or whatever. I didn't take playing music seriously until I joined Runrig.'

As with The Electric Ceilidh Band, Malcolm engaged in a great deal of stage-front staring with his soon-to-be colleagues. But he was not, he sternly insists, a fan. 'I suppose I saw Runrig as more of a good-time dance band.'

Spot the gnome. Malcolm in Steve Hillage mode

A heavily disguised Blair, knocking out a few hymn tunes at his one-man Evangelical meeting outside the Free Church, Portree

As a competition-winning piper, musical connoisseur, guitarist and close follower of fingering at live performances, Malcolm was well known to Calum, Rory and Donnie – they had all lived around the corner from each other for ten years – and an invitation to jam with the band came at Christmas 1977. 'They asked me just to do a few numbers with them at a couple of dances in Skye. That was my first taste of playing music in front of an audience. I thought it was great, really tremendous. It was chalk and cheese to just listening to music.'

Having possessed an electric guitar for 'about a year' at this time, Malcolm was back on holiday from his first year studying Biology, Chemistry and Maths in Glasgow. 'I wouldn't say I was confident at all. As a guitarist I was extremely mediocre. But in the six months before I actually joined the band, I would say I came on twice as well as before. So if I was extremely mediocre at Christmas 1977, by the time I joined the band I was probably just mediocre!'

It was, inevitably, the beginning of the summer – when Calum and Rory knew they could get guaranteed gigs, by this time all over the North – that Malcolm joined officially, Blair re-joined and the big push for full-time status began. It wasn't easy.

Calum: 'The first thing we did was play Skye in the summer, and after the summer was finished we toured all over, the islands as well, Wester Ross, Oban. We tried to fill every date in the diary so that we could make as much money as we could to see us through the winter.' There were what could euphemistically be termed disappointments – like the gig at Dornoch, Rory's birthplace, where only five people turned up in what would forever be Runrig's smallest audience.

And there were problems. The classic living-in-the-van syndrome took its toll. Donnie was still half-yearning for art and teaching, and the decision to invite Blair back was not working out. 'Blair had by this time swapped his anorak for a leather jacket and was hovering on the verges of Celto-punk, the wild man of Skye,' says Rory. 'He'd get carried away on stage, down on his knees with this huge electronic accordion strapped around his chest – but the old problems began to resurface and there were continual arguments.'

But fun too. Malcolm's featured piping spot was usually greeted enthusi-astically, but never with the same hilarity caused one night when Calum and Blair opened a hatch in the wall above the stage during Malcolm's solo appearance and waved an old pair of underpants on the end of a brush through it. Malcolm couldn't understand why everyone was laughing at his piping.

'Blair seized the reins of the band that summer and pushed us in a harder direction,' says Rory. 'Some of the groundwork for the new set was worked out by him. He arranged numbers like Malcolm's *What Time?* along with an early version of *Gamhna Gealla* and the Irish song *Raglan Road*, and these and other tracks were ultimately demoed at Ça Va studios in Glasgow in November. It's always been a source of great loss to the band that we never got it together with Blair and so lost out on his immense talents.'

The *Free Press* pictured the youthful Runrig filming the opening titles for Grampian's *Cuir Car* at the pier in Portree

Money was running short and tempers shorter when a saviour appeared in the unlikely form of Martin Macdonald, now producing Gaelic programmes for Grampian Television. Donny Macleod had been preparing himself for future stardom in *Dotaman* with his sister Margaret and the rest of Na-h-Oganaich in a Grampian children's series called *Cuir Car* – a kind of Gaelic *Playschool*. 'It means "Turn Around!",' says Martin. 'Runrig were making an impact at the time, and Na-h-Oganaich had broken up, so I suggested to Grampian that they give them a try.' Rory: 'That was a real godsend. It saw us through for about a year and a half from September 1978 onwards. By that time we were down to £15 a week each.'

Many future Runrig fans must, as infants, have first glimpsed their heroes in bizarre dress, camping it up like mad for the cameras.

'I'm sure it was absolutely atrocious,' grins Donnie. 'We were playing music, and we had to do links in the studio into cartoons and little sketches. The whole thing was recorded as live, and you could only stop during a cartoon. If you made a mistake you had to go right back to the beginning and start again. I remember Rory once being dressed up as a teacher, and us both doing Rolf Harris-type paintings live.' There were hilarious moments. 'It was quite good fun,' he remembers. 'You were out on a limb.'

Blair did not enjoy being out on quite such a surreal limb, although he was only involved for the first series. Rory: 'Blair wouldn't say anything much in Gaelic at all. He just felt, "I'm a musician. I want no part of this".'

But Blair was in the band and he had to be given things to say. Martin remembers it all with amusement. 'Blair was very much his own man. You felt he was the odd man out, he wanted to play his own type of music,

Open-air session at the Oban Mod, featuring duelling accordions from Blair and Robert, with banjo from Donnie 'Large'

and you had that feeling. He was a fluent Gaelic writer, could speak conversational Gaelic, yet in the studio I couldn't get a line into his mouth. He just didn't like talking in a TV studio.'

Everyone involved remembers a famous incident where, after many rewrites by Martin, a script introducing Sam, the cartoon character of the day, was left with one line which had to be said by Blair. 'The line was "*Cai'l Sam?*", "Where's Sam?",' recalls a rueful Martin Macdonald. 'And eventually he was persuaded to do it, but it was like getting blood from a stone. Unlike Malcolm Jones, who couldn't speak Gaelic at all. You could give him whole lines of dialogue and he'd spout it out quite happily.'

Runrig's burgeoning reputation for being 'difficult' caused Martin no problems. 'I remember them as being very easy to work with. I know they had trouble at Scottish Television, because STV refused to allow them to pre-record their music. They couldn't reach agreement and that was that. The band were very very meticulous and professional, even at that stage.'

Attempts to unearth any tapes of *Cuir Car* have so far proved fruitless. Grampian gave copies of the programmes to Highland Regional Council for use in schools, but these too have disappeared. Donnie would love to see any that are still in existence, but the others would probably be just as happy if they had vanished completely.

What does remain, however, is an original script from the first programme of the series. Here, untranslated but self-explanatory, is a Runrig it is hard to believe ever existed . . . though it seems Blair had more to say than people remember.

CUIR CAR 1

1: Opening film

DONNIE: *Hullo. Is sinne Runrig. Is mise Donnie. Is sud Ruairidh.*
RORY: *Hullo, ciamar a tha sibh, agus Calum thall an sud air na drumaichean.*
CALUM: *Hullo, tha mi'n dochas gun cord am program ruibh. Agus sud Blair thall an sud air a' bhocsa.*
BLAIR: *Hullo, agus sud Malcolm.*
MALCOLM: *Hi.*

2: Runrig – *Air an Traigh* (8-bar intro)

RORY: *Air an traigh – a' cheud oran Gaidhlig a sgriobh Calum riamh. Bidh Calum a' sgriobhadh moran dhe na h-orain againn . . .*
CALUM: *. . . is bidh Ruairidh cur moran dhe na fuinn riutha . . .*
DONNIE: *. . . is bidh sinn uile 'gan seinn, ach an drasda . . .*
ALL: *. . . CUIR CAR!*

3: Cartoon

CALUM: *Ach de thachras ma dhuisgeas an dragon?*
RORY: *Feumaidh sinne falbh son mionaid neo dha ach chi sin an ceart-*

uair.

DONNIE: *Cuimhnich cha bhidh sinn ach mionaid. Feuch gu fuirich sibh ruinn!*

Break

DONNIE: *Ah sud sibh. Tha mi toilichte gun do dh'fhuirich sibh rinn.*
(Knight in armour clanks on)
RORY (to DONNIE): *Co idir tha sin.*
BLAIR (knocking on armour): *Bheil duine stigh?*
MALCOLM (in armour): *Tha.*
CALUM: *Co th'ann?*
MALCOLM: *Mise?*
RORY: *Ach co thusa?*
MALCOLM: *Tha mise. MALCOLM!*
DONNIE: *Hud Malcolm le chleasan a rithist.*
RORY: *Ach sud an seorsa aodach a bha saighdearan a' cleachdadh uaireigin. Iarunn a bh'ann agus bha e gan cumail sabhailte.*
CALUM: *Agus bidh iad ag cuimhneachadh air na saighdearan sin fhathastann am baile anns an Eadailt a h-uile bliadhna. Cuir car agus chi sibh.*

4: Jousting film

(Malcolm is stabbed by a bass)
DONNIE: *Ach caite an dh'fhag sinn Sam?*
CALUM: *Agus an dragon?*
BLAIR: *Agus Sir Eachunn?*
RORY: *Cuir car gu faic sinn.*
ALL: *CUIR CAR!*

5: Cartoon (Part 2)

RORY: *Nach e Sam am balach! Ach a nise oran – 'Sguaban Arbhair'*

Recording *Cuir Car* 'as live', at Grampian Aberdeen studios

6: Song – *'Sguaban Arbhair'*

DONNIE: *Chi sinn air an ath sheacdain sibh, is cuimhnichibh . . .*
ALL: *. . . CUIR CAR!*

The end

Thus began – and possibly ended – the careers of five unpromising young actors.

The Oban Mod fringe in October 1978 saw some prophetic signs of what were to be outrageous scenes the next year in Stornoway, but nothing much more than enthusiastic acceptance. Things were becoming untenable with Blair and in January 1979 he left the group, to return only as an occasional guest.

'We felt we had a direction to go in with the band, and Blair wanted to do his own thing,' says Calum. 'He decided to quit, so we continued as a four-piece – just Donnie, Malcolm, Rory and me.'

There were some great memories, though, of the times with Blair, perhaps none more surreal than an open-air rehearsal at Braes, on a beautiful summer's day when the Royal Yacht *Britannia* suddenly appeared in the Sound of Raasay. The band burst into a heavily amplified and tongue-in-cheek version of *God Save the Queen*, which echoed across the glassy water to the seaborne royals, whose ancestors' marines had once landed at Braes to pacify the rebellious crofters.

Malcolm remembers some of the venues played around this time as being bizarre in the extreme. There is a long list: the hold of a car ferry sailing round Oban Bay ('smelly'); a farm byre in Broadford with the mains unearthed ('smelly again'); the band's first outdoor gig proper at Ruthven Barracks, near Kingussie, in June 1979 – 'A power generator had been provided, but it was producing nearly 300 volts. So after we struck the first chord, all our amps blew up, with smoke and flames shooting out the back of them.' A year earlier in Lochaline, a bar-room fight broke out during the set ('straight out of the wild west'). Runrig kept playing until their nerve snapped and 'we started looking for the nearest window to jump out of'. At Kintail the sound had to be mixed from the hall kitchen, penetrating the hall via a small serving hatch. And on 2 February 1979, Runrig managed to play two concerts in one night. 'We did 9 p.m. to midnight at Stornoway Town Hall, packed up and raced to Ness, set up and played until well after 3 a.m., then packed up again and raced to catch the Ullapool ferry, leaving at 5.30 a.m. and driving all the way back to Portree and bed.'

Increasing fame would, however, bring other pressures – like the end-of-term extravaganza at Heriot Watt University the band almost cancelled when they discovered a supposed stripper was on the bill with them. Soothed by the assurances of an entertainments convener that 'she's just an exotic dancer', Runrig agreed to perform. The 'exotic dancer' duly

This page and over: Concert for Inverness Rugby Club, Bught Park, Inverness, the summer of 1978

arrived, with a companion who almost, by their own admission, scared Donnie and Calum out of the building. Sharing a dressing-room with a giant python had never been a problem in Skye . . .

But desperation was now setting in. It was winter, the band's ace accordionist and most recognised musician had left, and money was getting tighter and tighter. Only *Cuir Car* was keeping the wolf from the band's door, and they had all moved in together in Dalkeith. The next step was, as Rory and Calum admit, a desperate gamble. Had it failed, Runrig would have crumpled into bankruptcy. But it was all or nothing.

'We had gone so far, and we were down to our bottom drawer anyway, so we decided to go for it,' Rory says. 'We decided to record another album, and pay for it ourselves.'

His brother was totally in agreement. 'We sat down in this flat we had with Malcolm and started working. It all happened very quickly.' Rory: 'It started in February. By March or April 1979 Calum and myself had a few songs together and we started writing more and more songs on the spot. We were determined, too, that from that point on, the dances were finished. We would simply perform the record. That was the start of having a real set. We didn't play for dancing. We had a set of our own songs.'

As if this was not enough, the band's nerves of steel were called into play once more. 'We decided,' says Donnie, 'that Lismor hadn't really done justice to what we were trying to do. So we set up Ridge Records and borrowed the money from the Royal Bank in Portree.'

Thus was founded Ridge Records – and £8,000 was borrowed to make what would become *The Highland Connection*, some of it from the Royal Bank, some from friends and family.

For Malcolm Jones everything was happening very quickly indeed. 'There was the leaping for joy on first joining the band, and then there was the recording. The development was so quick. It was obviously a turning point, going again for the Gaelic songs as opposed to a full dance album.'

Rehearsals took place in the lounge of the band's house in Dalkeith, with Calum's drums draped in towels to deaden the noise, and a studio was booked for June. It had a name destined to figure heavily in Runrig's future – Castlesound – and its owner and engineer, Calum Malcolm, would become an integral part of the band's recording team. He was then on tour with the Edinburgh pop band the Headboys, so, taking control completely, Runrig decided to produce the album themselves, with engineer Phil Yule instructing them in the finer points of flanging and slapback EQ. Gone were the summers of fun touring in the isles. The summer of 1979 was essentially one of recording, worrying and sweating. Everyone knew it was make or break.

Recording *The Highland Connection*

CHAPTER FIVE

CONNECTION

The recording of *The Highland Connection* took place partly at Castlesound's Edinburgh premises and partly at the old school in Pencaitland, just outside Edinburgh, later to become Runrig's recording home. The move was made halfway through the recording, causing the by now somewhat hyper band an even greater increase in tension. And if it was a rush to record the album, it was even more of a sprint to bring it out in time for the Stornoway Mod. That against-the-sun cover shot was taken not in the Highlands but on Arthur's Seat in Edinburgh to save time. Indeed, the gathering gloom which hides Calum, Rory, Malcolm and Donnie also hides the appalling tartan jackets they were, for some reason, wearing at the time.

The Mod was the ideal launch pad. Donnie remembers it as 'the first time there had been a real determination to create a successful fringe event', although the band had played the previous year at Oban. It was a success beyond anyone's fantasy – if somewhat controversial.

Runrig had been booked to play two shows a night at the Seaforth Hotel

Mixing *Connection* at the Castlesound studios in Pentcaitland – the first record ever made in the East Lothian village

Publicity shots for *Connection* – overlooking Portree Bay

for four nights in a row. Rory: 'It was a turning point for us after all that had happened. If it hadn't worked then that would have been it – finished.' There was a new excitement in the air that Mod, a stirring in the sleeping language. Donnie: 'We were aware that there was something happening in Gaelic, especially given the Mod fringe. There was a huge buzz about the band.' 'It was as if it had just started to happen, and there was that kind of political arousal too, and we were involved in it. Suddenly there was a very, very conscious attitude towards Gaelic, and towards encouraging new things to grow.'

The *West Highland Free Press*, by this time something of a radical institution, had played its part in that slow burning revival, that reclaiming of Gaelic by the young. Donnie: 'The paper definitely created a new awareness of things that we had really seen before but just not understood. I can't stress enough the difference the paper made to Skye. For the first time you could find out what was really going on through some tremendous investigative journalism. Anyway, we made a very conscious decision that at the Mod we'd do nothing but Gaelic songs, that we'd perform totally new Gaelic music. That was definite.'

So the band took the Seaforth stage, fuelled by all the pent-up tension and frustration of the past six months, with something to prove – and £8,000 of *Highland Connection*-induced debt to get out of. The presence of the young Malcolm Jones, playing then with a precocious ferocity, added to the effect, which was shattering. Suddenly, Runrig were dangerous.

'It was the first time the band really expressed themselves on stage,' says Rory. 'We were really physical on stage for the first time, jumping about, and there was a real cutting edge to it all.' Donnie remembers seeing Brian Wilson leap up to dance – 'the only time I ever saw him be first on to the floor' – and then the roof fell in, metaphorically speaking. It was a splendid controversy, the 'no dancing' tiff, which hit the national newspapers and brought Runrig some welcome national publicity. For Donnie it was 'just silly'.

'It was a situation where I think the proprietors of the Seaforth Hotel were worried about the numbers in the lounge, all laid out specifically for

Let's get physical: Mod Fringe, Stornoway

'drinking. It has to be said that was for maximising their profits, and the fact that people would actually get up to dance was perceived as in some way limiting the capacity to sort of stand and drink at the same time. So whether it was that or some safety aspect that escaped us, they had this silly ruling that nobody could dance.'

Instructed by the Seaforth management to tell the audience that dancing was not permitted, Runrig did not react positively. Douglas Lowe of the *Glasgow Herald* described the scene. 'It was like a red rag to a bull, turning the mods into rockers. The next evening a space was cleared for dancing.'

This was Runrig's first major triumph, and the album appeared on a wave crest of mild controversy. What could be better? Douglas Lowe anchored his review of *The Highland Connection* on his news story about the riotous goings on in Stornoway. 'Runrig, who were victors in the "no dancing" row at the National Mod, have released their second album . . . quite apart from the high standard of the numbers, it is a fascinating tribute to the band's concept of musical evolution in Gaeldom. Indeed, revolution might be a better way of describing it.'

Simon Jones, later to champion the band with *Folk Roots*, was then writing for the tiny *Southern Rag* magazine. 'Their music puts Gaelic society in your front room,' he wrote. 'Pure heaven – they'd set Cambridge alight.' Al Clark in *The Scotsman* picked out *Fichead Bliadhna*'s comment on the poverty of most young Gaels' education in their own history, but found the inclusion of *Loch Lomond* puzzling. 'Could this be designed to catch the tourist's eye?'

The Irish *Southern Star* drew pertinent comparisons with both Moving Hearts and Horslips, while Stewart Ross in the Aberdeen *Evening Express* was reminded of 'early Thin Lizzy before they lost sight of their folk origins' and Alain Stivell.

As one might have expected, the *Free Press* went to town, Aonghas Macneacail terming *Fichead Bliadhna* 'best track of all – I'd almost say song of the century'. 'Runrig's new album well and truly connects young Gaeldom with the mainstream of contemporary music,' he wrote. 'The idiom is modern, the beat is black, but melodic lines and themes remain true to the band's melodic roots.' *Loch Lomond* had been 'released from MacKellaritis'.

Aonghas welcomed the inclusion of three songs in English, although he felt the Gaelic material was by far the strongest. Waxing lyrical about the bitter *Fichead Bliadhna*, he said the song should 'challenge young Gaels to question the education they are receiving. It should also be a challenge to those who have no Gaelic to learn enough to discover what Runrig are singing about. For they also, if they live in the Highlands, are victims of deprivation.' Having said all that, amongst the influences he identified on the band were 'Simon and Garfunkel, Incredible String Band and the Everley Brothers'.

Today, *Highland Connection* stands up well. The band's own production is light years ahead of the Black Gold-produced sound on *Play Gaelic*, and

no one could have any doubts: describing *Play Gaelic* as rock seems ridiculous nowadays. *Highland Connection* is as raunchy as John Lydon's sneer. It's a record with attitude.

The traditional *Gamhna Gealla* kicks things off in a welter of distorted guitar, courtesy of the band's new young blood. Malcolm is omnipresent on *Connection*, sometimes making up in digital dexterity for a youthful lack of restraint. But then, this is not a restrained album. Very Steeleye Span meets Gary Moore, *Gamhna Gealla* is a shock to the system after *Play Gaelic*'s timidity. Calum and Rory's *Mairi* which follows, couples a typically singable Runrig melody with emotive, romantic lyrics, and then Malcolm lets loose with the fast and furious *What Time?*, a frenzied excursion into neo-traditional guitar pyrotechnics. It's still impressive, if showy compared with the exacting subtlety the Runrig guitarist strives for these days. The title stems from the band's encounter with a hard-of-hearing gentleman on Barra, who, when asked any question would shout in reply, 'What time? What time?'

Fichead Bliadhna is the most significant song on the LP, perhaps a little too consciously so. It has a great melody and Rory's lead vocal, harder and bleaker than Donnie's more dulcet tones, suits the unforgiving lyrics well. Even in English, the words carry tremendous weight.

From the 'Highland Rock Is Here' poster – the band at Quiraing, Skye

Shadows lookalikes at Quiraing

FICHEAD BLIADHNA (*Twenty Years*)

(Translation)
Freedom of the moor
Freedom of the hill
And then to school
At the end of a summer
Children, five years of age
Without many words of English

Here is your book
Here is your pen
Study hard
That's what they told me
And you will rise up in the world
You will achieve

I learnt many things
The English language
The poetry of England
The music of Germany
The history of Spain
And even that was a misleading history

Then on to further education
Following education, more education
Like puppets
On the end of a string
Our heads filled with a sort of learning
And I did rise in the world
I found my suit
I found my shirt
I found a place in the eyes of men
Well away from the freedom of the moor

But why did they keep
Our history from us?
I'll tell you they are frightened
In case the children of Gaeldom awaken
With searching
And penetrating questions
Twenty years for the truth
I had to wait
I had to search
Twenty years of deceit
They denied me knowledge of myself

(© *C. & R. Macdonald, Storr Music, 1979*)

Musically, the acoustic backing, interspersed with intrusively complex Jones guitar licks, doesn't quite match the epic put-down of the lyrics, a kind of Gaelic *Another Brick in the Wall*. However, the song is followed by Malcolm's finest moment on the LP, the astonishing *Na Luing Air Seoladh*. Here the slow, stately, multi-tracked guitars assume an enormous melancholy and scale, and give the clearest signs of the influence Malcolm's piping had on his guitar style.

Loch Lomond sounds weak compared with the two later versions committed to vinyl – the Chris Harley-produced single of 1983 and the tour de force on *Once in a Lifetime* – and there are some ill-advised touches like the bizarre hand-claps in the outro. However, *Na H-Uain A's t-Earrach*, my own favourite from the LP, opens side two with a juddering, syncopated rhythm, Malcolm's guitar stuttering and growling away. This is very Fairport/Steeleye Span, full of urgency and with a touch of post-Dr Feelgood punkiness about it. It celebrates the joys of youth but, unlike the 'hope I die before I get old' sentiments of the *My Generation*-for-Gaels it tends towards, a cautious nod to the need for responsibility is included.

Foghar Nan Eilean deals ironically with the end of the island summer when the tourists leave. Despite its aggression, *Connection* is an 'end of the summer' record, very much about breaking free of irresponsible youth into self-realisation and awareness of culture, though fun is not forgotten. On *The Twenty-Five Pounder* Malcolm lets loose a cannonade of over-the-top guitar, bagpipe, goose, drum and tambourine, to enjoyably loopy effect.

Going Home, the oldest song on the album by far, works all the better for its contrast with the harsh sentiments expressed elsewhere. It's a classic song, simple and unashamedly sentimental, and the deliberate lyrical clash with *Morning Tide*, about sailing away with 'a burning heart that keeps tearing me away', is reinforced by that song's odd pure pop bounciness.

The album closes with *Cearcal a Chuain*, and the acceptance of natural processes of change presages 1991's epic *The Big Wheel*. Change is what *Connection* is all about: changed attitudes to the past, to culture, to roots. It's the rawest, the most restless of all Runrig's albums, and it touched a nerve among young Gaels. It still rings with emotion and urgency today.

Prince Charles Edward Stuart liked it too, and offered to manage the group – or at least become involved as promoter. It all started with a telephone call from England. The mysterious and then anonymous caller said he had to meet Runrig, as he had important proposals to make to them. He was met at Waverley station by Donnie and Rory, who took the ordinary-looking young man for a meal. But who was he? A record company scout? An agent? He revealed nothing, other than making cryptic remarks about 'things not being what they seem'. Eventually, asked to reveal his identity, he told a story about Bonnie Prince Charlie's flight from Culloden and a supposed illegitimate Stuart child, and Donnie twigged. 'You're a descendant of that child!' No. Then after much cryptic banter the staggering truth unfolded. 'You *are* Bonnie Prince Charlie!' Yes, came the reply. 'We'd been expecting Harvey Goldsmith,' says Donnie, 'and we got Bonnie Prince Charlie!'

The Prince wanted to utilise Runrig's new-found power and fame to generate support for his cause. His plan was to appear on every Runrig poster, and at every gig, sweeping silently and mysteriously on stage. He had been to the islands, he claimed, finding his journey marked by white silk handkerchiefs hanging on washing lines . . .

He was put up for the night at the band's flat in Dalkeith and sent home the next day, but not before an unsuspecting Calum had been introduced to Charles Edward Stuart and numerous jokes made about 'a boat with four trustworthy men waiting to row you to the bus station in the morning'. The Prince, needless to say, has never returned.

More recently run by Calum, in earlier days Ridge Records involved every-one. It was Donnie who initially set up the distribution network to retail shops, and for his sins retained responsibility for keeping the VAT office happy. Ridge was a wing-and-a-prayer organisation in the grand tradition of independent record companies. 'We were doing everything ourselves,' Donnie says. 'When *The Highland Connection* came out there was this really strange network of people, it was like cells scattered throughout Scotland. They were basically friends all over who would go down to their local record shops and make sure they were stocked up. It was a totally inefficient system, but it served a purpose at the time. We distributed the records ourselves, parcelled them, posted them, took orders, all that kind of thing.'

A year from release, the money borrowed to make *Connection* had been paid back. But by then, Runrig had achieved their biggest ever success and, rumour had it, almost broken up. It was an odd time.

Their popularity and professionalism had been growing steadily. On 16 November 1979 the band had hired a PA rig for the first time in their career, a 1kW affair from Les Honeyman Soundhire in Perth who had been recommended by an Aberdeen music-shop owner who couldn't herself provide a PA at that time. Her name was Marlene Ross. 'They phoned the shop and we didn't have enough equipment to sort them out, so I put them on to Les and Ivor Johnston.' That was the future Runrig manager's first contact with the band which was to take over her life.

Ivor Johnston remembers the gig. 'It was in a horrific gymnasium-type place – but you could realise their potential right away. They had that ability to get across to people.' Donnie remembers finding Les Honeyman, sound engineer, asleep on a bench at the back of the hall, amid humorous suggestions that he'd been there since the third number of the set. At the next concert Ivor and Les did the now legendary Eden Court Theatre night at Inverness with the band, and potential started to move towards fruition. 'It was after the Stornoway Mod,' Rory says, 'and after all that fantastic success we decided to go for Inverness where we'd never really played before. It was a big step for us.' According to Iain MacDonald, 'This was *the* big gamble. It was at their own initiative and their own risk, and Eden Court held something like 900 people at that time.'

Perhaps it was the influence of punk's go-for-it mentality seeping through, but Eden Court was another example of the band's hell-bent make-or-break philosophy at the time. 'If you talked to them then, there was a degree of swithering about whether they were still going to keep plugging away,' says Iain, 'whether or not they could make some break-through that would basically justify the kind of expense there was going to be, touring a band of that size. There were some very sweaty palms and maybe a few trouser changes because they frankly didn't know if they would get bums on the seats for that night.'

It had all been Donnie's idea. 'I said, "Let's give it a try", because I'd lived in Inverness and we'd never done a sit-down theatre venue before. So we phoned Eden Court and they weren't interested in putting us on, so we had to hire the place ourselves. It was a huge outlay for us at the time – they certainly safeguarded their own financial situation – because of the level of production, support acts, PA, lights and the like.'

With everything once again on the line, every stop was pulled out. A support line-up was booked which included Christine Primrose, the Wallochmor Ceilidh Band, and compère Aonghas Macneacail. Blair was invited back for a solo spot, and fly-posting was employed to such an extent by the band members that, says Calum, 'we got into trouble with the council and had to take them down again'.

Eden Court's management, dubious as to the pulling power of this unknown bunch of Gaels, got an embarrassing shock. 'Tickets just began flying out the door,' remembers Donnie. 'It sold out very rapidly indeed, and the theatre management started coming back and offering us deals, suggesting we might come back and do one for them.'

The gig itself was a storming success, packed as the theatre was. Jim Love, now assistant editor on the *Inverness Courier*, was then writing for the *Press and Journal* and inadvertently came up with a Highland equivalent of John Landau's 'Rock 'n' roll future' quote about the young Bruce Springsteen.

Headlined ' "Beatlemania" for Run Rig', the *P & J* review identified 'the two most stimulating developments in Gaelic recently' as the TV programme *Can Seo* and Runrig: 'It was Beatlemania, Celtic style when the Skye rock group made their debut at Eden Court, Inverness, on Friday night. Young Gaels clearly identify with the band and everyone in the capacity audience must have felt the same sense of pride and achievement as the fans of three other successful local groups – Sunshine, Colorado and The Tools.' Despite such, with hindsight, invidious comparisons, Jim recognised Runrig's uniqueness: 'Fine though these outfits are, Run Rig stand alone as the most original band working on the Highland popular music scene.'

Almost immediately, there surfaced an are-our-boys-getting-too-big-for-their-boots response from Skye, in the form of a good-humoured, tongue-in-cheek caption in the following week's *West Highland Free Press*: ' "Beatlemania for Run Rig" ran the headline in one newspaper the morning after the Skye band's late-night concert at Eden Court last week. For

Rory, 1980

those of our readers too young to remember, the symptoms of Beatlemania included a form of hysteria induced by a brand of music which appeared to have an immediate relevance to the audience of the time. We're not sure about the hysteria, but Runrig's brand of rock music clearly appeals to many young (and not so young) Gaels.'

A comment from Rory that hopes of doing more such gigs certainly did not mean the end of village-hall appearances ('they're great fun too') inspired a wonderful Chris Tyler cartoon which today, given the fleet of trucks which accompanies the average Runrig tour, seems doubly ironic.

'I'm sure they would identify that concert as a milestone,' says Iain MacDonald, and indeed they do. Donnie: 'It was extremely significant. It's all a sort of confidence boost if you like, but there are a lot of things along the journey. It's like you reach a situation where there's a wee rise, and you stand on it and look ahead and it just gives you that extra vision to go a wee bit further. It's been like that all the way along the line – the little things have spurred us on.'

'This was the beginning, the early years of the Gaelic renaissance,' says Martin Macdonald. 'Suddenly, there was this huge impact Runrig had on Gaelic-speaking kids, a sort of validation of their own language. Suddenly there were representatives of their own people "up there".'

It was a great way to end a decade, but as the '80s dawned, Runrig were not in the best of fettle. Money was tighter than ever, with Donnie and his wife Teresa's first child on the way, so, Donnie says, 'we decided to sort of stand back a wee bit and look at things, to go back into other employment and carry on working part-time with a view to recording the next album.'

Only Malcolm continued to practise full-time when the band was off the road. The continual lack of money affected everybody, with Rory 'on nothing but liver and turnip for six months'. According to Malcolm, 'There was a lot of risk-taking at that time, doing our own concert promotions in the cities and trying to keep the band afloat on a part-time basis. Inevitably, the aims of the band became less focused, but despite the financial situation I don't think we ever said, "Right, in two months' time we're going to pack it in".' Despite rumours to that effect running up and down the West Coast like wildfire.

The gigs in the Highlands continued, sometimes with disastrous or near-disastrous consequences. 'We had done a date in Fort William,' Calum remembers, 'and afterwards some of us travelled back to Edinburgh. We arrived at 4.30 a.m., with Rory driving. He dropped everyone off and rushed home to his bed – but he forgot he was driving a high-sided Luton van. So he took a short-cut home, went under a low railway bridge and ripped the top of the van off like a tin of sardines.' On another occasion, the band were coming into Lochearnhead. 'There was a big hill,' Calum recalls, 'with a cliff-face on one side, and a huge drop on the other. We hit black ice and the van was all over the road for 100 yards. I had to decide whether to crash into the rocks or over the drop. I chose the rocks. It was a very lucky escape.'

But perhaps this period is best symbolised by a concert in Kintail which sticks in Ivor Johnston's memory. 'This was when they were still encoring with *Statesboro' Blues*. The whole PA rig went down in the middle of a set, and we were madly checking wires and fuses when someone shouted "Has anybody got a 50 pence piece?" And that's what it was – we had to sit and feed the meter in the hall all night.' Ivor also had a famous encounter with Donnie's mother in Skye, when the PA system went dead during a support spot by Blair Douglas. Running backstage, breathing fire and brimstone, Ivor discovered Donnie's mum had unplugged the PA so she could make tea for everyone.

Playing cost money, and the money just wasn't coming in fast enough. However, self-promoted nights were organised in Glasgow and Edinburgh, and the 'Celtic Rock Nights' sold out, just as the Inverness event had. The problem was that one concert of that type could only be played in each big city every few months.

'The first of our own promotions outside the Highlands was at the Astoria Ballroom in Edinburgh,' says Calum. 'We couldn't believe how many people turned up – and that was another major turning point.'

'We had a few bizarre situations with those,' Rory remembers, 'like taking on the management of Tiffany's in Glasgow. We were promoting everything ourselves, remember, and we discovered the bouncers were holding back tickets, reselling them to the punters outside and pocketing the money.' On being informed by a friend of the band that this scam was being practised, an irate Rory tackled the more than intimidating bouncers

– though he admits it was rage rather than courage which enabled him to do it. 'Five minutes before we were due on stage I said, "Excuse me," to this enormous guy, "I believe you are reselling our tickets!" "Say that again, pal, and I'll break every bone in your body," he replied. We went into the manager's office and he sacked those responsible on the spot. But as soon as we were out of the way they were back on the door.'

The revolving stage at Tiffany's in Glasgow also provided a hilarious episode during a benefit gig for An Commun Gaidhealach. Due to the actions of what dark mutterings from Donnie indicate was an overly refreshed accordionist in another band, the lever operating the revolving stage sent Runrig spinning into the audience's view and then off again – twice – playing all the while. And in Glasgow, fly-posting could be a dangerous business. A hasty retreat had to be beaten from Bridgeton when exception was taken by some Rangers supporters to the phrase 'Celtic Rock Night' on a poster. Somehow, though, everyone did survive such events without requiring hospitalisation.

Despite it all, the determination was there to keep on going and to produce another LP, so from the spring onwards Calum and Rory began writing the pool of songs which would eventually be sifted through for *Recovery*. As the gigs continued in fits and starts, Calum began to recognise his own limitations. 'I knew within myself I wasn't a drummer, not really. If the band was going to progress, then it needed a better hand than me.' So, towards the end of 1980, a year of stock-taking, trying to earn money to pay bills and care for babies, rents and overdrafts, they took another gamble. A young, brash, very talented and somewhat abrasive drummer was recruited from folk-rock band New Celeste . . . but to a band that was not full-time.

Iain had not, to say the least, been a Runrig fan. In November 1980, when he phoned Malcolm and said, 'I hear you're looking for a drummer', Iain Bayne was 20 going on 21, and had been playing the drums for over a decade. 'When I was nine I used to just sit and watch all these older guys playing in the pipe band in St Andrews where I was born and brought up, thinking "I'll never be able to do that".' But at 13, exposure to pop music convinced him that his future lay in music, and a year later he was playing drums for a professional theatre company at the Byre Theatre – 'the first time I'd ever played a drum kit in my life'. So he and Calum had one thing in common – they both played drum kits for the first time in their first appearances before an audience. Calum had not, it must be said, also won the Scottish Junior Snare Drumming Championship in his youth.

Nagging his mother into buying him an old Carlton drum kit ('£65, and it's still here today'), a series of teenage bands with names like 'Nebulous' took Iain towards the cash-only world of cabaret and Scottish dance music. 'Before I left school I was playing with this accordionist called Billy Anderson, who was quite well known within the Scottish music scene, and I'd been down to London and all over the country doing cabaret. I left school in 1977 and went straight into that.'

Margaret Macleod from Na-h-Oganaich, who had already played a significant part in the Runrig story, became an employer, so Gaelic began to make its own musical impact on Iain. As did Shetland dialect, during an eventful seven-month engagement in a duo with Alan Clarke on the Aberdeen to Lerwick ferry *St Clair*. The 14-hour crossing between Scotland and Shetland features a band or duo every night during the spring and summer. 'That was six nights a week for 30 weeks,' groans Iain. 'I reckoned if I could do that I could do any job. It really did your head in, like some of those demented oil workers who couldn't come down on the plane because the weather was bad. Some nights on that boat it was blowing so bad we shouldn't have been out on a pond, let alone the North Sea.'

Taking three days off from the sea-sickness, the 18-year-old drummer recorded 14 songs for an album by Margaret Macleod, before returning to work live with her. 'That took me up to 1980, and then in January of that year I joined New Celeste.'

New Celeste were at this stage a veteran folk-rock band with ambition and a large European following. A previous incarnation had produced one of the finest folk-rock albums ever made by a Scottish band, the never-released-in-Britain *On the Line*. That had featured a young Graeme Duffin – more recently the fairly famous 'unofficial fifth member of Wet Wet Wet' – who had been replaced by Nigel Clark – more recently the fairly famous guitar player with Hue and Cry.

'It was through Nigel I joined New Celeste, who at that stage were doing festivals in Europe.' Nigel had played with Iain in Margaret Macleod's band, so they knew each other well. New Celeste had always flirted with jazz-fusion musicians like Messrs Duffin and Clark, so Iain's complex style fitted in well. For a time. 'We did two three-month tours in that one year, plus a couple of six-week tours at the end of it. It was so intense we wanted to kill each other afterwards, and that was November 1980.'

But Iain didn't like Runrig, or so he had insisted on telling, at length, in depth and in explicit detail, two girls called Sylvia and Debbie the previous year. Both were mad keen Runrig fans, and Debbie just happened to be Rory's girlfriend, now wife.

'I'd played a show with Runrig in 1979 in Glasgow with Margaret Macleod, and I saw them somewhere else as well. I wasn't too enamoured with what I heard, or with what I saw anyway. I was at this party and I just started to slag Runrig something terrible, and Sylvia, who was one of their most avid fans, was shouting me down and calling me everything under the sun. Debbie was trying to be diplomatic, and I was arguing every point and being totally rude.'

Never one to let such a minor fracas bother him, Iain, out of a job, quite happily swallowed his artistic pride and phoned Malcolm to see about an audition. He was in France, fulfilling a last New Celeste date, when he phoned again to be told he was the new Runrig drummer.

'I finished with New Celeste, and I had six days to learn 19 songs with Runrig for a gig at Tiffany's in Glasgow. I think they just felt they needed somebody with a wee bit more technical ability than Calum – as good a feel as he's undoubtedly got. They needed to progress, to get new ideas

Iain Bayne

The young, innocent Iain Bayne. He was auditioned along with the now legendary Mr Boom, Andy Munro

and new drive behind them.'

Calum admits that 'At first I just thought, "Oh no",' and Iain remembers 'it being a bit strange. I took over Calum's role completely and he was left to shake the odd tambourine, and the rest of the time just sit at the side of the stage. That really felt like a waste of someone's musical input. So that's when we started building up a new percussion section and getting him far more involved with that.'

Iain was quickly absorbed into the family of Runrig, despite receiving a very poor reference indeed when Debbie recognised him. 'You're not getting him,' she told Rory. 'He's that horrible guy who was slagging you off!' But Iain found them 'very very friendly. When I'd met them before they had seemed very stand-offish, which I don't think was intentional. They probably just thought I was chancing my arm a bit. But when I joined they were very friendly, no airs and graces at all.'

And in due course he underwent something of an artistic conversion. 'As far as the music was concerned I felt there was a lot of power in it and I saw then the real potential that the band had. I suddenly realised that the band was going to develop into something. It was totally different to anything I'd ever played, so simple and straightforward. It was no major challenge in a technical sense, but the challenge came in expressing it in the way they wanted. My style of drumming was completely wrong, and it was a case of re-educating myself into their style. Ninety-nine per cent of what I was doing at first was wrong – far too busy.'

'Initially there was a bit of a mish-mash of styles,' says Calum. 'Iain was very busy and flashy, and he had to fit in with the style of the band.'

What Iain did not find it easy to fit in with, however, was the style of a part-time outfit. 'It was like that for two years, and there I was waiting for them to make the decision to go full-time, and pushing for it. I had been on these European tours as a full-time musician since I'd left school, so for me sitting around idle and doing nothing . . . I was getting really itchy feet. I couldn't understand it.'

There was a great deal of rehearsing for *Recovery* in the early part of 1981, in an attempt to integrate Iain's style fully. Finding the money for a third album, the second with Ridge, proved a problem.

'We were desperate,' Rory admits. 'We needed £15,000 this time, and then this guy called John Mayer offered to come in with us on a 50-50 basis. He owned a record shop called Phoenix Records in Edinburgh. We were very stupid because for providing his 50 per cent, he was to get 50 per cent of all the profits. What actually happened was that he didn't have to put his hand in his pocket at all because *Recovery* made its money back immediately, and from then on he got half the profits.' He shakes his head in despair at one of the classic Runrig business blunders. 'We bought him out a few years ago. You might say we were very naive, but we were desperate, and when someone says, "There's half the money, lads, but I want half the profits," you say, "OK".'

The recording was to take place at Castlesound in Pencaitland, with Calum Malcolm engineering, and a producer who seems, in retrospect, more than a little odd. The Blue Nile had still to produce their stunning debut single *I Love This Life*, and one Robert Bell was at a loose end.

'Robert didn't really like the music, and just took a back seat,' says Rory. 'He was basically there to look after John Mayer's interests, and jumped to his feet every time John came in the control-room. We got on fine with him – it was just that he didn't do much.'

The indisputably cool Robert Bell, now hailed as a member of one of the world's most sophisticated modern bands, experienced severe culture shock, according to Donnie. 'It was really funny, because the Blue Nile are seen as such a classy band, so enigmatic. But thinking back, the first time we met Robert Bell we were rehearsing in an old potato shed in East Lothian which had been used at some point as a stable, and only the bottom half of the door opened. It was just terrible, a stinking place. The first night Robert came to meet us, we were playing away, and he had to crawl in underneath this old stable door and fight through this old carpet we'd hung up to keep the drafts out.'

Recovery was another gamble – although it was not to prove as big a one as had been anticipated – and a far-sighted bank manager might have saved the band from the financially ruinous deal with John Mayer. 'It was a hard time,' Donnie remembers. 'I was teaching at Leith Academy and when I finished at 4 p.m., I was coming out to the studio to continue the music; we did all-night sessions sometimes. It was hard on a personal level because by the end of 1980 we'd had our first baby, and I didn't have a lot of time . . . it wasn't a satisfactory situation. But we all decided that we had to do it again, if we were to be really serious about it. In spite of the commitments of paying rents, supporting families, we would have to try.'

CHAPTER SIX

RECOVERIES AND RELAPSES

The dream of the Runrig which might yet be, continued to haunt Rory and Calum in particular. The audience was still growing in both quantity and fervour, and rather than try to extract the last penny's profit from live shows, money real and projected was ploughed into the creation of a bigger, better band.

The commitment to a full sound and lighting team, not to mention support bands and discos, made previously profitable tours in the islands increasingly marginal in financial terms. In an interview with Brian Wilson for the *Free Press*, Rory pointed out that the expenses alone for a Stornoway gig were £900, 'and though we had a 300 crowd at Dornie, which was very good, we didn't make a penny out of it'. On the other hand, bigger events in 1980, such as the 'Celtic Rock Nights', had led to a major Astoria Ballroom appearance during the Edinburgh Festival Fringe. All this had whetted their appetite for more, but ambition was one thing. Achieving such status on a regular basis was another.

They were in a very strange position. They had a large and vociferous cult following, but no major record company backing to underwrite tours. The received knowledge was that major bands did not make money touring, but were subsidised by the profits from selling records in the places they played. Runrig were trying to tour profitably, yet put on shows equivalent in scale to major-league rock attractions.

Marriages, births and personal poverty were going hand in hand with a constant growth in the scale of risks taken, hopeful investments in the future like Iain Bayne, making records, big production shows. The demand was there, they felt, for their music, but they couldn't afford to fill it in the way they wanted to, and no major record company wanted a 'teuchter rock band'.

'Inevitably that has fuelled production at the West Highland and Island Rumour Factory,' wrote Brian Wilson. ' "They say they're breaking up." But the good news, *direach a beul an eich* (from the horse's mouth), is that there is no likelihood of this happening.'

So loins were duly girded up, breaths sharply taken in and, for the summer islands tours coinciding with the release of *Recovery*, a keyboard player was sought.

'I'd never heard of them,' says Richard Cherns, the self-confessed 'first English Jew of Russian extraction ever to play in a Gaelic rock band'. 'It's only a band like Runrig who could advertise for a keyboard player in the Edinburgh *Evening News*. They wanted a folk-rock keyboard player, I had

At the Skye Folk Festival, with Iain Bayne on drums and, invisible, Richard Cherns on keyboards, 1981

a history of playing in both folk and rock bands, so I thought, well, I can do this.'

Asked to audition, Richard feverishly tried to collect the Runrig record output. Obtaining a pre-release copy of *Recovery* immediately impressed the former Finn MacCuill and Medium Wave Band member. 'As soon as I played it I thought it was one of the finest records I'd heard. In fact, some of the tracks – *'Ic Iain 'Ic Sheumais* and *The Old Boys* – were very moving and I was very keen to join the band. There are sounds on *Recovery* I don't think they've capitalised on fully, even yet. Anyway, they seemed keen on having me.'

August 1981 saw Richard in Portree, an Englishman in the Gaidhealtacht, rehearsing synthesiser harmonies with Malcolm's pipes – 'we never did that again' – and trying to sing harmony vocals in a Highland accent. And there were also a few problems of integration, some clearly fuelled by Richard's tendency to smoke a cigar on stage while wearing a plastic fluorescent stars-and-stripes jacket and a baseball cap – 'I don't remember being greatly encouraged in this. Indeed, I believe there were mutterings and I quietened down very quickly.'

From working part-time with Theatre Alba, Richard graduated to payment by the concert with Runrig, doing better out of it than anyone else, he believes. 'I was getting £70 a night in 1981, on average two nights a week. This was wealth beyond my dreams. That lasted for four months, and then one day in the van Rory chimed up with, "Haven't you told him yet?" and back came the answer, "No." I was asking what was going on and Rory and Calum were just saying, "You say it." "No, you say it." "No, you, on you go." "Ach, let's forget about it." So eventually I turned round and said, "What are you talking about?" And Calum gave a wry smile and said, "Congratulations on your new appointment – you're now a member of the band." That meant I was immediately reduced to £80 a week from £140. From that day on we never got a rise. Despite the amount of money coming in, the overheads were so colossal that we couldn't change this pattern of expenditure through all the time I was in the band. It really was a very hard time for everyone.'

But the band were now a potent force live, reaching for the big music that Calum and Rory had perhaps always heard internally when writing the songs. Richard's first show was at the Skye Folk Festival, and Runrig were to play more and more folk festival dates both in Britain and abroad over the coming years. Live, their performance was anything but woolly-jumperish. On record, however, *Recovery* seemed restrained, more acoustic and traditional than the ferocious *Highland Connection*. Few doubted that it was the band's best effort to date – but were they showing signs of growing up?

Jim Wilkie had remained in close touch, but even in 1980 had been unimpressed by the live shows. 'The response they got was amazing, the phenomenon was really beginning to pick up, but musically I still didn't think much was happening – although the public obviously did. It was *Recovery* that really did it for me. I well remember being at a party with

The new line-up recording for the BBC programme *Aibisidh*

a guy in Stornoway and he was singing 'Ic Iain 'Ic Sheumais all the time, and it was like a bolt from the blue to me. I thought, "This is what the whole Gaelic thing is about. This is the essential appeal." They were really getting to Gaels through popular music and that was the first time I saw its real importance.'

The album sold like the proverbial hot doughnuts, causing immense frustration to the band, who saw half their profits disappearing towards the oddly named Shaughnessy El Fakir Perkins Le Fevre Goldberg and Co. Ltd (trading as John Mayer [I Saw It First] Productions). Not only did John Mayer have half the UK profits from Recovery, he also negotiated exclusive foreign licensing rights for The Highland Connection, and 25 per cent of all foreign royalties. As Alistair Moffat, programme controller with Scottish Television and master of the one-liner, was to say to Rory a decade later about a different negotiation: 'You'll be driving that old Saab of yours forever if you keep offering deals like this.' The band bought out Mr Mayer's interests in their products eventually, but Runrig's business naivety, harnessed as it was to a fierce ambition, was to cost them even more dearly, long before they became the Saab-driving supergroup which was to produce Scottish TV's City of Lights.

Meanwhile, Aonghas Macneacail had switched to the Oban Times for his typically detailed – and less breathlessly vivid than of yore – assessment of the band's third LP. 'There are many fine images and turns of phrase which transform Calum Macdonald's words into something more than simple song lyrics,' he wrote. 'They are poems, and convey the ambiguities and truths that only poetry can convey. Take the final chorus of the final song Dust, which could be described as a presbyterian negro spiritual.' The title track he found 'perplexing at first', as the tempo was slow, 'the mood tentative'. But listening further, 'the chorus ends with the words, "here I am, recovering" – still a bit unsteady on the feet.

'Recovery is the theme and mood of the album as a whole. Recovery for Gaeldom, our music and traditions. Runrig themselves are in no need of "recovery". Musically they are in the bloom of health, able to look back and out with a clear and steady eye.'

At the other end of the UK, Simon Jones of Folk Roots was still pleading for someone to bring Runrig to England. While 'not having the out and out power' of Highland Connection, Recovery 'is far more subtle, perfectly arranged and an overall improvement. Most of the lyrics are in Gaelic, but grab it anyway . . . if Stivell represents the thoughts of Bretons, then Runrig must speak for the Scots Gaels.'

Today, Recovery remains the most listenable of the first three albums, courtesy of a warm, ear-friendly production which may or may not have anything to do with Robert Bell, but certainly owes a great deal to Calum Malcolm's mastery in his Castlesound studio. An Toll Dubh, however, which opens the LP in all its waulking-song-derived mixture of regret and defiant hope for the future of Gaelic, is deliberately rough and as tra-ditional-sounding as any finger-in-the-ear merchant could wish. (Runrig members, incidentally, always favoured the much cooler cupped-hand-over-the-ear method of hearing what they were trying to sing in the midst of howling on-stage feedback, although this has been largely abandoned in the face of improved monitor technology.)

Rubh Nan Cudaigean displays the new technical assurance of the band, with classy drumming and Malcolm's guitar beginning to establish the unique style which was to become such a Runrig hallmark. Gone is the nasty gritty fuzzbox sound. Instead, a valve-driven warmth is obvious. *'Ic Iain 'Ic Sheumais* is outstanding, the first of several songs dealing with war and its implications. But the traditional tale of Donald MacIain and his dreadful wounding at the Battle of Carnish is furnished with superb organ from the temporarily returned Blair Douglas, and a truly great solo from Malcolm, combining extravagance with discipline.

Rory sings lead on three and a bit of *Recovery*'s songs, and the sound of both his voice and Donnie's is massively improved over the previous two LPs. Rory's treatment of *Recovery* itself, backed by his own playing on accordion and guitar, plus Ronnie Gerrard from New Celeste on fiddle, is stunning. The lyric, too, is an emotionally draining masterpiece, based as it is on the unrest on 1880s' Skye over land tenure surrounding John MacPherson, the Glendale Martyr, the Battle of the Braes, the rent strikes and civil disobedience, which led in 1884 to the sending of a gunboat to the island by a fretful government. Two years later the Napier Commission's report led to the Crofting Act, and a genuine victory had been won.

Moody in woolly jumpers: the band in 1982

'It would be as easy to stop the Atlantic Ocean as to stop the present agitation until justice has been done to the people,' said John MacPherson in 1884, quoted on the sleeve of *Recovery*. But Calum's lyrics are not a simple history lesson. The chorus relates not just to the Victorian crofter but to the 1980s' Gael. As the men of Braes and Glendale saw hope of recovering their land, so the Gaels of 1981 saw the beginnings of their own recovery of language, culture and heritage – even if, as Aonghas Macneacail wrote in the *Oban Times*, they were 'still a bit unsteady on the feet'.

Meanwhile, Malcolm Jones's *Instrumental* almost has the ring of high quality TV theme music, while the traditional urgency of *'S Tu Mo Leannan/Nightfall on Marsco* lacks the integration later to be displayed in the *Once in a Lifetime* version. Malcolm's excellent *Breaking the Chains* segues into the album's lament for the exploitation of the Highland footsoldier, *Fuaim A Bhlair*, a polyrhythmic showcase for Iain's percussive skills which again is a little too ambitious in structure for its own good. Still, the instrumental coda is immensely powerful.

Then it's the political protest against militarism *Tir An Airm*, a great song of splenetic anger which still manages to use some beautiful poetic imagery and effective shifts in historical perspective. Resonance is the order of the day.

TIR AN AIRM (*Land of the Army*)

(Translation)
Come along with me, my young lover
To the peaceful, happy land
And you will see the sight of soldiers
Running through the beautiful, wild moorland flowers

And you can look out on peaceful mornings
To see the dark evil birds
Ploughing the skies above us
Making for Stornoway at high speed

Now read your history, open your eyes
To every generation and to the ways of the military
Stamping on the seed of the corn
The young lives of the Uist boys

But I cannot go 'for the king'
I cannot fight any more
The deceit of London, the treachery of Great Britain
I can only fight for the preservation of these islands

Horo horain O
Welcome to the Land of the Army
Horo horain O

(© *C. Macdonald, Storr Music, 1981*)

The lyric shows Calum's poetic gifts beginning to flower fully, with the rooting of modern political issues such as the lengthening of the Stornoway airport runway to accommodate NATO bombers and the huge military presence at Benbecula with the 'ways of the military' down through history. Opening one's eyes to history enables present-day political issues to be seen in a more realistic light, he argues.

The Old Boys, a tribute to champion of Gaelic, Colonel Jock Macdonald, looks back to the World War Two engagement at St Valery in France, and the passing of 'the old boys', the heroes of yesteryear. It falters slightly in its lyrical sentimentality, but any weakness is immediately forgotten as the amazing closing track takes a grip on the listener.

Dust is a visionary song, applying the Old Testament image of the scattering of the Children of Israel to the Gaels, and carrying all the awesome weight of a scriptural prophecy. The hypnotic, psalm-like tune adds to the effect, as do Rory's keening-off-the-Cuillins vocals, joining both Donnie and Calum on the track.

On the whole, while *Recovery* features songs of tremendous power and sees a huge advance in Calum's lyric writing, it is not the edgy rock-folk onslaught that *Connection* was. It is reflective, measured, even mature, seeing a delving into traditional music and Gaelic history applied much more creatively to the issues of the 1980s than Runrig has previously achieved. A quiet step forward.

Eden Court Theatre brought a victorious end to 1981 in a sell-out concert featuring Binn Cheol and Dick Gaughan. There were a few queries about

Piped music at
Tiffany's,
Glasgow

the new line-up and overbearing sound in the press, but even the staid *Inverness Courier* was swept away with enthusiasm. 'If even 60 per cent of the audience knew what they were singing about, then An Commun should have few worries about the future of Gaelic.' Both the *Courier* and the *Highland News* reviewers complained about the volume. 'Unfortunately or otherwise,' said the *News*, 'quite a few fans of the group left early due to the discomfort of their eardrums . . . "But how else can a rock band function!" comes the cry of the ardent fan!'

In 1982, the decision was taken to go full-time again, much to the delight of Iain Bayne, who had been keen on such a move since joining the band. 'It had almost been semi-professional in its approach,' he says, 'and I couldn't understand why they couldn't commit themselves to going full-time. I couldn't understand their reluctance.'

But it was a serious gamble. The first European dates encouraged the move, and shows in England – though mostly to Scottish expatriates – proved viable. Money was starting to come in from merchandising as well. Iain 'T-shirt' Macdonald had arrived on the scene, and was becoming a regular fixture at gigs with his stall of Runrig souvenirs. He remembers selling £73-worth of T-shirts during one gig at Glasgow University Union, 'the most they'd ever sold – they were just cock-a-hoop about it, saying they'd have to start doing it regularly'.

'Going full-time was just desperation really,' says Calum. 'It was just a question of getting everyone together and making sure we were all committed to it. Even up until the last moment Donnie was still swithering.'

Wages were at this point distributed in different amounts, depending on dependents. 'We knew money was tight,' Donnie says, 'and we basically said to each other, what do you need to survive? We all had different needs.'

One need the band felt was for a hit single, and the idea of re-recording *Loch Lomond* for Ridge came up. 'It was deliberately commercial,' Rory admits, 'very much so. But it had been going down so well live, and we genuinely liked the song. It's a really good song, and largely misunderstood. We did get a lot of criticism at the time.'

Loch Lomond was Runrig's first studio outing with Chris Harley, the man who would be so crucial in fashioning the mature Runrig sound on record, at the helm. Chris had by this time had a successful career as a performer under the name Chris Rainbow, recorded with Stevie Wonder's band and producers in Los Angeles, had been a member of the Alan Parsons Project and Camel and had generally been a fixture in the music business. By 1982 he was still inexperienced in big time production, but he had Skye connections – and a house near Broadford.

'We had originally wanted Chris to produce *Play Gaelic*, simply because he was the only person we sort of knew who was remotely connected with the rock business then,' Calum remembers. 'But in 1982 we went to him for the *Loch Lomond* project.'

'We'd met the year before, and had one of those evenings,' Chris recalls. 'I've a feeling Calum and Rory just wanted to pick my brains, and find out how they could take things a bit further.'

The mooting of the *Loch Lomond* project was something of a shock to the Harley system. 'Rory phoned me up, and asked would I produce a single for them. I said I'd love to – what is it? There was a little pause, and then he said, *Loch Lomond*. I was just astonished. I mean, everybody's covered *Loch Lomond* – it seemed a really weird choice. So I just said, "Why?" He replied that he just thought it was a really great song, and so I said OK.'

Working with the band was strange, Chris remembers. 'We went to Castlesound, the first time I'd ever worked there, and it took us two days to form even a new structure for the song. Then it took seven to record. It was a culture shock for me. They played in a very different, very Scottish manner. The drums were like a marching band, the guitar like bagpipes. It was very straight ahead and very strange. The whole thing was close to a pipe band, very strict.'

That first experience did not instil in Chris the confidence that Runrig would someday be a major force, and it was not until he saw the band play live at Caol village hall that their potential hit him. 'It was packed out. I had time to stand in the wings and watch the audience reaction, and it struck me then that they could be a stadium band. They were still very Scottish – Donnie hadn't crafted his stage technique at that point – but it was evident at Caol that this band had that little thing that takes a group out of the parochial domain and into the world market.'

Ridge Records, meanwhile, had to sit down quickly in the small Dalkeith flat headquarters and play big time. An imaginative marketing campaign was mapped out which involved an incredible workload for the limited company personnel. They were to be record reps, pluggers and designers, and, in week two of the campaign, set off in separate cars to tour the UK radio stations, turning up on the doorstep, presenting the single and offering to give interviews.

The single, released with *Tuireadh Iain Ruaidh* on the B-side, cracked the top 50 in January 1983, if you believe some contemporary press reports, although the official highest placing was 72 nationally. Nevertheless, it achieved heavy Scottish sales and airplay, and was briefly featured on Radio One. But it was a victim of the bias against localised sales which still plagues Runrig's relationship with the national charts. Promotions in London did see the first glimmerings of southern interest in the band, and as Rory says, 'It was very successful because it broke us through to an audience in Scotland we didn't have before. The people who had no connection with Gaelic were suddenly being exposed to us in a big way.'

Despite the historical credentials of *Loch Lomond*, there was a degree of moaning in the Highland press and from long-standing fans about selling out – a phrase which was to haunt Runrig on and off for years, until they became so popular it was irrelevant. While the band admit that *Loch Lomond* was a consciously commercial tilt at the charts, the strength of the song can be judged from its continued presence in the live set to this day, and the fact that it has now become almost synonymous with Runrig, rather than the bekilted masters of tartan tat who once soaked it in warbly sentimentalised gloop. Runrig, if you like, have reclaimed *Loch Lomond*, brought it home where it belongs.

But Runrig were in a strange position. Given a reasonable gap between concerts, they could sell out major venues in most Scottish cities. The European market and the English folk-festival scene was about to open up to them, and they'd released three albums which had been successful. But that elusive hit single hadn't materialised, despite *Loch Lomond* gaining them a great deal of recognition, and they were full-time but poverty-stricken. What they needed was a manager.

Enter, stage left, Messrs Myles Cooney and Roger Ferdinand, alias Top Concerts. Enter – or rather, re-enter – stage right, Ms Marlene Ross of Aberdeen.

Runrig were looking for someone to look after them. Les Honeyman, who had been recommended by Marlene to Runrig in 1979 for a PA hire, duly repaid the favour during 1982. 'The band wanted to go full-time,' says Marlene, 'and they asked Les Honeyman if he had any ideas for a manager. I was promoting gigs and managing bands at the time – I'd promoted two Runrig gigs at the Ritzy in Aberdeen, and they'd been impressed – they'd gone well – so he suggested me. Those Aberdeen gigs made money, and that impressed them even more.'

Marlene met the band, and the band duly asked her to be their manager. It was a marriage made in hospital. 'I've always been one for challenges,' Marlene smiles, 'that's the whole history of my working life. I had a nursing background, and I was a nursing sister when I was 22, so I've always accepted whatever challenge was going and, whether it took a long time or a short time, I always got there. I knew it was going to be a tall order, and my goodness, it certainly has been.'

Marlene and her husband Graeme were running a company called Abbotsford Acoustics which in 1982 began providing sound and lighting equipment for the band's Scottish gigs. Graeme was to work with the band on the road for several years, providing valuable service as a lighting engineer. But Marlene's management relationship with Runrig was a personal one. 'I just fell in love with their music – and with them as people. I just found them so sincere. I liked what they stood for – just everything about them appealed to me. And they didn't have this immature rock aura which other bands I'd managed had. So we decided to give it a bash.'

'Giving it a bash' in the short term meant, for Marlene, handling Runrig's tortuous day-to-day finances. 'There were six of them, and they all required a salary. We just sat down and worked out everybody's situation – Donnie was the only one at that stage with a family, so he was the only one requiring a reasonable amount of money! I'd never done anything like it before. I'd approached record companies for other bands, but suddenly there I was, maintaining six guys' mortgages or rents or whatever.'

But was keeping a six-piece, full-time, big-league band on the road without record company subsidy feasible? 'No, it wasn't feasible at all. But they came to me at the end of the summer of 1982, so I could see that we'd have a run up from September through to December, your university prime time for freshers' gigs and all the rest of it, so I thought well, maybe. But it was all really a sort of gamble. They said, "Well, OK, we'll try it", and I thought, "My goodness, once having said that, you'll do it!" But it was a tall order.' Nothing was put down on paper, and Marlene's percentage was what it remained for years: absolutely zero.

Meanwhile, the Myles and Roger show hit town. Titillated by the media success engendered by *Loch Lomond*, they took Runrig up to a high place and showed them the riches of the earth. They waved a career plan about, which included such richly promising phrases as 'to launch Runrig in the European and American market' and 'to extend the potential audience of Runrig in the UK', and in addition offered an exclusive management deal which would have sealed Runrig's fate to theirs for five years.

Myles Cooney was then the king of fly-posting in Scotland, as he still is, masterminding the appearance of posters on empty buildings and disused hoardings throughout the country and used by every major record company and promoter, not to mention every struggling pub band. Together with Roger Ferdinand, he set up Top Concerts as a promotions and management agency, Roger having worked extensively in London's rock scene as an agent. They wanted Runrig, and went all out to get them.

'The two of them approached us initially with a view to a tour of Scotland,' says Rory, 'but the first time we met them, at a hotel in Dalkeith, Roger actually had a contract in his hand. After we'd known him for 15 minutes, he wanted us to sign a management contract.' Calum: 'They were desperate for us to sign, but initially the carrot was this tour of Scotland, which was to be the biggest tour ever. We wanted them to prove themselves to us as promoters first. Only then could we look at the whole management picture. So we agreed to do the tour.'

January 1983 arrived, with *Loch Lomond* still in the nether regions of the charts, Myles and Roger promising the earth and Marlene having kittens in Aberdeen. 'Myles and Roger did a hard, hard sell to the band, and I strongly advised the boys not to do it. I thought Myles and Roger were the wrong type of people for Runrig to be involved with, and I was strongly against having anything to do with them. But then again, I'd just come into the picture myself, I hadn't had time to make any great impact, and I think the boys just felt, well . . . no harm in doing a tour with them.'

Top Concert's projected accounts for the tour made attractive reading. It would last 14 days, with 12 dates. If gigs were 100 per cent sold out, there would be a net profit of £20,804, with Top getting 30 per cent – £6,241. If only half the total seats were sold, the band would still come out with £2,941, Roger and Myles with £1,260. It seemed daft to turn it down.

'We made a total profit of £69.12,' Marlene remembers. 'It was a complete disaster, and it totally destroyed the band's earning potential in Scotland for an entire year because we couldn't go back to any of those places and play, and make the money that I had anticipated making so they could survive. It was a hell of a dent. It nearly blew the whole thing off the face of the earth.'

'Yes, it was a total disaster,' Calum admits. 'They thought they could impress us with a taste of the high life – a luxury minibus, booking us into really good hotels, rushing us in the back doors of gigs saying, "There's your towels, lads."' Rory: 'If the tour had been well run, it would have made money. But it wasn't and it didn't. I mean, there were great nights, like at Tiffany's in Glasgow. But then there were places where Runrig didn't have a following, like Arbroath. There were so few tickets sold for the Smokey's gig that they had to go out in the van and try and sell them round the pubs. They ended up giving them away and there were still only a dozen people there.'

Iain 'T-shirt' Macdonald was merchandising on the tour, which he remembers as a nightmare. 'Marlene was pretty upset, though I didn't know it at the time. It was obvious that Roger and Myles were trying to oust her, and she'd already put in a lot of work for very little reward. They were trying to dump her, basically.

'The tour started OK because they were in safe places like Islay and Campbeltown, and then it just started going from bad to worse. There was a terrible tension. Roger was tour manager and everybody fell out with him – he was a really difficult guy to work with, and the crew had a lot of barneys with him. The concert at Arbroath had about 13 people there. They were going round the pubs and chippies giving out tickets, and Smokey's must hold nearly 1,000 people – it's a huge place. That part of the country had never heard of Runrig – they hadn't even played in Dundee at that time.'

Arbroath also featured the worst hotel anyone in Runrig could remember. 'Brian Freel was the support act, and I remember him running up and down the stairs shouting that there were bedbugs, and sure enough the sheets were nearly running down the stairs themselves.'

When the nightmare ended, Runrig's prospective bread-and-butter income for the next four months had all but vanished. 'It was a really pitiful time,' says Marlene, still angry at the memory. Thanks to Iain Bayne's previous escapades with New Celeste, a lucrative appearance was fixed up at the Roskilde Festival in Denmark, and also at the Nyon festival in Switzerland. That, plus a famously controversial gig with Alain Stivell at the Edinburgh Playhouse – Stivell, ostensibly the main attraction, insisted on going on first because of the baying hordes of Runrig fans present – brought in some much needed cash. ('I remember the Playhouse staff were astonished,' says Iain T-shirt, 'because the band were actually carrying equipment themselves, and they'd headlined a sold-out gig.') The concert garnered a rave review in the good old *Free Press*, along with a description of Runrig 'being greeted like latter-day Beatles'.

Perhaps to Sgiathanaichs, but not to the inhabitants of Arbroath. It had been a bad year, that first period of mature, counting-the-cost professionalism, and there had been very few consolations. Things, however, were about to get much, much worse.

CHAPTER SEVEN

THE WORST OF TIMES . . .

Against Marlene's better judgement and advice, the band continued to work with Myles Cooney after the disastrous tour of February 1983, although Roger Ferdinand was unceremoniously ditched.

Marlene Ross

'But we felt that Myles was a grafter,' says Rory. 'He worked hard and we felt he could be of some assistance, so we kept up the relationship on a sort of guidance level.'

'Ferdinand was given the order of the boot, because he was the one everyone had taken an instant dislike to,' Marlene remembers. 'The band thought Myles was OK. His selling point was that he had worked a lot with the London end, with record companies, and the band thought it would be a good idea if he came in to help me with that side of the business while I did all the hard work and attended to the practicalities of keeping the whole machine going.'

Rory remembers it somewhat differently. 'Marlene was very reluctant to assume the role of going down to London and start passing around demos, feeling that we were not yet at that sort of stage.'

'Marlene was going to keep us in wages, initially,' says Calum, 'keep the wolf from the door.'

But there was one wolf even the redoubtable Marlene would not be able to shoo away from the Runrig portals. Indeed, she was taken in along with everyone else as enthusiasm mounted for some kind of national break-through, and a large hairy beast called Simple Records was welcomed with open arms.

Calum: 'We always did believe that we could sell some of our records elsewhere, because the audiences were increasing and we were getting a bigger and better reaction all the time.' Rory: 'Thereupon we took the second step downwards. We tried every company going for a deal but we only got one offer.'

'Myles set us up with Gordon Simpson of Simple Records,' says Marlene, 'and that was the last thing he did before we got rid of him. He introduced us to Gordon. So we were away from Myles, but we had this proposition of doing a record with Simple, and we fell for it, the lot of us. The result was absolute chaos.'

There is still a lot of bitterness over that Simple Records fiasco, which at first sight was the classic case of a naive young band being taken for a ride. But Runrig were not teenagers any more, and had surely been exploited sufficiently in the past to have bred some caution. However, a national record company had offered them a deal, and the stars sparkling

Signing with Simple. On the
left is Calum and Donnie's
Portree High classmate,
solicitor Roddy John
Macleod, with Gordon
Simpson on the right

in their eyes were too big and bright to be ignored.

'Besides, we had the contracts fully checked out by our lawyers,' Rory points out. 'It was a terrible mistake,' says Marlene, 'but it was an area I had no experience in. I got various solicitors to check it out, and anyway he seemed like a genuine guy to us.'

Gordon Simpson, the 'genuine guy' in question, first arranged to meet the band in Scotland and then failed to turn up. On 14 March 1984 Runrig were playing in London at the Venue, and this time Simpson did materialise. Next day, he invited the band to his office and a deal was discussed.

Two months later, Simpson and Phil Scott, then doing A&R (Artistes and Repertoire – essentially scouting for new talent) for Simple, came to Edinburgh to see Runrig at the Caley Palais, 'to assess the live potential'. Next day they offered the band a contract which they wanted signed on the spot. After legal checking, a clause was changed which Runrig thought would allow them a degree of artistic control over master tapes. On 30 May the contract was signed. Depending on how you looked at it, it was a five-year deal with Simple having the option to drop the band after a year, or a one-year deal with three 16-month options available to Simple for its extension. It had the framework of a standard record company contract, but its details gave Simple an option on Runrig's soul. And no one associated with the band noticed.

Chris Harley was kept well out of the picture by Simple, who refused to have him involved in any production work. Instead, Englishman Jeremy Green was contracted to produce the planned first single for the company, *Dance Called America*. Castlesound was agreed for recording to start on 18 June. Except it hadn't been booked. Gordon Simpson apologised, apparently sacked A&R man Phil Scott, and booked Surrey Sound studios in London, scene of the Police's early successes but an alien environment for Runrig. Later Simpson admitted that he was now 'getting his own way by default'.

Recording began on 25 June, with pressure being brought to bear by Simple that as little time should be taken as possible. A successful appearance at the Cambridge Folk Festival brought a smile to critic Simon Jones' face, after all those years of pleading that the band play there, and then it was back to recording. After a move to Wessex Studios, *Dance Called America* was recorded, along with two potential B-sides – *Na H-Uain A's t-Earrach* and *Ribhinn O* – by 4 July. Next day, in the unbelievably quick time of ten hours, all three tracks were mixed down. Gordon Simpson expressed himself 'delighted' at the result.

The first fists in the air. The beginnings of a student following, Aberdeen University, 1983

At the Cambridge Folk
Festival, 1984

For a little while. Then he decided he was unhappy, and demanded a
remix from one Derek Lawrence. The band were not involved and, when
they heard the remix, were horrified. 'We also discovered,' Calum recollects
with some pain, 'that by the time it reached Derek Lawrence, the master
tape had been stretched, causing a marked fluctuation in tempo and pitch.
In addition, an effect had made the rhythm guitar sound out of tune.' The
band urged the immediate enlistment of Chris Harley for a salvage job.
But Gordon Simpson confidently informed them, 'We have a hit record on

our hands.'

Dance Called America was, in the classic phrase, not so much released as allowed to escape. To the relief of the band it gained little attention. 'It was dreadful,' says Rory. 'Just a complete thrash,' says Richard, although he did like the seven-inch's B-side, *Na H-Uian A's t-Earrach*, while according to Calum, such fans as obtained the record – and not many did – were unimpressed. The 12-inch also included *Ribhinn O*. 'I think we did it in an afternoon,' says Richard. 'It was one of the few times that the keyboards were allowed a great deal of space.' Even in Scotland, the single disappeared virtually without trace, and listening to it today it was just as well. A classic song had been dealt a wounding, if not fatal, blow.

But worse was to come. Next on the cards was the recording of an LP, and Chris Harley's name was again put forward by the band as producer. Again he was turned down. The only two names acceptable to Simple would, it seemed, be Derek Lawrence, the man responsible for remixing *Dance Called America* – it later turned out that he was doing A&R for Simple – or one Alan O'Duffy. But a compromise was agreed and a single (*Skye*) would be recorded with Alan O'Duffy to ascertain his suitability for the album. And the band did have hopes of him, as he had worked on Horslips' brilliant concept album *The Tain*, an album which pioneered Celtic rock music.

Things then started to get silly. In August, Runrig were due to play the Tonder Festival in Denmark. Having stressed that O'Duffy should at least hear them live before recording them, the producer agreed to come to Denmark. Simple said no. Runrig pleaded, even offered to pay O'Duffy's fare. No again. After bizarre negotiations with Simpson and O'Duffy, which included being given an ultimatum that O'Duffy would only work with Runrig if compromises were made on arrangements and material, recording began on an unlucky 13 September. A week later, Alan O'Duffy hurriedly left. The recording was unfinished, with only hastily overdubbed guide drums. Yet on 5 October the band received rough mixes of the supposedly finished tracks for their comments. Not only had they been remixed, but new instruments – including a synthesized bass line – had been added.

'We were horrified,' Calum says. 'What had been done to the songs was totally out of character with our music.' Simple's response was to cancel a booking with Castlesound for recording the LP. 'This was financially crippling,' he continues, 'because it meant the earliest we could begin recording was March 1985, and the original recording dates had been integral to our plans for 1984. We couldn't arrange alternative live gigs at such short notice.'

A panic meeting was arranged in October with Simpson and Shirley Stone, the other director of Simple. The only solution, the band felt, was to call in Chris, salvage the single and continue with the LP. Simpson replied that he had total faith in Alan O'Duffy and that 'We've got a hit single on our hands'. Trust me, boys, he reportedly said. Trust my judgement. No, the band said. They were then allegedly told that what they felt 'was of no account'.

The poverty-stricken Runrig then offered to pay for the remixing and fixing up of *Skye* themselves. The offer was refused and tempers became frayed, Simpson stormed out when Marlene demanded the advance due for the release of *Dance Called America.*

By November, Marlene was informed by Simple that the unfinished, unapproved single was being released, and was 'a potential hit' in which 'several Radio One producers' were interested. They were also, Calum remembers, 'curiously confident that *Skye* would chart by Christmas'.

That fateful 1984 December swept in, with an astonished Calum hearing the finished mix of *Skye* for the first time on Radio Scotland's Tom Ferrie programme. 'We felt our career was now in serious jeopardy. The song had been remixed with new parts added, other parts edited and completely altered beyond recognition, and we felt we could in no way associate ourselves with it.'

There was a scathing media response. Tom Ferrie told the band – off the record, so to speak – that if he hadn't had so much respect for Runrig's past achievements he would have binned *Skye* immediately. But it took old pal Campbell Gunn, writing more in sorrow than derision in the *People's Journal*, to say what everyone, including the band, thought.

It was a mystery how a band like Runrig 'who are absolutely stunning when playing live, and who can produce such excellent album tracks' had failed to crack the singles market, Campbell wrote. 'This latest, titled simply *Skye*, is in my opinion the worst single, and possibly the worst track, they have ever recorded. According to the press release along with the record, "this Celtic dance track moves along with grace and pathos". Pathos is generally defined as that quality which raises pity. It seems a pity that this is the best Runrig can produce.' There was more, including a plea for a return to the innocence of earlier days. But the most hideously embarrassing thing was when Campbell Gunn, whose credentials in Gaelic music were impeccable, pointed out that the B-side *Hey Mandu* had been credited to Calum and Rory as writers. 'That will come as something of a surprise to many folk in the islands who knew the song long before the lads were born,' he wrote, adding that it had already been recorded by 'virtually everyone with pretensions to Celtic rock'.

Things could only get better, and they didn't. Furious, the band demanded that the mistake about *Hey Mandu*'s origins be corrected. No worries, Simpson assured them. And no correction either.

Horrified, embarrassed, yet unable to ignore this mutation which had been let loose on the public in their name, Runrig spent the last month of 1984 watching the charts. Astonishingly, the single charted in the national top 200 at 108, with Simple promising it would go to the top 100 by January. Instead, *Skye* was removed from the charts altogether by compilers Gallup, amid allegations of chart rigging. The band could hardly believe it was happening, but a tirade of press, radio and television coverage, putting Runrig in the worst possible light, confirmed it was true.

Runrig were cleared of any involvement, Simple denied all knowledge of such a scam, and blame fell, according to the British Phonographic Institute, on a young boy and a couple who had been travelling around the South-West of England buying two or three copies of *Skye* at a time. They were possibly 'misguided fans', the BPI said.

Marlene was then called by Gordon Simpson. Considering the success of *Skye*, he said, he was prepared to let Chris Harley produce the album. Innocent, he claimed, of any chart rigging, he asserted that the single would have been in the top ten had it not been removed from the chart. Calum: 'His justification for this was that he had received inside information from an employee at Gallup regarding the computer read-out.'

Never mind, said Gordon, claiming that *Skye* had been 'a great success'. A budget of £25,000 was agreed for the album, a £2,000 advance was paid to Chris, and everything was ready to go on 27 March 1985.

'During all this time,' Calum sighs, 'we were committed to recording, rehearsal and planning, incurring great expense and without any possibility of doing live work – our only source of income.' Runrig was slithering towards a sticky end, it seemed – but it was felt that the record might save things.

Then Simple simply pulled out of the album project, refusing to confirm the already agreed budget. 'What we didn't know,' Rory says, 'was that they were already going into liquidation.'

The band discovered that Gordon Simpson had slipped into Edinburgh on other business, and on 11 April they confronted him in La Sorbonne, a Grassmarket nightclub. 'He was totally unwilling to discuss anything with us,' says Calum, 'and he assured us he would see us the following week.' They never heard from him again.

Perhaps that was something to do with Marlene. 'I told him where he could stuff his contract. We could have walked away from that contract any time we liked, and that is exactly what we did.'

'Of all the people I've been involved with,' says Donnie, 'that whole episode is still the one that really, really hurts, not because they didn't deliver. We were,' he says with no trace of irony, 'all very simple people in a sense, and we dealt with people genuinely. That was the first time I think we ever met people who were unwilling to deal directly with us, but really we'd checked them out as much as we could, vetted them through the bank, and we were the first band on their books, so we thought maybe they'd really go for it.'

A legacy was left with the band, not of intuitive mistrust, but of never again taking people at face value. 'If you're let down once, you can't carry that around with you,' Donnie says philosophically, 'but if someone becomes involved now, offers us something, we always look at it and say, well, what is it they really want? Because very few people want to give you something for nothing. But we have made very bad judgements. We've made mistakes.' Ever since, and contributing to that mildly 'difficult' reputation, all Runrig's decisions have been mulled over in band meetings, looked at from every angle, and made cautiously.

When they weren't taking yet another mammoth gamble, that is; and that's exactly what they did next.

Simple was to come back and haunt Runrig, over the next few years particularly. The rights to Runrig's recordings for the label were sold off, and the appearance of *A Feast of Scottish Folk – Volume One* on Alba Records caused much wringing of hands in the Runrig camp, featuring as it does *Skye, Na H-Uain A's t-Earrach* and an early version of *Lifeline*, all as recorded for Simple. Washing away the taste of the previous recordings demanded that the songs be done again, and done properly. And so *Heartland* was born.

Marlene had by this time assumed a degree of authority in the band set-up, and 'it was the first time I was getting to do anything without outsiders' interference. We'd got rid of the dross, we were in control ourselves, in command . . . really, it was like when you know something's wrong, that it's going to be a complete disaster, and you can't convince six people but you love them all so much, you love the music and you love what they're doing, and you won't walk away.

'It would have been the time for me to say, "Look, I've told you what I think. If you're not going to listen, I'm out." But it's like your kids. You try and advise them and all the rest of it, but you don't disown them just because they won't listen to you. You just sit there and wait, and then you pick up the pieces. That's what I've always done.'

The band themselves are fully aware of the debt they owe to a woman who has become something of a legend in the Scottish music scene. 'I know a lot of managers,' says Calum, 'who have mortgaged their houses for a band they believed in, but Marlene has mortgaged her whole life for us. There were weeks when we had to go on to half wages, and weeks when we had to go without. She did the same. We owe her an enormous debt. She's perfect for us because, like ourselves, she doesn't quite fit the bill as far as the normal way of functioning within the music industry is concerned. Contrary to the belief of many, who have felt the cutting edge of her extraordinary negotiating abilities, she's really a big softie – a generous, warm-hearted woman with strong beliefs and an infectious sense of humour.'

Getting them on the right path involved getting hold of a vast quantity of cash to record the album which would set the dubious record(s) of the past year straight. The amount needed was staggering. 'About £40,000,' says Marlene. Donnie and Calum would dress up in suits and visit bank after bank. 'We had some surprising interest from merchant banks,' he says now. But no cash. In the end, it was down to Marlene. 'I went to my own accountant, who suggested I try this manager in the Bank of Scotland. So I went to him, and he said if I could get everybody, all my friends and family to act as guarantors, they would do it. They gave us some and the rest came from gigs. *Heartland* was done in bits and pieces, because we didn't have all the money all at once.'

'We decided we were not going to be held back,' Calum says. 'We'd be in the studio, and then at lunchtime Donnie and I would leap out with suits on and tackle banks for loans. But nobody wanted to know, even though all our records had made their money back. It was getting really, really bad.'

Stumbling from studio to studio (*Heartland* was recorded at Castlesound, REL in Edinburgh and ÇaVa in Glasgow) but with the unifying force of Chris Harley at the production helm, the summer of 1985 was some way removed from the glorious carefree days in '70s' Skye. However, a tour of Denmark with erstwhile heroes Fairport Convention not only brought in much needed cash, but renovated the band's studio-bound soul.

'*Heartland*,' Malcolm remembers, 'was a hard album to do. It was like getting blood out of a stone, because of all the nonsense that was going on while we were in the studio.' But somehow, the slow climb out of the slough of despondency went on. Live work was crammed in, and Marlene admits now that it was inviting criticism. And there were encouragements, like the review in *Melody Maker* of the Queen's Park gig. Runrig were later to be the only band during my four years with *Melody Maker* who ever wrote to thank me for writing about them.

'We were forced to do a lot more live work than would have been advisable in overall career terms,' Marlene admits. 'I had to think not so much in career terms as in terms of getting them a reasonable wage – because by this time more had acquired wives and children, and we had to get the money matters sorted out. People who sat on the sidelines and said we were doing too many live gigs didn't understand that there was no pile of money backing them, no pile of anything behind them. So we had to do things differently. Everything had to be made to pay.'

But £40,000 for *Heartland*? Could it possibly work? Had Runrig's recent escapades alienated their record-buying public, and would the record, produced as it was under severe emotional and financial strictures, be any good? Would anybody like it?

After the Aalborg Festival,
Denmark, with Spic, Ivor and
promoter Jan Vinter, 1985

CHAPTER EIGHT

LIFELINE

'The technical turning point was *Heartland*,' says its producer Chris Harley in all modesty, and he's absolutely right. From the album cover – with its superb photographs front and rear of Laxay's Donna Ferguson, one by Gus Wylie, the other by Sam Maynard, (and bearing a graphic resemblance to Springsteen's *Nebraska*, much to the embarrassment of the designer, one Roderick Macdonald Esq.) – to the production, this was a quality item.

It was four years since the release of *Recovery*, which with *Highland Connection* had by this point sold some 40,000 copies, and the demand for the Runrig product had increased vastly. 'It sold like hot cakes,' Calum remembers, 'it was the first album which really crossed over into the Lowland Scottish market.'

In the press, reception was, with one notable exception, enthusiastic. A major feature by Brian Wilson in the *Free Press* of 6 December 1985 gave Donnie a chance to set the record straight on the events of the previous two nightmare years. 'We were lucky that we were strong enough in ourselves not to be totally dependent on Simple,' he said. It was the understatement of the decade. And explaining *Dance Called America*'s lyric, Donnie told Brian, 'Calum read in a book that the aristocracy had a dance at the time of the Clearances called *America*, in which they mimicked the people going away.' In live shows, he went on, 'I dedicate it to the sheer arrogance of those individuals. When I sang it at a festival in the grounds of Dunrobin Castle I was able to dedicate it to the man on the hill [the statue of the Duke of Sutherland above Golspie].' While defending the increase in English content on *Heartland*, Donnie argued, 'While language is vital to a culture, we would put forward that the strength and identity of all our music comes from the same area of feeling, whether it is in English or Gaelic.' All involved with the record were very pleased with it, Donnie concluded; it was 'a catching up on what we've been doing over the past few years'.

Brian Wilson's carefully written feature was something of a warning to Gaeldom that Runrig were moving on from being simply a private Gaelic property. The last paragraph spoke volumes.

> Over the years, Runrig have become a well-respected institution within this, their area of origin, and well beyond. But like all worthwhile institutions they have kept developing, progressing and opening up new frontiers with their work. The thoughtful, radical lyrics and exciting sounds on *Heartland* deserve all the success they will undoubtedly achieve.

Under canvas at Cambridge

A relieved Campbell Gunn went to town in the *People's Journal* after his sorrowful savaging of *Skye*. 'Runrig have come up with what is arguably their best album to date,' he opined, 'and, just to show that the poor quality of the singles *Dance Called America* and *Skye* was not their fault, the band have included them on the LP. It is hard to recognise that they are the same songs, especially *Skye*, which now emerges as a first-class piece of work.' The album was duly awarded 'eleven out of ten'.

The *Stornoway Gazette* simply hailed it as brilliant, adding, 'although *Heartland* does not contain as many Gaelic songs as some Gaels would have hoped for, this album will be enjoyed throughout Gaeldom and beyond'. Meanwhile old champion Simon Jones loved the songs but the seamless rock production was too much for his folk-educated ears ('note to the man behind the console – Runrig are not Big Country') and there was, he felt, a lack of passion and edge. However, *Melody Maker* gave *Heartland* a page lead and a picture – along with some unfortunate phrases such as 'positively yells "MacSpringsteen" ' – and the Aberdeen *Evening Express* also provided a thumbs up. Even the record industry trade paper *Music Week* advised dealers to stock this 'most compelling album', and Brian Wilson also provided the *Glasgow Herald* with a similar article to the one already published in the *Free Press*.

On the beach, Lorient

Ah yes, the *Free Press*. Even today Calum still smarts at the review which came a week after Brian Wilson's feature. 'That was the second great stab in the back from the Gaelic establishment,' he grimaces. 'I'll never forget that review – "Runrig are losing their Highland connection" – not because of any musical criticism, but because of a totally negative parochial vision on behalf of the writer. It was like the first time we played the all-Gaelic set. The home side just couldn't accept what we were doing. "That's it!

They've stopped singing in Gaelic!" It was a really scathing piece of writing, and after all we'd been through to put that record out . . . we just felt like throwing up.'

What the headline actually said was 'Are Runrig in danger of losing their Highland connection?' Iain Maciver, then a Gaelic youth broadcaster for the BBC, wrote as an activist in the gathering lunge for Gaelic unilateralism. He attacked the inclusion of the re-recorded singles as 'astounding and disappointing', and was 'to say the least disappointed' about the inclusion of only four Gaelic tracks. He liked *Air A Chuan*, but found *O Cho Meallt*'s attack on people not a million miles from Simple Records an unendearing tissue of excuses – although, peculiarly, 'it is a fine song and well performed'.

The rest of the review represented a strain of parochialism which dogs Runrig to this day – the Gaelic version of the Scotland-wide 'Aa' Jock Tamson's bairns' syndrome. 'The rest of the album is,' Iain thought, 'the group's pandering to the whims of the Lowlands and beyond . . . I fear that Runrig have decided they should extend their frontiers and woo audiences who will hopefully pay the bills better and not insist on long and expensive ferry trips and other discomforts for the privilege of entertaining them.' And there was much more. Hopes were expressed that Runrig 'haven't forgotten their real heartland' and the inclusion of *The Everlasting Gun* brought a passing reference to its alleged Falklands War content – 'as good a bandwagon as any nowadays'.

No wonder palms were sweaty in Dalkeith. It was a deliberately provocative review, an agitprop statement by a committed individual, and it came directly from the heartland itself. It felt like betrayal; it certainly provoked a response. Although the armed guards on Mr Maciver's home were to prove unnecessary.

Letters flowed in to the *Free Press* offices defending Runrig against every real and imagined slur. In the end, the real record buyers in the Gaidhealtacht understood, as they voted with their wallets in shops from Stornoway to Mallaig.

How does *Heartland* sound today? Better on CD than on vinyl, for one thing, partly because there's too much music – six substantial tracks a side – for the full dynamic to be contained on plastic grooves. The other reason is more esoteric, but involves the original mastering of the LP in Glasgow, at hi-fi manufacturers Linn Products. Linn's purist mastering techniques, which allowed for no equalisation or 'tweaking', usually resulted in albums of unusual clarity. Or it could, in squeezing large amounts of music on to plastic, result in a slight reduction in sheer rock 'n' roll oomph.

That aside, the record is the first Runrig waxing to be given a proper pop production. The drums sound like the drums on big, expensive records, and the playing has a discipline and precision completely absent from previous LPs. More to the point, the vocals just blossom under the tutelage of Chris Harley, a classic and severely underrated pop stylist in his own right. Never before had Rory and especially Donnie sounded so good. Malcolm's guitar playing lacks the ragged glory of *Highland Connection*, but makes up for that in subtlety and resonance – *Dance Called America* showing it was possible to out-Adamson Big Country without using the motorised plectrum called an E-bow.

Malcolm, perfectionist as ever, sees the weaknesses in the album which could, he says, 'have been the first recording to capture all the best elements of the band. It just didn't have the right overall feel. There were basic faults but it still had a lot of good moments.'

There are the great, classic songs, such as *Dance Called America* and *Skye*, and the astonishing, brooding *Cnoc Na Feille*, with a lyric which reeks of supernatural and natural menace in a way quite unlike anything Calum has done before or since. There is a real sense of Springsteenian triumphalism about the likes of *Lifeline*, but who can begrudge that when the band were emerging from the long dark night of the past two years – and rescuing *Lifeline* from its fate as a rejected Simple B-side?

One wonders if writs might have flown had *O Cho Meallt* been given an English translation on the inner sleeve, as all the other Gaelic songs were. The translation has always posed difficulties for the band, who have never been happy with the transference of the song's strong sentiments into bare English.

O CHO MEALLT *(excerpts)*

(Translation)
We left the islands of the west
Began playing throughout Scotland
And all things were fine and well
Until the big man from London arrived

'I like the music you have here
Why don't you come along with me
We can make great progress
Just sign your name at the bottom of the page'

But all we heard at the end of the day
Were lies and empty promises . . .

. . . The world can be a deceitful place.

The nearest comparison, apart from the Byrds' *So you Wanna Be a Rock 'n' Roll Star* or Buffalo Springfield's wonderful *Broken Arrow* is John Fogerty's merciless attack on his former manager Saul Zantz: *Zanz Can't Dance* from the LP *Centrefield*. That song resulted in a major lawsuit and the withdrawal from sale of an entire pressing of the LP.

In the end, *Heartland* stands today as an almost great record. The production was just about there, but Runrig had not yet grown confident enough to rest easy with it. It was like seeing a man, proud of his Armani suit and sharp haircut, looking great but not quite sure if the jacket's really meant to hang like that and shuffling about worrying if that haircut's just a wee bit too posy. This was Runrig's first real big-time rock record. All it lacked was the sense that the band believed they really *were* big time rock 'n' roll.

'You could put a knife in their career at that time and say "From here, it's only upwards".' Iain MacDonald of Radio Scotland had mixed feelings about *Heartland*. 'In pure theory it's a very bad album, because there's too much on it. In musical terms and in terms of what had gone before, though, it's superb. It was well produced and well put together, plus they got a large sympathy vote from the Highlands because a lot of people knew what had gone on with Simple and DJs like Tom Ferrie were pushing them harder and harder.'

So was Marlene. 'I was saying, "Forget about the record company side just now. We have to go into other markets. We know the live side works, let's expand on that." So we built up the European profile – Germany, France, Denmark – and started thinking about Canada. Everything still had to balance out, or be subsidised by something else that made money.'

But as the touring accelerated and increased in scale, the band's sole Englishman began to get restless. Always less committed than the others to the notion of rock success, Richard had other musical ambitions he wanted to fulfil, particularly in the realms of composition.

Today Richard Cherns is a successful freelance composer, responsible for pieces of music like Radio Scotland's theme tune – with Malcolm Jones on guitar – and musical director for the Brunton Theatre company in Musselburgh and Theatre Alba.

'I learnt so much through Runrig. Even now, we share something which

Producer Chris Harley,
with Robin and Les

Recording *Heartland* at Ça
Va, Glasgow, with engineer
Robin Rankin, and co-
producer Les Lavin

binds us together in a positive sense. There were some painful moments, but it's been a very important chunk of my life. Since then I've written for vocal, orchestral and Celtic ensembles and, though the link may not at first be obvious, I've found that my time with Runrig has provided directly valuable experience.'

Richard had been signalling his desire to leave since well before the recording of *Heartland*, but had agreed to stay on until a replacement could be found. He admits now that 'I was never particularly happy about the conscious attempt to make the music more accessible to a wider number of people – and I think the band has gradually learnt to produce what they feel happiest with.' But the final nine months were 'a happy time for me' he says, with his own writing for the theatre taking off and Runrig's recovery from the disasters of Top and Simple relatively assured. 'All the arrangements we were trying seemed to work so well, and yet I couldn't afford to miss the boat as far as my own writing was concerned.' Despite the potential problems Richard was causing, there was little tension. 'I can think of other rock bands who are internally destructive, colossally so, but Runrig were not like that – they are good people whose hearts are in the right place.'

So in February 1986, Richard left. The memories still linger, though. 'I remember "hunt the drummer" after several gigs . . . breaking down in the depths of November on a deserted road in Harris . . . after an hour we saw cars approaching, and Iain Bayne was out of the door like a jack rabbit in case it was girls . . . and it was, and they whisked him off to Stornoway for some serious beer-patrolling while we slipped quietly into hypothermia . . . a *Blues Brothers*-type concert in Lewis with people trying to kill each other in the bar and then under the wheels of the van . . . a taped music intro breaking down at Barrowland . . .'

His own regrets relate to the way he believes Runrig have recently begun to integrate traditional elements into their music in a way he longed to participate in. 'We could have done more music like *An Ubhal As Airde* earlier if the band hadn't wanted to cross over to reach a wider audience. That would have given me more scope to help make the music soar. While I enjoyed the other aspects, perhaps that's where my contribution belongs most. I think we could have allowed ourselves more room to experiment and fail, if only to speed the evolutionary process, but it is difficult when the pressure is on.'

'I remember saying to Iain Macdonald, when we were at college together,' says Peter Wishart, ' "Who's this band 'Recovery' then?" because he had on this Runrig T-shirt from the *Recovery* era, and that was my first intro-duction to them. Iain was always going on about them.'

Born in 1962 in Fife and brought up in the village of Kingseat near Dunfermline, by the time he was at Moray House studying Community Education, Peter Wishart had already supped briefly from rock 'n' roll's glamorous teacup. From a family background in Scottish music – his father was a semi-professional accordionist – Peter had graduated through

Peter, when he joined Runrig

'playing David Bowie songs on an old Yamaha home organ' to the local gig circuit at 17 with his brother Alan.

'Stuart Adamson had been playing with the Skids, and the band I was in with my brother – Subject, we were called – had played a few concerts with them. Just after the Skids broke up, Stuart decided to form a new band, which myself and my brother joined. That was Big Country.'

Peter and Alan spent a year with the band, rehearsing the songs which would surface on *The Crossing* and, for a brief period, take this small country by storm. Support tours with Alice Cooper were 'great fun', Peter says, and then music-biz muscle moved in on Big Country's homespun Dunfermline line-up.

'The management and record company insisted on a new rhythm section, a new drummer and bass guitarist. My brother was playing bass, and there were arguments – so I left at that point because I didn't really want to pursue it without my brother playing. Just after that Big Country went on to huge, massive, things.'

Regrets, there were a few. But then again . . . 'There was a part of me that did regret leaving when I saw how well the first album did. It was one of the major sellers of the 1980s. There's always that thing . . . maybe I should have tried to make it up, bite my lip – but I still see Stuart quite a bit. He still stays in Dunfermline.'

The Big Country connection did Peter no harm at all when Iain T-shirt mentioned his name to the band. 'Hearing Big Country was a very significant moment for me,' says Rory. 'I can remember thinking, "This is what we've wanted to do all along." ' If Runrig had been any kind of influence on Big Country's music – and while admitting that both share common roots, Stuart Adamson denies this – Big Country certainly gave Runrig a model for what scale of success might be achieved. Donnie still recalls an early Big Country gig as 'possibly the most exciting live concert I've attended, even now'.

'The band were very much fans of Big Country,' says Peter. 'What they had achieved Runrig wanted to emulate, and my connection did give me a head start.' He identifies a two-way sharing of influences between the bands. 'Runrig had that definite ingredient of the Highland guitar sound, but Big Country were able to present it a bit better during that period. Runrig had been focused on what was basically an electric folk market; Big Country went straight for the kids.'

So did Stuart steal his guitar style from Malcolm, as many have alleged? 'No, I wouldn't say that at all,' Peter states categorically. 'They developed differently, and I know Stuart wasn't aware of Runrig until well after the Skids, when he already had that type of approach to the guitar.' Malcolm can't even see much of a resemblance. 'I've always been a bit puzzled by that, because in purely musical terms I can't see a close connection. Playing the pipes has influenced my guitar, along with other things, and I think our styles have developed separately.'

Stuart Adamson himself admits that seeing Runrig in 1984 was 'a revelation – I'd taken a lot of abuse in the music business for playing

contemporary music that was aware of its roots, but I think that's what everyone wants to do – and it's certainly what Runrig do.

'As to whether Runrig were any influence on Big Country, I don't really think so. Since the Skids, I've had a fairly unique guitar style, just something I developed. I've never had any guitar lessons, and I think that was quite important to the sound. Everything we've ever done has been from a songwriting point of view, not a novelty one, and that is something we share with Runrig, and maybe is the cause of some comparisons.

'I think Runrig and Big Country share some ethnic roots. Having said that, a lot of the chord structures I use are country-based rather than folk, which tends to be the case with Runrig. Also, I started out in a cover versions band, which means my voice is a lot less folky than Donnie's.

'The other major difference is the language barrier in that I'm not a Gaelic speaker. But the fact that Runrig still perform a lot of songs in Gaelic is one of the things I respect most about them. A lot of people say that by doing that they are being parochial or whatever – but I think it is exactly the opposite. I think they're trying to be forward-looking.'

So that's settled, then. And so was Peter. After a mere three auditions ('We seemed to hit it off quite well') he left the children's assessment centre he'd been working in since graduating from Moray House – where he'd been something of a political activist and president of the Students' Union – and became a member of the extended Runrig family.

'I was thoroughly delighted to be given another chance at being a musician – though it was a wee bit of a culture shock seeing them the first time in a half-empty Barrowland. What with Calum coming up to the front of the stage and hitting a pair of spoons to a Scottish dance tune.'

Peter also brought with him the Big Country attitude to record deals and rock music. 'When I joined they were still perceived as a folk-rock band and the projected image did the band no favours at all. I thought if something wasn't done about the folk tag, we would not get that larger audience. Little things would be annoying, like not finding the records in the general sections of record stores but tucked away in the folk section, and advertising by European promoters describing us as Scotland's Gaelic folk group. As for recording contracts, they basically weren't interested. After Simple, they were very suspicious of record companies and it took much debate before the search for a deal would begin again.'

Peter's first concert with the band remains a vivid memory. 'My future wife came up with me to Fort William for it. I was extremely nervous, physically shaking – it had been a year since I'd been on stage, and it was always going to be difficult. I remember sitting there in Fort William, looking up at the hills and thinking, "Can I really go on and do this?".' Which he did, finding thereafter that it took 'some time to get rid of the feeling of achievement'.

Any pride soon took a tumble, though, at Peter's first Edinburgh concert, when one of his keyboards fell from its stand. 'I had to grab on to one while members of the crew held on as I was playing it. The embarrassing thing was that my mother was there – the first time she'd seen the band and me playing . . .'

Marlene, by this time, was making things pay, and Ridge Records was spilling out of Calum's flat in Dalkeith. 'My wee flat in the High Street was just overflowing with boxes, floor to ceiling,' Calum remembers. 'It was like living in a record shop. The lorries turning up outside were getting bigger and bigger, but we were beginning to make money from the LPs and it was a much healthier situation.'

Marlene's firm hand on the financial tiller had also meant a smoother course was now being steered through the live scene, and income for each band member had been regularised. The profits were split equally, and Peter was a beneficiary of the new steadiness. 'At that point it was probably better than it had been in previous years, but it still wasn't very much at all – enough to pay the rent on a flat and maybe get out at the weekend – but that was it.'

But demand from England was increasing, and trips to London became a regular occurrence. Calum: 'It was very exciting, going down and playing pubs in Putney, Hackney, the Sir George Robey . . . everytime you went there, you felt you had something to prove, you'd really want to go for it.' That attitude, he believes, stems from the chip-on-the-shoulder sense of insecurity Runrig took with them from their island background. 'From the moment we started playing in Inverness and the south, that's where the passion developed from, because we always felt that we had a job to be accepted because we were always this teuchter band. You had to go out

there and really prove yourself, and, apart from the emotion in the music, it manifested itself physically as well. I have always felt a strong similarity between music and sport in terms of sheer sweat, performance and general relationship with an audience.'

Recording the video for the *Alba* single at Calton Hill, Edinburgh

It was just before the band were due to leave for three London gigs in April 1986 that tragic news reached them. Their former accordionist Robert Macdonald had died in Portree after a long battle against cancer. He was just 32.

Robert had become a much-loved and highly respected teacher, and had been head of the history department at Portree High School until 1985, when his illness forced him to give up work. Still a close friend of the band, the death of their former member came as a major blow to Rory, Calum and Donnie in particular, although it was not unexpected. 'We were just thankful that we were all able to share a lot of his last days with him in Edinburgh, where he was attending hospital,' says Rory.

Iain T-shirt, a cousin of Robert's, remembers what happened with vivid clarity. He was due to travel with the band to London to do the merchandis-

Van trouble: Sunday, outside
Hamburg, on the way to
Lorient

The saga continues

Breakdown vehicle number two

This is the way to travel . . .

ing when a distressed Calum phoned to say the mini-tour had been cancelled. A few hours later there was a change of plan. 'Apparently all the tickets had been sold for the London dates,' says Iain, 'so we went to London, and then Donnie, Calum, Rory and myself came up in a car to Edinburgh, where we got another car up to Skye for the funeral.'

There was another London gig that night, so the car was abandoned in Skye, and a flight from Breakish airstrip to Edinburgh arranged. From there it was a shuttle to London. Iain remembers the whole experience as dislocating in the extreme.

'The flights were about an hour and a half late, so they almost missed the concert. I remember they walked in to the Half Moon in Putney, the three of them, and the crowd was going daft. It was an amazing reception.' But one Rory, Donnie and Calum found difficult to cope with. 'It was the gig they'd least wanted to play, and they were obviously very upset. But they played.' 'It was,' Calum says briefly, 'one of the strangest nights of our lives.'

The hectic programme of concerts continued, with Peter settling in very quickly. A disastrous tour of England was best remembered for a bizarre gig in Workington, the only appearance in the north after four in the south and south-west. One of the agents, a lovably ethnic folkie, Joey James, had assured Runrig – after the Danish husband and wife support group dropped out 'because the audience intimidated them' and the venue in Bristol burnt down – that Workington would be great. Not only was it near Scotland, but it was a good area for the band 'wot wiv all these mountains and fings'. Fourteen people turned up in a 400-seater venue.

The reason for the band's presence in such a bizarre place soon became clear, when an attractive woman attached herself to the previously mentioned lovably ethnic folkie. 'We were there so that he could spend a weekend with a lady friend,' says Peter, 'and entertain her with his favourite "Scotch" band.'

The Isle of Skye Music Festival in July was a major homecoming triumph, however, and the *Free Press* almost made amends for that scathing review of *Heartland*. 'Skye's own Runrig were clearly the biggest attraction for many, and their set – including *Dance Called America*, highly topical in this centenary year of the Crofting Act – was a hard one to follow. Rock band Nazareth, who topped the bill, gave it their best shot and had a big following. But there can be no doubt that the buzz of energy and enthusiasm engendered by Runrig faded when they left the stage.'

The summer accelerated into Europe, with two major festival appearances, one at Skanderburg in Denmark, the other in the Celtic festival at Lorient in Brittany. What happened was vintage Runrig stuff. The band left Skanderburg in two groups. Donnie, Peter, Iain, Marlene and the road crew took the minibus, while Calum, Malcolm and Rory went in the transit van with all the equipment. Rory takes up the story: 'We left on Sunday, and we had to reach Lorient by Tuesday, where we were headlining the main Lorient concert with the Pogues. First of all we had radiator trouble, at a German farm, then outside Hamburg on the autobahn. None of us

Opposite:
Edinburgh Playhouse:
the first sell-out

spoke German, we had no German money, and anyway there were no
garages open on Sunday.

'We tried to hire another van, but no luck. Then we eventually found a
garage and got going, only to break down again. We stayed the night in
Germany, then got going again at lunchtime on Monday. We were having
to rush by then, so we tried to drive through the night, but in the end we
had to rest in a French border town . . .

'Next day, Tuesday, we were making good time through a deserted area
of western France, when we heard a large explosion. The van shuddered
to a halt, leaking oil and steaming all over. We had to run miles across
fields to get help, trying to avoid guard dogs at various farms. And we
couldn't speak much French. Eventually, we got a breakdown wagon out,
but by now we had a feeling we might miss the show. Visions of financial
disaster loomed large.'

Marlene was, with some trepidation, telephoned – 'she was in a state of
panic' – and then, suddenly, the van was fixed. According to Rory, 'we
drove 80 miles in 55 minutes to get the gear set up ten minutes before
show-time.'

Lorient had always been an event where things happened to Runrig, and
they played the Breton festival several times. On one occasion, angry fans
protesting against the loudness of Runrig compared to the acoustic traditionalism of another band invaded the stage during a sound-check.
Defending his territory, Rory manhandled a voluble Frenchman off the
stage, loudly. He later discovered, in Donnie's words, 'he had just thrown
the mayor of Lorient, our host, off the stage'.

Less traumatic was the Commonwealth Games concert, broadcast by
BBC TV and featuring old pal Freeland Barbour and the Wallochmor
Ceilidh Band.

Self-inflicted wounds being something of a Runrig speciality, though,
1986 could not be let lie without another disaster, albeit one without
serious consequences. In retrospect, the saga of *The Work Song* is hilarious,
involving another onset of that Runrig curse: the mysterious machinery
breakdown.

With any follow-up album to *Heartland* impossible before mid-1987,
the idea of recording a quick, cheap, and hopefully successful single was
appealing in the autumn of 1986. After all, it would capitalise on what
had been a successful year's live work. Or so it seemed.

Another van, another low
bridge: the infamous driving-
home-late-at-night incident

The Work Song had already been demoed at home by Calum and Rory
on their trusty Portastudio, and its poignant tale of youth, employment,
unemployment and the West of Scotland work ethic was familiar Runrig
territory. A quick, producer-less recording session was mooted on cost
grounds, as was the decision to use Pier House Studios in Edinburgh, a
much less upmarket operation at that stage than REL or Castlesound.

A backing track was recorded, and then the band, acting as their own
producers, decided on a shift to Hart Street studios – 'might be good for
the atmosphere of the track'. Everything was moved, the recording began,
and the mixing-desk immediately broke down. Engineers from England

repaired it. It duly broke down again, this time terminally. Another move seemed advisable.

So off Runrig went to Craighall, another studio used mostly for demos, with their alter egos, the ace producers, in hot pursuit. Craighall was famous for recording pipe bands and accordions. It only took a few days for the mixing-desk there to disintegrate in the jinxed presence of the Runrig contingent. The band were running out of studios.

Next they moved upmarket to REL, where the studio engineer, Beeg Al, kept a nervous eye on his mixing-desk, and finally the recording was completed. The only problem now was that having used four studios, nobody could remember what was recorded on which bit of the multi-track tape. And the ace producers hadn't taken a note.

An understandably exasperated Calum Malcolm of Castlesound was then faced with pleadings that he try and salvage something from the complex mess. Somehow, he managed to mix *The Work Song* into a surprisingly cohesive whole. It's not a bad single. The B-side, the lovely *This Time of Year*, was lifted from material previously recorded for *Heartland* at Ça Va in Glasgow, meaning that six Scottish studios had been used to make one single. 'Is this a record?' the band asked. No one seemed to be sure if *The Work Song* was, in fact, much of a single. It was released in December and received 'absolutely no critical acclaim and flopped disastrously', says Rory. Old pal Campbell Gunn wanted to like it, though one wonders if his *People's Journal* comment that 'the words come over loud and clear in what is an excellent mix' was a bit of an in-joke. However, 'it takes several hearings to impress itself on the mind'.

The band were unperturbed. Ridge Records were by this time turning over a reasonable profit – although Calum and Donnie had been hauled up to Portree by the Royal Bank of Scotland to account for the band's ever-increasing overdraft. They did allow themselves the luxury of one final dip into 'Fisher's Pond', as the account had affectionately become known – named after Mr Fisher, a very sympathetic manager – to hire the fastest and most luxurious motor possible for the journey to Skye and the impending High Noon.

Meanwhile, back at *The Work Song*, 'We decided in our collective wisdom,' says Peter, 'to press up extra copies to cope with the inevitable rush of orders – about ten times the actual number required.' 'Even today,' he continues, sorrowfully, 'band members' homes are littered with small boxes of *Work Song* singles. They have been employed as all sorts of useful household aids . . .'

It was not a hit, *The Work Song*. Not even with the burglars who broke into Runrig's Aberdeen office the following year. Finding several boxes of the record amongst their swag, they duly returned them all anonymously. It was not a popular record but it is still available – indeed, a cupboard in REL studios is reputedly still filled with unsold copies.

And so the year ended and 1987 began in spectacularly uplifting style, with the BBC's Hogmanay concert, featuring the irrepressible Andy Cameron. The new year was to be a watershed.

Iain keeping time

Getting ahead in Calgary, Canada

Left:
Malcolm jamming with
Charlie and Mark from
Capercaillie, backstage
at the Winnipeg Folk
Festival

CHAPTER NINE

AN UBHAL AS AIRDE

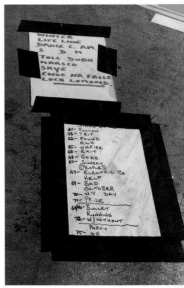

A tale of two set lists, Murrayfield

For the band, 1987 was a year of live success beyond their wildest dreams, a year when the word 'Runrig' became better known outside Gaeldom as a band than as an answer to a crossword clue about land tenure.

If an ideal strategy had been planned out for the eventual release in December of *The Cutter and the Clan*, the album that was to change everything, it would have differed little from the actual events of the year. In the early spring, the band began recording at REL Studios with Beeg Al engineering since Castlesound, by then one of the hottest studios in Britain as a result of the Blue Nile's success, was booked up. Chris Harley had once more been enlisted as producer, a task he was by now relishing – although he admits that working with the band has not been the easiest of jobs.

'It can be problematic, but it isn't caused through bloody-mindedness, it's caused by an anxiety, mainly from Rory and Malcolm, to get things right. There is a real perfectionist streak in the band, and it takes them a long time to trust anyone because they've been betrayed so much. We've had many heated arguments in the studio, but in the end they've not found it hard to trust me, because I'm dead straight with all of them.'

The sessions for *The Cutter* were almost the first since *Highland Connection* to open without the sense of imminent financial disaster hanging over the band. Confidence was high, and when the time came to break off in the summer for foreign touring, it was even higher. Things had gone well. 'With the energy that there was then, people were definitely starting to view us more as a rock band,' says Donnie, whose on-stage confidence and sense of security with his role were both growing by the day. 'This was the first time the band was really confident. We often look back on things and that's an attitude we still have that's a real leveller, and I'm glad we have it. Rory especially has it, and it's useful when you're in situations that are greater or grander than you might have thought you would ever have been in.

'In some ways it's a negative trait, a Highland trait, where you sort of put yourself down before anyone else does – where you say "Och, maybe we will . . ." but it's a self-protecting modesty. You tell people they won't like something before they've a chance to knock you. It's possibly a historical throwback – the whole history of the Highlands displays that attitude. But in 1987, with *The Cutter and the Clan* and everything, the performance was as individuals with determination and there was an obvious personal commitment, because we'd gone through all this stuff on a personal level.'

'It all came from within ourselves,' says Iain Bayne, 'but I think in particular Donnie gained a lot of confidence in terms of performing, and as a singer.' The studio work with Chris Harley had a lot to do with this, as can be heard in the vastly increased Munro range on *The Cutter*. 'Donnie is the actual sound of the band,' says Chris. 'He has to carry the songs – but the songs are the important part. The shows are the band's face and, of course, their funds.' And with no longer any need to use his guitar as something of a shield, the sight of Donnie in air-pummelling front-man mould began to carry the songs to the furthest reaches of the biggest venues imaginable. Such projection proved necessary.

The shows in the summer of 1987 were bigger and scarier than ever before. The band were ready. First there was a successful tour of Denmark, which had become something of a happy hunting ground, followed in the same country by Midtfyn, a gigantic festival which saw the unlikely head-lining combination of Runrig, Lou Reed and Chuck Berry – and the biggest-ever Runrig crowd, some 60,000 people. Then came the first tour of Canada, which proved to be an important springboard for the band and the whole experience a well of inspiration for songs which were to appear on the *Cutter* album. There was an air of real optimism at long last, with everyone feeling very positive and stimulated. The tour included a late-night slot at the Winnipeg Festival, which Calum referred to as 'probably our best performance to date, despite the pouring rain – or maybe because of it'.

The night after Runrig played, Donnie was backstage with Scots-Australian folk singer Eric Bogle, watching ageing starchild Donovan mesmerise the huge crowd with memories of flower power and lurve. 'I remember Eric Bogle peering through this tiny chink in the backstage curtain at Donovan as he sang these songs of peace and love, and him growling, "Get that hippy bastard off of there!" ' It brought back long-buried Munro memories of the '70s, when Donovan had a retreat on Skye. He and his manager, Gipsy Dave Smith, were met by a youthful Donnie Munro, for some reason 'riding a horse from a farm to some stables'. Donovan and Gipsy Dave were most impressed by this display of rural ethnicity, Donnie remembers. At Winnipeg, he happily informed the well-preserved trouba-dour of their previous meeting, and of Donovan's greatest moment of fame – opening a sale of work at the Skye Gathering Hall. 'He was horrified.'

But for the home market the key was the support to contemporary superstars U2 at Murrayfield in August, a marriage made in heaven and in part courtesy of Simple Minds' Jim Kerr, who sang the band's praises to close friend Bono, but mainly by a titanic piece of management by Marlene. She deflected and ducked blow after blow from the London music biz heavyweights and refused to give in until the band had secured their place on the bill, making sure that any subsequent Runrig promotions would be adopting a greater sense of fair play in respect of support bands and artistes. As the size of venue increased, Donnie wrestled with the political stance of the band, pondering whether or not overt statements were the key. The words of *Cuir Car* producer Martin Macdonald remained with him. 'I'd said to Martin, "I think we should maybe be much more political", and he shook his head and said, "You're political by the mere fact that you as a band exist." '

Murrayfield itself was another step onwards and upwards. Bob Flynn was reporting on the event for *NME*. 'I remember the effect they had, and it seemed to be something of a watershed for them. They were the first band on that day, and they were way ahead of all the other supports. People were just hanging about the stadium and milling around until Runrig started, and then they just appeared from all over the place to converge on the stage . . . and they played brilliantly. Blowing Love and Money, the Mission and the Pogues off stage was no small accomplishment.'

Runrig's next appearance was somewhat different. A converted army hut in Aultbea was, says Donnie, 'just as good in many ways'.

On something of a high, the band returned to the studio as the summer slipped into autumn, and October saw *The Cutter* being mixed for release before Christmas. A pivotal television outing also raised the band's profile, not to mention establishing a working relationship which would eventually bear more extravagant fruit. *Mod for Rockers* utilised a pun which had been in existence since the Skyevers as the title for a Scottish Television broadcast of a Runrig concert from that year's National Mod in Stirling. But there was still bad feeling from some traditionalist quarters about the exposure given to nasty old rock in an environment more attuned to kilts, frilly blouses, choirs and 'proper' music – and it hit the press. It all seems rather silly nowadays, when traditional Gaelic singers use the Runrig canon as a source of material.

Alistair Moffat, now head of programmes at Scottish Television, remem-

The crowd at Murrayfield

The *Cutter* tour

bers the programme well. He was already a Runrig fan, his first task on joining Scottish in 1982 having been what he calls 'probably the worst job in the world' – making a film about the Mod, then being held in Fort William. 'I knew more about Geordies then than I did about Gaels, and I found it quite extraordinary – all these wee lassies singing the same song and things like that, many of them unable to speak Gaelic, having just learned the songs phonetically. I couldn't make head nor tail of it. Then I came across Runrig, who were performing there, and I thought they were wonderful – they were so incredibly different.' He had no direct input in *Mods for Rockers* five years later, 'but I was keen to do it – I liked the title. It did really well, and I began to understand this phenomenal support the band had.' The Scottish Television connection would eventually lead to the sumptuous *City of Lights* film, of course, but the lower-budget outside broadcast *Mods for Rockers* impressed many neutral non-Gaels with the band.

Just before *The Cutter* was released, an emotional return to Skye saw the band participating in what, according to the *Free Press*, 'many thought was one of the most entertaining evenings the Skye Gathering Hall had ever seen'. Included were many stars of the Gaelic firmament such as Arthur Cormack, Mary MacInnes and Blair Douglas, in what turned out to be a very moving tribute to the late Robert Macdonald. There was also a televised version later shown on BBC Scotland.

The concert was in aid of the Robert Macdonald Memorial Trust, set up to help young people in their musical education. A memorial library at

Portree High School today reflects Robert's contribution to both music and to Gaelic history.

The Cutter and the Clan was the subject of much pre-release discussion, specifically about the title. Peter and Iain felt the use of the word 'clan' reinforced the stereotype of a tartan-tinged band which should be dispensed with immediately. ('I still don't think it was the best title for it,' says a mildly mutinous drummer today.) Iain T-shirt Macdonald, who at this stage became involved full-time doing the band's press and publicity, remembers the stushies. 'There was a lot of argument. Both Peter and Iain were very strongly against that title, but Calum and Rory loved it. They were trying to push the idea that it was "The Clan", the international family.' Rory and Calum won the day, and *The Cutter* arrived in its splendidly poignant McIlroy Coates cover, complete with Red Indian symbols, already exuding the transatlantic emigrant-homeland atmosphere which pervaded the music.

Everything was poised for the big push. The indefatigable Iain – now swapping his 'T-shirt' soubriquet, necessary to distinguish him from Scotland's many other Iain Macdonalds, for the middle initial 'D' – took on the role of press representative with enormous enthusiasm and energy, sparking the already-fuelled press interest in album number five. 'It was a really exciting time, it was great. There was a real buzz about *The Cutter* and we felt it would do well – although I don't think anybody expected it to do as well as it did.'

'We felt it had worked for us as an album,' says Rory. 'What happened was that we had a good collection of songs, but there was an atmosphere. It was dramatic, and there was that feeling of confidence.' Iain Bayne concurs. 'I felt Calum and Rory were saying something really, really strong

Left:
Party at the end of the *Cutter* tour. Chris, with Peter's mum and Marlene's son, Gordon

Right:
Partying

The *Cutter* and the cake

on that album.' And Donnie, whose vocals caught fire on *The Cutter* in a new, wholly assured way, was surprised at his own reaction. 'For the first time, I sat down with an album we'd produced and said, "Well, there's a kind of completeness here. There's a feeling from the band of something quite powerful." Before *The Cutter* there had always been powerful songs – I've always had a high regard for Calum and Rory's songwriting – but there was something about these songs which did not reflect just a concept but really connected through the band for the first time. There was something about *The Cutter and the Clan* which was quite irresistible.'

It was also a time for Peter to make his mark. He was afforded a lot of space musically which he was to utilise with a freshness and directness of style which greatly enhanced this and future album projects. Peter adds, 'I thoroughly enjoyed the experience of my first studio recording and I was determined to put my stamp on it, and feature the keyboards prominently in the mix. The bands I had been listening to prior to joining had been the big sounds of Simple Minds, U2 and early Big Country. It was this dimension I wanted to bring to our recording.'

'As is often the case in recording,' adds Donnie, 'certain tracks take on a life of their own. This was certainly true of *Alba* to which I must confess to being an initial doubter, and *An Ubhal As Airde* which was to be one of the most fortuitous, spontaneous and compelling moments in my experience with the band. These sessions were filled with a passion which I hope we will never lose.'

The mainstream tabloids were beginning to catch on to Runrig's huge following, and so even the mass-circulation *Daily Record* gave the album space. Initially, pop writer Billy Sloan had taken an idea for a Runrig feature to his editor, only to be told that 'Runrig were thought of as too faceless and anonymous'. The problem at first, says Billy, was that 'Runrig are not really weird enough or different enough for a daily newspaper'. Things were changing fast.

The reviews were astonishing. Bob Flynn gave them a virtually unprecedented score of ten in his *NME* piece, and favourable reviews followed in all the major rock weeklies. A pop column syndicated to English regional papers, supposedly by Radio One's Simon Mayo but actually ghosted by journalist Mike Davies, raved about the band, apparently to Mr Mayo's initial confusion. It was a time when the Proclaimers were bringing Scottish pop gutteralism into fashion, and the whole roots-music boom was in full swing. No wonder, then, that firmly London-based papers like the *Guardian* and the *Independent* began taking an enthusiastic interest. If it was cool to have roots, then Runrig's remained untinted . . . well, almost.

Back at the root of the roots, the *Free Press* took a leisurely (March 1988) look back at *The Cutter*. Torcuil Crichton's 'personal reflection' on the album was a fascinating assessment by one of the rising stars of bilingual Scottish journalism, and someone who understood not only rock music, but the demands of the Gaidhealtacht, thoroughly.

'Commercial success is initially what I thought the album was all about,' Torcuil wrote. 'The music struck home as a rather bland and shallow carbon of former Runrig albums. I hated it before I'd listened to it properly.' But on reflection, what was wrong with popular music? Torcuil pondered. And 'the fact that it contained only two Gaelic tracks' might not be just 'an indication of the album's wider sales pitch'. Why, as the band themselves asked, 'write or sing in Gaelic for Gaelic's sake if it's not good?'

But *Alba* and *An Ubhal As Airde* were both OK, with the latter singled out for praise in its 'haunting employment of Gaelic psalm singing in the arrangement'. While 'religious music, or rather religious-sounding music – from the *muezzin* calling the faithful to prayer to the *eildear* leading the psalms – succeeds in transcending cultures to provoke a response, a series of images translated from a distinctly Gaelic background into an English song do not.' In this category, according to Torcuil, was *Worker for the Wind*. 'Imagery, words and experiences which would mean everything in Gaelic are left fallow.' *Pride of the Summer*, however, 'captures perfectly the first rush of young love in Portree or anywhere else for that matter. It may be that it works because adolescence was experienced with an English consciousness while the croft was much earlier, and always Gaelic.'

The rest of the review trashed *The Cutter* and *The Only Rose* ('interesting, but nothing more than that, not even musically'), liked *Protect and Survive* and loved *Our Earth Was Once Green* and *Rocket to the Moon*. Having said all that, accusations of 'sell-out' were inappropriate, Torcuil insisted, and the effect of the album overall was to destroy scepticism. 'Play the tape at full blast on a car stereo or a Walkman while heading north across Rannoch Moor. That always works: there's nothing like coming home to Runrig.'

It was a very significant review, by a young Gael on the crest of the Gaelic renaissance's new wave, unwilling to treat Runrig as either sacred cow or turncoats. Instead, Gaeldom's greatest suffered an intellectual dissection by a sympathetic fellow-Gael who had, unlike Calum and Rory, returned to live and work in the heart of the heartland. Never had their urban exile shown so clearly.

But it was the first time a dispassionate, critical overview of the band's work had been undertaken by someone who knew what was going on in both English and Gaelic. The fact that, in the end, the record's sheer emotional pull drew Torcuil into identification with it perhaps displayed the central fact about Runrig for Gaels in particular and Scots in general: we live in a context which makes the music's feel and the lyrics' content irresistible. We understand what we sometimes do not comprehend, and respond to what we may not think we ought to enjoy.

Three and a bit years on, *The Cutter and the Clan* still stands as Runrig's finest album prior to *The Big Wheel*. The production takes off from *Heartland*'s smoothness into a big, reverberant spaciousness reminiscent of Simple Minds or U2. Only the hard edge left around some high frequencies makes you wonder what it would have sounded like if it had been made at Castlesound.

Alba, released as a single by Ridge as a taster for the LP, might have

Barrowland dressing-room, before recording the live album, Christmas, 1987

been a hit in its single form, if — and it's a shame to say it — it had not been in Gaelic. In English, it might have been too overtly political for the playlists anyway. Its prophetic vision draws on Calum's increasing Christian commitment, and in one verse completely on the prophet Isaiah. The integration of the returning exile, the warmth and beauty of the land, its rape by the rich, and urban economic downfall, are beautifully accomplished and carry real spiritual power. But what did Bishop Desmond Tutu make of it? He borrowed the single from a Runrig-loving development worker in South Africa, having been captivated by the strangeness of Gaelic rock music. 'The thought of Bishop Tutu bopping around at home to *Alba* is an interesting one,' grins Donnie.

The affectionate, but melancholy *Cutter* itself is a brilliant story song, a sketch of the real-life Johnny Morrison, as featured in Scottish Television's *Playing for your Country* film. The irony of the successful exile in Canada who comes home to cut his mother's peat every summer is wonderfully reinforced by the music, which captures both the joy and sadness of the situation.

Donnie in full flight

Pride of the Summer and *Hearts of Olden Glory* provide side one with another two songs of enormous quality, the latter's effortless imagery of Christian renewal blending with both the description of fading photographs and a much more primitive, pagan form of rebirth than that signified by 'a cross for your people'. *Worker for the Wind*'s potent loneliness improves with every hearing, while *Rocket to the Moon* – written on a Winnipeg bus – pays tribute to the emigrants who became immigrants in America and Canada, and *The Only Rose* spells out disenchantment and desire, a straight love song. Christianity surfaces again in *Protect and Survive*'s storming anti-war sentiments – again, lyrically too strong for the playlists, perhaps, when it later failed in the singles stakes as remodelled under Chrysalis – and also in the environmentally friendly *Our Earth Was Once Green*, although one wonders what those without a serious Sunday school background make of the line 'Romans One facing Satan's stare'. Nothing can be said about *An Ubhal As Airde* that remotely conveys its staggering beauty. Unashamedly religious – Donnie describes it as 'inspiration . . . an expression of faith' in *City of Lights* – it will forever remain one of Runrig's finest songs. And the use of the sound of Gaelic psalm singing – amazingly enough, entirely created by multi-tracking the band's own singing in the studio – simply bowls the listener over. It did (and does) this one anyway.

The Cutter and the Clan became the fastest-selling LP ever in Scotland, selling 30,000 copies in just three weeks before Christmas. Despite this, however, it failed to chart because of 'weighting' – an attempt to stop the buying up of singles into the top 50 by localised fans – descriminating against sales in any one region and sparking off the rumblings of discontent with natural chart policy which had begun with *Loch Lomond* and has ended with the setting up of two new Scottish charts over the last two years. And still no one's happy.

For Ridge Records, still being run from Dalkeith but using Iain D. Macdonald's tiny Leith flat as a warehouse, this was more of the big time than could comfortably be borne. He remembers that period with a mixture of pride and horror. 'The warehousing was an absolute nightmare.' The street where Iain still lives is absurdly narrow, a single-track dead-end and constantly swamped with parked cars. 'At one point we had three trucks up in the street with neighbours wanting to get their cars out. I don't know how people put up with it.'

A launch party had been arranged at Edinburgh's Calton Studios, but the records did not arrive until the night before. 'They arrived at the flat at four in the morning – 7,000 of them – and they had to be loaded in from the street. For a month and a half the whole house was full of boxes. They come in cartons of 40, with three of those in a big box, and they were piled right up my stairs, all the way to the top. One night I was going out and I slipped, fell right to the bottom of the stairs and brought half the records crashing down on top of me. I was lying at the bottom, I'd had hardly any sleep, and I just sat there and cried for about two minutes.'

Calum too had his burdens to bear. 'I remember driving the first consignment of *Cutter* to the back door of Virgin Records in Edinburgh, only to be met by a very surprised manager, saying, "Good grief, are you still doing this?" He was expecting the band in later that morning for a signing session. However, a cup of coffee and a quick wash did the trick.'

But it wasn't just records. There were cassettes and, for the first time, CDs. And also for the first time, the press were chasing the band rather than vice versa. 'We arranged signing sessions at record shops wherever we went. There were press conferences and tremendous press interest, so it became almost a case of servicing people rather than chasing them up. People were calling us.' It was then that the decision was taken to treat all requests for interviews equally, giving the same co-operation to local newspapers and radio stations as to national media. And the policy has paid dividends for the band, as journalists have moved up the promotions ladder and taken their affection for Runrig with them.

As sales of *The Cutter* increased, it grew harder and harder to ignore the need for a major record company. Peter Wishart and Iain Bayne had always been keen on tackling the big London companies, but had failed to convince anyone else; the memories of Simple were too fresh.

'We just felt very hurt after Simple and thought, "Oh no, I'm not going to let them do that to us again",' says Marlene. Finding the record company which would take on board the mature, successful, confident yet wary Runrig was never going to be easy.

'Runrig are a very difficult body of people to manage. They're great guys, but they've all got strong, definite views, all six of them. And they had a way of life which I couldn't see fitting in with a normal record deal which demands that you're away for nine or ten months of the year touring around America. I knew they wouldn't do that because of their family commitments – it just wasn't the lifestyle they wanted. I always had it in the back of my mind that there were parts of a record deal they wanted, but other parts they wouldn't tolerate.

'The record companies I'd dealt with in the past had been used to young bands who lived in the back of Transit vans, who were ready to do anything for sucess, even sell their grannies for a deal. Runrig were not like that, so what I had to do was sift through all the record companies and try to find a bunch of people that had some understanding of the way we wanted to live and conduct our business.'

As 1988 dawned, there were signs that the big boys were at last taking an interest in this peculiar band which could sell 35,000 albums in two months from a tiny flat in Leith. A deal struck in 1987 with John Giddings and Graham Pullen of the prestigious Solo Agency in London opened a great many doors and began a relationship which was to be mutually beneficial in the years to come. 'They were instrumental in helping us get the deal, because they had managed and been agents for so many huge acts,' Marlene says. They handled, among others, David Bowie, Phil Collins, Paul Young, REM and the Blue Nile. She smiles. 'They just couldn't believe that we make money from live shows. Nobody else does at this level. They think we're absolutely unreal because we make money from gigs. Anyway, Graham and John have proved to be loyal, trusting and good friends, as well as business colleagues.'

Graham was manager of the Edinburgh Playhouse when he had come across the band in 1983, at the famous Alain Stivel Edinburgh Folk Festival gig where the band had ended up going on *after* the headlining act. 'There had been a bit of a problem with the finances, which I'd sorted out, and I built up my relationship with Marlene, because I was very impressed with the way she'd handled that situation. In the end I promoted them three or four times at the Playhouse, and every time the audiences grew and grew.'

But after five years in Edinburgh, Graham moved south to set up Solo with John. Then, late in 1986, a measure of success under their belts, the search was on for what he calls 'longer-term projects'. He remembered Runrig.

'I called Marlene and amazingly she was still at the same number. "Are you doing any gigs?" I asked, and she said, "Actually, we're playing in Inverness tonight" – and that we'd better get ourselves up there. And I said OK.' Graham and John then flew to Glasgow, from where they caught the Loganair flight to Inverness. 'It was this thing with four seats, in the middle of winter – it was horrendous. I've never been so scared in all my life.'

It was worth it, though. At Eden Court, he and John sat at the mixing desk, 'spellbound'. They flew back to London and 'promised to do something'. There was no formal agreement, no contract – just as there is none between Marlene and the band – and Graham displays a firm belief in the personal relationship he has with the band which would be pure showbiz if it weren't so obviously heartfelt.

'I still haven't got a formal agreement with Runrig. They and Marlene are people I have a great relationship with and I'm not going to mess them about. I take them as being exactly the same way with me. The day our relationship finishes, formal agreements go out the window anyway, and a piece of paper just becomes something to hit each other over the head with.'

It was the Solo people who advised a London showcase at the Town and Country Club, which in March attracted several A&R persons to view 'this Scotch band' at first hand. Most impressed were Virgin Records, and for a time it looked certain that Runrig would become part of the Branson empire. The Scottish press carried stories claiming that a deal was imminent. Ironically, Virgin's A&R man, John Wooler, had previously been managed by Marlene during his time as a blues guitarist with Aberdeen band The Sailing Shoes.

'It was almost going to be Virgin at first,' says Calum. 'The deal was on the table. Then, after a week, word came through that everything was off because Virgin's international department couldn't commit themselves to us. So that was it, back down again. But at this point I don't think we were even disappointed any more – it was just another setback.'

Not ones to let the small matter of having a longed-for major deal whipped away from under their noses at the last second bother them, Runrig returned in ironic triumph to Glasgow's Barrowland in April, where they recorded shows for a projected live album. This would eventually, with some tracks from Eden Court Theatre in Inverness, become *Once in a Lifetime*. Meanwhile, hunting as ever in packs, more record companies were sniffing around like pigs in search of truffles.

'Iain [D.] Macdonald had been mustering a lot of enthusiasm with

Chrysalis,' says Rory. Other record companies, trying to impress, had rubbed up the resolutely down-to-earth Runrig manager very much the wrong way. 'Chrysalis were really the first bunch of people I thought I could relate to,' Marlene says. 'Most of the record company people were folk you couldn't even be bothered having a conversation with. Considering the way I'd had to do Runrig's business for years, for me to go in everywhere and see smoked salmon, caviare and champagne being dispensed so flippantly just went against the grain.'

As the first company 'in which I could see a sign of just normal business practice', Chrysalis became hot favourites. Runrig were coming into the deal with a lot to offer. *The Cutter* would go to the new record company, as would the unreleased live album, so production costs would, initially, be low – although Runrig would not be coming cheap, it was stressed.

Come Mayfest, the band were playing at Govan Town Hall, and a Chrysalis contingent flew up to Glasgow for the occasion. However, as happens when one company becomes enthusiastic about a group, other A&R men flocked to the venerable building. There, all of them, including the Chrysalis representatives, were very swiftly put in their place. Marlene is unwilling to tell the story, but Calum and Rory aren't.

'Marlene insisted that all the record company people go into this one tiny room to wait, one by one, without knowing the others were there,' Rory says. 'I'm sure every A&R man thought that they were the only ones

Marlene with Graham
Pullen of Solo

who were going to be there.'

The atmosphere in the room was strained, to say the least, when the door flew open and Marlene, in Rory's words, 'made her grand entrance'. Calum: 'She said, "Right, gentlemen! You can all get your cheque books out now!"' It was an act of considerable style.

Solo's contacts with record companies had been crucial in drumming up interest in the band, and Graham Pullen remembers the famous Govan Town Hall incident well, with the record company A&R men almost driven to palpitations by being left alone together, as he says gleefully, 'in a room without even a bar'. The moment when Marlene brutally asked one Scottish talent scout 'where the heck he'd been all his life' vastly amuses him still, especially as the word used wasn't 'heck'.

One David Belcher of the *Glasgow Herald* did not like it at all, and said so in print, provoking a storm of protest from fans and beginning something of a war of attrition between Runrig and the paper's 'thinking popster'.

Peter Robinson, the A&R man who signed Runrig to Chrysalis, was also there with colleague Stuart Slater from the company's publishing arm. 'I was just totally amazed,' he says, 'at the atmosphere and the fanaticism that was evident amongst their audience. Neither Stuart nor I had ever seen anything like it before.'

It was Solo who organised the Fulham Greyhound gig in London which eventually convinced Chrysalis to sign the band, and Graham still stresses the importance of the Runrig live performance in obtaining that deal. 'This band will sell more records by working live. Lots of bands will sell less by working live because they haven't got the talent. This band is really talented, both collectively and as individuals. They're a phenomenon.'

'We were excited about Runrig,' says Peter Robinson, 'as we felt that we could take their existing sales base and make it much bigger, and over the six or seven weeks after seeing the band we were talking to them and to Marlene. I think they liked and trusted us, and we felt the same about them. They're straightforward people, and Marlene is a straight-talking, inimitable manager. It's unusual in the music business to find a band manager who is so to the point and honest.'

Graham agrees. 'She is unlike any other manager . . . she has a way of dealing with people which is phenomenal. She motivates people to do things for her and entertains them while doing it. Once you establish a relationship with Marlene, you'll die for the woman. I know I would, and my partner would too. I mean, if we get calls in the office, we'll often say, "For God's sake, tell them I'm not in." But if it's Marlene . . . we've never done that with her.' And there can surely be no higher compliment than not having your call put on hold. On one occasion, however, Marlene put the phone down on Graham. 'They were at this festival in Denmark, and their truck arrived at the ferry terminal just in time to see the ferry steaming out of the harbour. So Marlene called me up and said, listen, we've missed the ferry. I said, oh my God, what are we going to do? And she said, I know, and put the phone down.' And what did the resourceful Aberdonian do? 'She phoned up the ferry and convinced the captain to turn round and come back for them.' Whether or not the captain came from Aberdeen is not recorded.

However, while realising 'Runrig were not a trendy band' and that there might be problems in promoting them, Chrysalis were most impressed by the band's following. 'In my A&R career I have generally signed bands without an eye to the size of their following, but in Runrig's case it was quite influential – as was the fact that I obviously liked their music.'

On 22 June the deed was done and Runrig capped an astonishing return from the near-death experience of Simple records by signing with Chrysalis. No one will spell it out, but it's reputed to be not only a very valuable deal, but one supplying more than the usual amount of artistic freedom. But then, one would expect that.

One person who was extremely pleased was Skye salmon farmer and front man of Jethro Tull, Ian Anderson, whose relationship with Chrysalis went back 20 years. 'We'd written to him way back in 1982,' admits Donnie, 'and we got this very nice letter back saying he admired what we were doing but he didn't feel in any way inclined to contribute financially because he felt that being hungry was part of what brought about the determination to make things happen for a band. But after we'd signed with Chrysalis I found out that the actual day we signed, Ian Anderson had seen us on TV and he had phoned Chrysalis immediately and said, "Look, there's this Scottish band you have to sign," and Peter Robinson said, "We have." '

'When we signed, all the financial hardship was more or less over,' Marlene says. 'We had become quite established, and we were earning good money live. What we required from the deal wasn't so much a major advance as to get the records pushed out to bigger markets. I have to say that Chrysalis were impressed with what I'd achieved, and consequently I'm held in quite a lot of respect now, which has been beneficial to me because the whole area was one in which I didn't have much confidence myself.'

Chrysalis Publishing, meanwhile, signed a deal for the Calum and Rory songbook. Storr Music was no more and, while the pre-*Cutter* albums remained on Ridge, an independent era had passed. 'It was really exciting,' Calum says, 'but there was a feeling of reluctance, too, because we'd been with Ridge and put so much work into it, taking care of every single aspect of the process over the years . . . suddenly giving that up and handing it over to somebody else was hard. It was the end of an era for us.'

Then it was a question of, so much for the Chrysalis – what about the butterfly? Things didn't take long to take off. To re-launch *The Cutter* in its Chrysalis format, it was decided to re-record *Protect and Survive* as a single, with Steven Brown producing. As in the great tradition of Runrig singles, it did not set the Gallup heather on fire, and in its 12-inch extended version, it also sounded distinctly odd, akin to some kind of attempted Celtic house-disco.

A bizarre August Bank Holiday weekend saw Runrig playing both the beer-can and dandruff Reading Festival and the evangelical Greenbelt Festi-

val – despite no one in the band holding a specifically evangelical Christian stance but Calum. 'It was a bit like being involved with Red Wedge back in 1986,' says Rory. 'We shared a general outlook. I didn't have any problems with doing It.'

Calum told the Scripture Union's 'yoof' magazine *Jam* of his faith, as well as giving the clearest description yet of the origins of the band's name: 'The run-rig system was an old farming system that was used in Scotland from the 12th century onwards, and it's still used in certain places today. It meant different things in different times, but in the Scottish feudal clan system you had an area of ground that was designated arable land for the use of the community, which was all sectioned off. This was called the run-rig system. In other areas it was used as a drainage system whereby the land was very poor and had to be drained. The "run" was the drain and the sown part the "rig". The name came from the past, it came from the earth, and it sounded quite modern too . . .' So now you know.

The rest of the band were cautious about the risks of being identified with fundamentalist Christians – but Donnie was happy to admit to *Jam* that Reading had not been a good experience. 'Our impression was that there was a lot of sadness around that site, whereas at Greenbelt there was a lot of happiness.' This was a band who had played a concert in pre-Perestroika East Berlin for the Young Communist League – Peter Wishart's favourite gig memory – and the entirely relaxed form of liberal, flexible, non-dogmatic Christianity found currently in various corners of Runrig would probably not pass muster now with the likes of *Jam* or its bigger cousin *Buzz*. Runrig, these days, are a broad church.

Religion was not heavily discussed in September at the Belfast Folk Festival, at least not on stage. There were curious encounters, though.

Donnie was informed by the promoter that two people were waiting at the stage door of the theatre and wanted to speak to him. He advised caution. In the alley behind the theatre, two young men waited in the shadows. They shook hands with Donnie. 'It's great to meet you,' said one. 'I love the band, love your music.' Donnie remembers the younger of the two nudging the other, saying, 'Go on, tell him.' And eventually the older of the two did. 'Your records are banned in Long Kesh,' he said. 'I had mine confiscated.' Donnie was stunned. 'I just didn't know what to say. It turned out he'd been in Long Kesh for eight years and had only got out two weeks previously. He'd been caught planting a bomb, and he was obviously a member of an IRA cell. The prison authorities thought our Gaelic lyrics carried republican sentiments.'

Donnie pleaded with the two men to give up violence, but to no avail. 'No doubt I was grossly inadequate, but I felt I had to say something. I pleaded with them never to do it again, to use any political means, and they just said, "No way. We'll win." ' Donnie, with a relative actually serving in the security forces at the time, found the whole encounter bizarre in the extreme. 'They were really nice guys, very friendly. And when they left, they asked if we were staying in the Europa Hotel (the most bombed hotel in Belfast). I said yes, and they just said, "Don't worry, we'll see you all right." It was a really eerie feeling.'

Many other meetings with the indefatigably humorous Belfast public and friends on that trip helped inspire the heartfelt *Eirinn* from *Searchlight*. 'It was a privilege to be in that atmosphere,' Donnie says.

October saw satisfying sessions at REL with Pete Wingfield (progenitor of the cod-soul *Eighteen with a Bullet* many years ago) producing. *This Time of Year* eventually surfaced on the flip of *Every River* the following

Left:
The signing with Chrysalis

Right:
Limos all round, boys

year – having already appeared abortively as *The Work Song*'s B-side.

In November, *Once in a Lifetime* went on sale, and that same month Runrig began a support tour with Chris De Burgh. It was not a match made in heaven, but it was survived good-humouredly and exposed the band to vast numbers of potential fans. Seasoned campaigner and long-time Runrig sound engineer Billy Worton had seen it all before, having mixed Simple Minds, AC/DC, The Boomtown Rats and many other notables from rock's hall of fame, so his experience at this level was invaluable. For the rest of the crew the experience was an eye-and-ear opener, as it gave everyone experience of working in big-time concert venues. Perhaps the verdict on that tour is best left to the unsubtle, not to say blunt, columnist for the Belfast *Sunday World*, Ivan Martin. He began his column of 3 May 1989 with the immortal words, 'For me the only decent thing about the Chris De Burgh concert in Belfast was the support band Runrig.' But many De Burgh fans became Runrig converts and Runrig do not have a bad word to say about Chris, who on the last night of the tour appeared with the band in disguise to sing *Loch Lomond*. 'It was a really nice gesture,' says Iain. 'The boy done us proud!'

The band's first silver disc, for selling 60,000 copies of *Once in a Lifetime*, presented by Nicky Campbell

CHAPTER TEN

GLORY DAYS

Blessing Chris De Burgh's unbleached cotton socks for the chance to play to huge audiences throughout England, Ireland and Wales, Runrig set out on their 1988 pre-Christmas Scottish tour, which was inevitably sold out. The enthusiastic audiences now had an example of crowd reaction they could do their level best to surpass, in the form of the live album *Once in a Lifetime*, released in November, just before the tour began.

The live LP sold an astonishing 60,000 copies before Christmas, going silver on the back of a television advertising campaign and Chrysalis's superior marketing and distribution. Using tracks recorded in March at Eden Court Theatre in Inverness, scene of those early 'Beatlemania' reports, and at Barrowland in Glasgow the following month, the album met constant demands over the years for some kind of representation of Runrig's in-concert power.

'Most of the tracks were done at Barrowland,' says Rory, 'as we found there was a better atmosphere, on the whole.'

Critical response was essentially good from those who were aware of Runrig, although the mainstream music press was by this time having difficulty in coping with the band. 'It's a big struggle to get Runrig coverage in the music papers,' says Peter Robinson. 'I think they're perceived as being a bit safe and tame.' It wasn't always so – but coverage depends on having a champion at court, and not only had Runrig's fans at *NME* and *Melody Maker* moved on to other things, but their increasing profile removed the cult tag which had once made them novel. Sneers at 'Celtic pomp rock' became common in the inkies, the weekly music papers which were by 1989 locked in a desperate struggle to survive, facing downwardly spiralling circulations and a race for a downmarket, teenybop readership. Acid House was a long way from Runrig.

But those who understood proclaimed their fervour. An increasing fan base in Ireland was reflected in reviews such as that in the magazine *In Dublin*, which called the LP 'undeniably effective' and added, 'the result is something comparable to the displays of energy and excitement Horslips used to generate in Belfast'. Surprisingly, the folk magazine *Broadbeat* voted *Once in a Lifetime* their album of the year, and Chris Simmonds belligerently demanded: 'So what if they lean more towards rock music these days? At long last here is what every Runrig fan has wanted for years – a live album, and as it covers all five previous recordings it safely doubles as a "best of" as well.'

At Newtongrange   Perhaps not quite – *An Ubhal As Airde* had not been played live by the
                     time of *Once in a Lifetime*, and personal favourites are in the end just that.
                     Given the immense quality of the overall Runrig canon, any 'Greatest Hits'
                     collection would have to be arbitrary – or perhaps thematic.

                     Which *Once in a Lifetime* certainly is. The first side moves through
                     History (*Dance Called America*) to War and Destruction (*Protect and
                     Survive*), before anchoring both in the individual islander's life and love
                     slipping away (*Chi Mi 'n Geamhradh*, superbly updated from *Play Gaelic*
                     a decade previously). The acceleration away to exile (*Rocket to the Moon*,

intensely moving with its ragged crowd-sung chorus) fades into the relief and simple attachment-to-place of *Going Home*.

Side Two is anchored solidly in geography, celebrating and meditating on the images of Marsco, Skye and, of course, *Loch Lomond*. It is about place and its meaning – a theme later to be explored more fully and mystically on *The Big Wheel*.

The end result is more than just a cobbled-together live album. *Once in a Lifetime* distils central Runrig themes out of a decade's recording, and reworks them into a new whole. Apart from anything else, the record captures the sound of the band with a clarity and depth missing from almost every other live record in existence, save perhaps the astonishing Van Morrison double set *It's Too Late to Stop Now*. The playing is a revelation throughout, particularly Malcolm's. The guitar ebbs and flows throughout the record, flooding or trickling as required to wonderful effect, the occasional flurry of feedback only adding to the huge sense of occasion generated by the crowd, whose presence is welcome, never too intrusive. Chris Harley, REL, Beeg Al and Billy Worton, the band's regular live sound engineer and co-mixer of the LP with producer Chris, all deserve accolades.

The relationship between a band and its record company is like a mar-

The Dirty Harry look: Runrig just back from their first Kirk session meeting

Great Linford Manor,
where *Searchlight* was
recorded

riage: there can be good ones and bad, stormy and serene. Mr and Mrs
Runrig-Chrysalis was a wedding of convenience, respect and even affection,
but there were still, as in any union, pressures and demands. January 1989
saw a London concert at the Dominion which sold out – the first time the
band had achieved that in England. But that same month, bowing to
demands from Chrysalis, the band began rehearsing their new album with
a producer unknown to them, Richard Manwaring. Castlesound was Runrig's choice of studio, but Chrysalis were determined to move the band
south.

'It was one area where Chrysalis wanted to give us a new start,' says
Rory, 'you know, a new producer who would try out different things. So
we said OK . . .' Calum: 'They wanted us to record outside Scotland. They
just had this feeling that really we'd been too cosy all these years recording
up here. It was an idea which really didn't work out too well. Apart from
anything else, we were keen to support the Scottish end of the music
industry, which we knew was facing difficult times, but we acquiesced.'

The fact that Castlesound, now regarded as one of the UK's top studios,
was only a few miles from most band members' homes cut no ice with
Chrysalis – but a compromise was reached, with *Searchlight* eventually
being recorded partially at Castlesound and partially at Great Linford
Studios near picturesque Milton Keynes.

Everyone wanted to do their best for the new record company, so in the
summer – that near-holy time when Runrig were usually out and about,
busily wielding instruments in front of live audiences – *Searchlight* was
being sweatily finished off. The album was mixed in central London during
one of the longest, hottest summers anyone could remember – or maybe
it just seemed that way. 'The only time it rained was when we went home

Tea and tarts on the lawn,
Great Linford

Mairi Macinnes, Karen Mathieson and Anne Turner recording *Every River* with Rory

Dinner at the studio, with producer Richard Manwaring and engineer Tony Harris

Outside the London studio where the orchestral parts for *News from Heaven* and *That Final Mile* were recorded, with string arranger Fi Trench and Captain Manwaring

Donnie tearing down these walls

Live at the Queen Margaret
Union, Glasgow, 1988

to do the video for *News from Heaven*,' complains Calum ruefully.

The album was launched with two sell-out shows at Barrowland in September, complete with massive searchlights outside the dancehall, scoring the cloudy sky like Batsignals and generally spreading fear and alarm amongst Glaswegians who remembered the Blitz. In its first week *Searchlight* grossed more than 60,000 sales, going straight into the national LP chart at 11, although it quickly fell back as the infamous regional weighting took hold. The 48-date tour which followed, taking in major European cities as well as England and Scotland, witnessed scenes of sheer pandemonium as the scrabble for tickets in Scotland reached fever pitch. Edinburgh Playhouse was sold out seven weeks in advance. The George Square Hogmanay show, welcoming Glasgow's reign as City of Culture, saw Robbie Coltrane famously blotting his ample copybook and gave the tabloid press another change to drag 'the-famous-band-that-will-only-go-on-after-midnight-on-Sunday' stories across their pages.

The band knew it was different but still thought it stood up well. Rory: 'I like it, I like the songs, but it's more of a collection of different songs rather than an album with a thematic or musical link.' For the fans it became a firm favourite, a collection of powerful songs which have benefited from their live format and many still feature in their present concert set. *News from Heaven*, released as a single – that fatal Runrig format – failed as usual to catch the public imagination, even as CD, 12-inch, limited-edition picture disc *et al*, although fans were delighted to acquire *Chi Mi 'n Tir* and *The Times They Are a-Changing* on assorted B-sides.

'Our attempts to break the singles market have all failed fairly ignominiously,' says Peter Robinson. 'We haven't been happy with the videos. Looking back on *Searchlight*, the most disappointing thing is that it didn't produce a hit single, although it has gone gold now, selling 100,000 copies.

Opposite:
Country boys

In musical terms, I think it was a very good record – my only reservation about it was the lack of up-tempo songs which *The Cutter and the Clan* had more of. It was definitely biased towards ballads and mid-tempo tracks, which made it quite a gloomy album in terms of mood.'

Erstwhile *NME* writer, now *Guardian* correspondent Bob Flynn, a fan, was unimpressed. 'The records in general don't come near the live sound. If I go to a great concert I'll often go home and put that band's record on and with Runrig it's always an anti-climax. They've never managed to capture that enormous energy and passion that they have live. They need to do what U2 did – get a level of production which is going to lift the vinyl up nearer the live sound. *Searchlight* had some of their best material, but it was so light compared to *The Cutter*, where I think they came closest.'

Stephen Pope, author of the first English national newspaper piece about Runrig, in the *Independent*, was less charitable. 'I particularly liked the stuff from *The Cutter*, and *Searchlight* seems to be a fall-off from that. It sounds in part as though they've tried to water down the Celticness a bit. I also hope that they don't stop writing about Scotland. There are some of the new love songs which don't seem as rooted in that Highland background.'

Scottish Television's Alistair Moffat – the man told by that unlikely figure, Michael Forsyth, that Stirling's Tory scourge of anyone left of Mrs Thatcher was a closet Runrig fan who continually listened to the band's tapes in his car – was also less than certain about *Searchlight*. 'They snip the umbilicus with their roots at their peril,' he says, 'and on *Searchlight* there was the hint of that happening – except for *Siol Ghoraidh*, this blockbuster thing which is in my opinion the best thing they've ever done. It's an extraordinary piece of work.'

Ah, but.

> We're all still fired
> Old emotions still burn inside
> On solid ground, round the mother tongue
> A tower of hope, a joyful sound
> You take your time
> A hand of aces in a pack of lies . . .

(From *City of Lights*, © C. & R. Macdonald, Chrysalis Music, 1989)

It's too easy to dismiss *Searchlight*, partly because it's almost too easy to listen to. This is Runrig as a pop-rock, as opposed to folk-rock band, and the elements of country music identified by the band's critical *bête noir*, David Belcher of the *Glasgow Herald*, also surface. But it does feature some of Calum and Rory's finest songs. Sure enough, *Siol Ghoraidh* is a big huge stomper of a song, and hearing it – especially live – is like being run over by its '18 teams of horses'. However, *Tir A' Mhurain*, with its hints of psalmody, not only recalls the masterful *An Ubhal As Airde* but

the band's roots right back to *Play Gaelic* as well.

Can we really disregard *News from Heaven*, Calum's overtly spiritual look at the birth of a son, the real-life personification of all this generational continuum stuff he's been writing about for 15-odd years? I think not. Richard Manwaring's production may be super-clean, but try putting on *Heartland* in comparison and hear how much bigger, more expensive, this sounds. We are in purpose-built CD territory here. *Every River* may not have been a great choice for a single, but it's still a moving song working on both the physical and spiritual levels.

Frankly, I love *City of Lights*, written about the experience of taking music to live audiences, and hustling along at a rate of knots, tuneful as ever. *Eirinn* is an incredibly brave song, tackling the problems of Ireland from the position of a 'blood brother Gael', and succeeding in protesting

Round the old Joanna for a wee sing-song

against violence while understanding its causes. It's probably the only 'pop' song about the Troubles which refuses to take an easy, dogmatic, irresponsible political or emotional stance – like, for example, Paul McCartney's appalling *Give Ireland Back to the Irish* – and it manages that because of the understanding of history's importance which infuses it. *Eirinn* is probably the best Runrig 'issue' song not dealing directly with matters Scottish.

Tear Down These Walls is a classic call to arms, compromised not a whit by its big-budget sound and vibrant rock setting. It's a miracle Lord Burton didn't try to sue the band, or at least wave a shot-gun in their general direction. The country lilt of *That Final Mile*'s paean to love and marriage could almost be sung by Willie Nelson, while *Smalltown* – complete with 1978 audience response – shows the other side of the coin from all those 'long hot summers in Skye' songs. The dark side of drink-laden and blood-spattered country dances comes over in an almost shocking way, and Runrig sound more like the berserk pre-punk ceilidh band they once were than at any time since. And few can remain unmoved, surely, at *Precious Years*?

Donnie hanging out
with Bonnie Tyler,
Reading Festival, 1988

Something fishy going
on . . . Germany, 1990

Marlene and Meatloaf,
Denmark, 1988

Well, apparently some connoisseurs can – although having gone gold as it has, fans are obviously not complaining. The album's actual sound is great, if occasionally a bit too streamlined for the good of the content. I would have to argue for *Searchlight* as a less self-consciously significant album than *The Cutter*, less integrated surely, less conceptual. But just because it doesn't have a concept it doesn't mean it's a bad album. In the same way Runrig have managed to move beyond the expectations of the Highland home crowd who wanted to hang on to 'their' band, they have the right to produce songs simply about their present experience. *Searchlight* probably isn't as important as *The Cutter*, nor is it produced with Chris Harley's certainty of touch and sheer feel for the band, but the songs are wonderful and as consummate pop-rock still firmly anchored in the Gaelic heartland, I'll root for it.

Throughout 1989, various STV persons had been having lunches and making plans, and in December, at the pre-Christmas Barrowland shows, an eight-camera film crew descended, to begin shooting the single most expensive programme in Scottish Television's history.

Alistair Moffat, STV's director of programmes and executive producer of what would become *City of Lights*, laughs sardonically when asked about the budget. 'I lied prodigiously to get the money. Oh God, it cost a fortune – I'm not going to tell you what it cost because I lied about it at the time. It cost an enormous amount of money, partly because it was on film and partly because we shot for weeks in the islands . . . and then one night we got something wrong, so we had to hire the Barrowland and go back and do some extra shots. We got 1,000 people from the fan club to come along and be a crowd for us.'

The decision to shoot the film at all stemmed from Alistair's increasing involvement in the world of Gaelic broadcasting, which eventually led him to the dizzy heights of an O-level in the subject. Gaelic, that is, not broadcasting. Barrowland was crucial to the film's success.

'We wanted to do a Barrowland concert because we wanted the sort of atmosphere of a benign tribe. The film works because that comes across – you really feel it. It's the only piece of work I've ever been involved in where the original notion actually came out of the other end of the tube.'

Director Graham Strong, who also produced the film with Seona Robertson, managed to come up with the kind of concert film-cum-documentary that many rock bands would kill to make. Occasionally tumbling into scenery over-kill and big statement-itis though it does, *City of Lights* sounds good, looks great and even, in the interviews with Donnie in Glasgow and a very cold Rory and Calum in North Uist, gives a real insight into the band's ideas and beliefs.

The North Uist filming took place in January 1990, giving the director and producers what they needed for their overall concept. 'The original notion,' says Alistair, was to do things which would contrast "city" and "home" using this kind of bleak moorland landscape. I don't know if you've ever been to North Uist, but that place wrote the book on bleakness.

It's a fairly common comparison to make, but we inverted it so that what you got was the Gaelic lyricism down in Glasgow and the driving rock 'n' roll up there. It works. You hear *Alba* and you see Uist; you hear *An Ubhal As Airde* and you see Glasgow. It's a simple technique but an effective one.'

It is too, although one old friend of Runrig was heard to exclaim: 'Who do those boys think they're kidding! North Uist? Their home was in Portree!' But she did admit that she liked the film.

City of Lights was broadcast in April, initially on Scottish and later on Grampian and Border. Alistair: 'It was absolutely the right time for the film. Sometimes you just get a hunch about these things – there was this rising, boiling tide of interest in Gaelic and the film just hit it. Getting a million people for a film about a rock band is unheard of – let alone a Gaelic rock band.' Its success prompted the ambitious programme *Playing for your Country*, in which various exiled Gaels, including Johnny Morrison of *Cutter* fame, got to choose their favourite Runrig tracks and explain their way of life, why they left the Gaidhealtacht, and what that particular song meant to them. In fact, it was a kind of *Deserted Island Discs*. Indeed, Runrig's involvement with television in the future is likely to increase, but only the right projects will be undertaken. Their importance as a televisual attraction is now immense.

When the *City of Lights* video was released on sell-through by Chrysalis/Channel Five, its sales surpassed anyone's imagintion. By Christmas 1990 it had gone considerably more than platinum, which in video terms means more than 50,000 sales. By staying in the national top ten for video sales for eight weeks, that figure has now climbed to over 70,000. 'Only *Scotch and Wry* has ever sold more,' says Alistair Moffat. 'Yet it had been on the telly in its entirety and people could have recorded it. It's extraordinary.'

As *City of Lights* continued to keep the band's profile at an all-time high, Calum and Rory began writing the songs which would eventually appear on *The Big Wheel*. A major influence on that writing was Neil Gunn's classic novel *Highland River*, with the album due to come out in his centenary year. But that would be 1991, and Chrysalis were keen to have a 'product' on the record-store shelves before then. And again, there was that hankering for a hit.

Chris Harley was by this time back in the fold, although he admits to feeling a trifle hurt at being sidelined for *Searchlight*. 'I was a bit put out at first in that I'd taken them studio-wise to that point. I was a bit sad. But it's important to stress that the deal was signed on the basis of the band's live side, and what happened was that once Chrysalis had put out a big sum, it was too risky to use a producer who hadn't any known track record.'

Searchlight itself, he thinks, sounds 'excellent'. If pushed, however, he will admit that, in his opinion, 'dynamics and feel are totally absent' although he pays tribute to Richard Manwaring as being 'a very competent producer'. At any rate, when the call came in May 1990, asking him to produce the *Capture the Heart* EP and then – if the EP worked out – *The*

And there was football, and there was Aberdeen . . . The end of the *Searchlight* tour

Filming *Siol Ghoraidh* for *City of Lights* with director Graeme Strong: Sollas Machair, North Uist, 1990

Big Wheel the following year, both at Castlesound ('the best studio in Scotland – and Calum Malcolm the engineer is a very sensitive person') he was ecstatic. 'I just went, "God, YES!" I mean, the reason I'm involved with this band is because I feel they are an important part of Scottish music, which has to be treated with care – for the sake of future generations.'

'*Capture the Heart* was a stop-gap,' says Calum. 'There's not much to say, really, except that Chrysalis were very keen to get it recorded.' Rory agreed: 'They were very keen to get a hit single, and basically that was it. Which is something we've never really had over the years.'

'We'd have been delighted,' his brother adds. 'It's never really been top of the priority list, but from their point of view, although they're doing well with us just now, they knew that if we had a hit single then album sales would double. Even by getting something into the top 40.'

Alas, it was not to be. The lavishly packaged four-track EP came out in September, with the lead track, *Stepping Down the Glory Road*, capturing a fair amount of airplay. In many ways its one of the classic Runrig songs, produced so as to kick heads in even over a trannie speaker, and indeed it sounds great on the radio. The lyrics, an ode to spiritual and aesthetic beauty and joy, were just about New Age enough to connect with southern urban sprawlees, but . . . the chart placing necessary to secure real daytime Radio One airplay was missed by a hairs-breadth.

Opposite:
Stepping Down the Glory Road

'It had a midweek position of 31,' says Calum. (Midweek chart placings are unofficial and not recorded for the chart which is released for general use at the weekend.) 'I was almost convinced it was going to reach the top 40, but it was just outside – at 49. Basically there were vast differences in where we were selling the records.' Weighting again. The introduction of new, Scotland-only charts are all very well, but the sad fact is that the main market they must conquer is in England. The Scottish charts may well be a useful money-making venture for those seeking sponsorship or a boost for bands, and yes, they may give a truer picture of what is actually selling in Scotland, but how many more records can Runrig sell here, and will a Scottish chart (or three) really help them reach a bigger audience than they already have.

Capture the Heart also features *Satellite Flood*, the nightmarish vision of a world horribly unified by the signals of satellite television, and *Harvest Moon* sees Calum replenishing his lyrical vision at the potent sources of Ecclesiastes and The Song of Solomon, utilising the imagery of the harvest to deal with both physical and spiritual love. Faith, and its insight into the arrogance of man, also infuse *The Apple Came Down*, but even an ardent Runrigophile has to describe it as musically kind of, well, odd.

'Frankly, *Capture the Heart* was a pain in the neck,' admits Rory, 'because Calum and I were working on writing the album and we got sidetracked by it.' As a tester for Chris, though, it was a success in Chrysalis's eyes.

Live work in 1990 had been limited, but prestigious. The week at Glasgow's brand new Royal Concert Hall had given even the band's sternest critics – as in Mr Belcher – cause to ponder their success, and the enormous Scottish tour in December – 30,000 tickets sold out completely in advance, a Runrig record – was a triumph, concluding with four amazing shows at the Inverness Ice Centre. Rest and recuperation over Christmas and New Year then saw a rejuvenate Runrig gathering in Pencaitland in early 1991, ready for the recording of *An Cuibhle Mor*. The plan was to spend three months on the LP but, in the event, *The Big Wheel* could not be finished before the end of April.

It was always seen as a crucial album – the record which would put the disappointments of *Searchlight* to rest. It was also Chris Harley's chance to show Chrysalis just what he could do with the band in the studio. And the record company wanted more. In Pete Robinson's slightly chilling words: 'It is our job to nudge the group in such a direction that will get Radio One interested, and that is something which I believe can be achieved with very little compromise on the part of the band. I hope we get a top-30 single, and I definitely believe that is achievable.' However, there is likely to be more pressure put on the band from Chrysalis in the future as Pete Robinson, essentially the Runrig champion in the company having signed them, left the firm's staff while *The Big Wheel* was being made. Nevertheless, he is still working with the band as Chrysalis's representative on a contract basis.

Opposite:
Capture the Heart

The early stages of writing *The Big Wheel*

For Calum and Rory, though, this record was to be a very special project. Thematically linked, the songs on *The Big Wheel* would mark a change in direction. The songs would not deal with specific historical or political events; nor would the references be localised. Instead, as in *Highland River*, the idea would be to root the entire aesthetic of the LP in their Highland-ness, their Gaelicness, in the landscape and the history of Scotland, but using those elements as the source for writing which would aim to be universal and spiritual

'It's probably a very spiritual album,' says Calum. He knows what comes next could lead to accusations from their die-hard Gaidhealtacht following of that perennial dismissal, yes, 'selling out'. 'It takes no parochial stance at all in that it aims to make the local universal. It's apolitical. There's no kind of stance at all. It's strongly spiritual.' Neil Gunn's book had served as a catalyst in the early stages of writing. In it Gunn uses the image of the river he grew up beside in Caithness, the source. 'He talks of the going away and the coming back,' says Rory, 'and there are lots of little images there which served as a catalyst. The finished album bears a resemblance to that.'

Uniquely for Runrig, the entire album was written as a single entity. 'Trying to work it through was almost like a film,' says Calum. 'We had a cinematic image of the whole thing.' But there is no question of self-indulgence, Rory believes. 'We're very excited. We've got a definite feeling about it, everything's going to be very positive. Musically it's harder, more

Donnie in a hat

Rehearsals

contemporary. The guitars sound much harder, tougher.' Calum: 'It's got a feeling similar to *The Cutter* – and hopefully there's a depth to this album.'

Meanwhile, in the midst of recording in February came sudden widespread publicity – for the band in general and Donnie in particular. It was announced that he had been nominated as a candidate for the rectorship of Edinburgh University, which came as something of a surprise to Mr Munro, who had been approached by students after one of the Inverness shows before Christmas, and hadn't quite realised what they wanted him to agree to. He had agreed anyway, though, and thought no more of it. However, when the news broke in Edinburgh University's student newspaper that he was a nominee, the national press descended on Pencaitland. Donnie's first inclination was to withdraw as gracefully as possible from the race for the post held previously and actively by Muriel Gray. After a few days, however, he changed his mind. 'I'd always wanted to accept the nomination – it was just I felt schedules were a bit too tight.' The fact that the band would not be recording in 1992 and that Chrysalis approved of lead singers becoming rectors swayed him. 'I will have time to do justice to the post,' he told *The Scotsman*. 'I just felt the students of Edinburgh University should have a wider choice.' He would also, he confided, do almost anything to prevent Margaret Thatcher gaining the office – a distinct possibility at the early stages.

As everybody knows, Donnie won that post and, like Pat Kane at Glasgow, is now a singing rector. But how many other lead singers could make a speech like the one delivered in Edinburgh that day when he actively committed himself to what is a highly visible post. His victory was, as he'd be the first to admit, Runrig's victory as well.

> *Tha e cudthromach dhomh an diugh gu bheil mi a toiseachadh nam briathran seo na mo chanain fhein, a Ghaidhlig, a Ghaidhlig Albannach. 'S i sin a chanain a cheud thug eolas an t-saoghail dhomh, agus a dh'innis mu dheidhinn gach dath is blas a th 'ann.*
>
> *A chanain a thug dhomh a cheud shealladh air caol agus air arach sabhailte. A chanain a chuir an teine beatha fhein n'am anam.*
>
> *Tha mi fo fhiachaibh mor ri mo dhualchas agus ri mo chanain. Airson an aobhair sin tha mi a toirt urram dhaigh an diugh.*

It was important for me to begin my address today in the Gaelic language for a number of reasons. Most importantly it was the language which first introduced me to the world, the language that first described its form, its colour, its music, and the language that showed to me the sense of worth in the support of the community which produced me.

It is something of a miracle that the 43rd rector of Edinburgh University is still at all capable of speaking Gaelic, given the history of institutionalised vandalism perpetrated against it, through the unspoken conspiracy of, at best, indifference; at worst, neglect. Education miserably failed me and many other young native Gaelic speakers in this way.

Not only did it deny continued meaningful contact with the language on a day-to-day basis, but it also denied us access to that other subversive force – the truth of Highland history. The truth about the history of our own people. The truth about John MacPherson of Glendale, the truth about the Land League, the truth about the Valtos men and the Braes people and many more, who all struggled courageously against the tyranny of their time.

It is not through me reflecting on a past grievance that the relevance of these denied truths now exists, but more because the result of the denial through indifference is as relevant to the present as it was to the past.

The language and culture were almost destroyed, and it remains to be seen whether new initiatives will prove successful in stopping the steady erosion. But as Murdo Macfarlane, the much-respected local bard of Melbost in Lewis, stated so defiantly: 'But still we sing.'

Many of the struggles and conflicts in the history of the Gaels were centred on the land as a resource for the common good. The land was a symbol of freedom, the bedrock of dignity and worth, which men like John MacPherson and those of the Land League movement fought hard to protect for the common people. The legacy of their example and courage remains with us today, for without the reforms they achieved there would be no people and no language in many of the places which still support healthy communities because people obtained access to the land.

While the atrocities of earlier days are behind us the power to dominate huge areas of Scotland through the ownership of land still lies in the hands of a few. They have usually gained it through inheritance or wealth rather than merit or commitment. Their right to control this great national resource will never be accepted by thinking people.

The power of landlordism is not just an evil rooted in the past. You can still find Highland landowners telling the local education authority that unless they stump up six-figure sums the ownership of some of their local schools will revert to the estate. You can still find homelessness in rural areas where no acre will be released for housing unless to the highest bidder. You will still find farms being taken over and shut down to make way for what they call sport.

The issue of land ownership should not be on the fringes of public debate in any society, but at the centre. By refusing to accord it that status we do not demonstrate its lack of importance but our own indifference to it . . .

I have pondered long and hard about what best qualifies someone for the role of rector, which I am informed is actually called Lord Rector.

We have a great love of titles in this country. The excellent advice of Robert Burns that 'the honest man's abune them a' is ignored as often as it is recited. We go further than any other society in the world by forming what is in theory the highest legislative chamber in the land exclusively from people who have been given titles by heredity or by patronage. It is scarcely surprising that they then legislate so assiduously in their own interest without a trace of embarrassment.

I recall one example from an earlier Conservative Government when they were having difficulty obtaining a majority in the House of Lords for the abolition of free school milk. A three-line whip was put out, and among those who responded to the patriotic call was one of our Scottish lords. For the first time in that parliamentary session he left his castle to play his part in the democratic process. He settled down to his first-class in-flight meal. On arrival in London he was driven to his hotel. The following day he attended the House. The Government won the day, the lord picked up his expenses and left us all safe in the knowledge that never again would some skinny waif from the urban wastelands get a mucky wee mitt around the top of a free 'Gold Top' . . .

Since my own education began in Portree High School, through higher education and my subsequent involvement as a teacher ended, many things have been and gone.

An Education Minister named Thatcher was elected leader and subsequently Prime Minister and embarked our country on the journey down the yellow brick road to the land of free enterprise and the promotion of values and ideas which would create a huge divide in society, across which was to span a great indifference to the hardship of those whose reality and hopes would fall victim to neglect. A society which would introduce new legislation on its most vulnerable young people which removed them from previous benefits. A society which would jeopardise the future of two of our most admired areas of our national provision – health and education – in an attempt to mimic the inferior but more commercialised American model.

On a national and international scale, indifference politically is inexcusable. But on an individual level, indifference is the indicator for the lack of real human love and caring.

These values, the background and ideas which infuse Donnie's rectorship with his personal story, his moral authority, are very much a part of the overall Runrig story.

CHAPTER ELEVEN

BELIEFS AND EXPECTATIONS

'History in rock 'n' roll terms is three minutes long and ends on a major chord.'

Iain Macdonald, BBC Radio Scotland

'There is a spirit of discontent all along the West Highlands at present and unless the government steps in and makes some concessions to the people by way of giving them the lands for which they are willing to pay, and fixity of tenure, they may be led to break the law, and there will result a spirit of discontentment such as no government could stop. So it is the wish of the people that their grievances should be remedied, in order to put a stop to the system of oppression and slavery under which they are labouring at present.'

Alexander Morrison of Stornoway. Evidence given to the Napier Commission, 1884

'We and our fathers have been cruelly burnt, like wasps, out of Strathnaver and forced down the barren rocks of the seashore . . . we have no security of tenure . . . we can be turned off our crofts without a penny compensation.'

Angus Mackay of Farr, Sutherland. Evidence given to the Napier Commission, 1884

'An instalment of justice . . . security of tenure and fair rents are lauded as if they were petty divinities which Highlanders ought at once to fall down and worship as great gifts . . .'

The *Oban Times*, commenting on the passing of the Crofting Act, 1886

' . . . it will be noticed that in all the Islands there are a great number of illiterates . . . English to them is unreadable . . .'

The *Scotsman*, 30 November 1886

'Identity is as important to us as industry and agriculture. If we don't have a strong sense of ourselves, how can we hope to develop as a community? Gaelic – the language, not its removable accessories – is vital to our sense of ourselves as Scots. The Highlands are part of every Scot's cerebral map, a spiritual umbilicus connects us to the north of our country. If Gaelic dies

then an active system for thinking about a necessary part of Scotland's identity dies with it.'

Alistair Moffat, controller of programmes, Scottish Television,
addressing the Royal Television Society, 1990

'Land ownership as an imposed idea has been the curse of the Highlands. It fathered the Clearances; the sheep farmers who turned fertile straths into glens of scrub; the shooting-tenants who came after to turn new wilderness into a playground for the new rich; the modern speculators in forestry and real estate . . . and land ownership as an ideal has infected even the Labour Party, judging by the 1976 Act.'

John Macleod, *The Scotsman*, 25 April 1991

'Owner-occupation of crofts appears to be spreading slowly but surely.'

Brian Wilson MP (a bitter opponent of the 1976 Act) on revelations in
April 1991 that one sixth of all crofts were privately owned

The way you sing will shine out
Illuminate the way you grow

From *Stepping Down the Glory Road*, © C. & R. Macdonald,
Chrysalis Music, 1991

Hugh MacDiarmid, great poet that he was, would probably have disliked Runrig. He hated the popularising of Gaelic and Scottish traditional song, taking the purist position in the 1950s that this was somehow to diminish the importance of both the language and the songs themselves. One of the prime movers of the Scottish folk song revival then was Hamish Henderson, illustrious writer of classic songs like *The John MacLean March* and *Freedom Come All Ye*, now retired senior lecturer at Edinburgh University's School of Scottish Studies.

'In the first three years of the People's Festival, which was organised in Glasgow by the Labour Festival Committee, we brought traditional Gaelic singers like Flora Macneil and Calum Johnstone in, the first time probably they had a chance to perform to that sort of audience. The folk song revival was really in its infancy, and this, a mixture of unaccompanied Gaelic song with the Scottish ballads, was a major stage. Hugh MacDiarmid stupidly started attacking all this. He was a great man but his position was stupid in my opinion. He thought it was just the resumption of the kailyard. It was strange he felt that way, but I think he has been proved wrong. From the very start I have been arguing with people who take a purist position about Gaelic song. These arguments have been around for a very long time, and I've always believed that the skies are the limits.

'There's no way that a tradition just marks time or, worse still, looks backwards. Any tradition worth a damn has to go forwards, and that is exactly what Runrig have done on the Gaelic side. They have taken it forwards and it's a marvellous thing to me that in this century there has been such a revival in Gaelic itself. There is the great poetry – Sorley Maclean, George Campbell Hay – and now Aonghas Macneacail and learners like Chris White are composing in Gaelic. This means that it is now a living organism. On the music side, Runrig have done just that. From their earliest days they have been composing good songs with fine lyrics, and adapting some of the old songs like *'Ic Iain 'Ic Sheumais*. They've done exactly what some of the purists said shouldn't be done.'

'Gaelic owes them a lot,' says Martin Macdonald. 'They broke open the old horizons completely.' Iain Macdonald of the BBC agrees, and argues that their English songwriting detracts not a whit from their Gaelicness. 'You'll hear some of the old diehards talking about selling out, that the band have sold out what with only having two Gaelic songs per album. But Gaelic owes them a great debt. You cannot accuse a songwriter who writes and speaks in Gaelic and continues to be a Gael of selling out because he writes some of his words in English. Every damn note you hear comes straight down a Gaelic pipeline. It's very clear, and some of the words are in English – so what? I think it's to their eternal credit that they've retained Gaelic and I don't think for one moment they've sold out to anybody.'

What was called 'the language of brigands, of popery, mischief and impiety' in the 16th century is now undergoing a massive renaissance, courtesy in part of the Highlands and Islands' councils, An Commun Gaidhealach and the Sabhal Mor Ostaig college in Skye. But Runrig's part in Gaelic's resurgence should not be underestimated, even though the band themselves are keen to play down the language issue as an *issue*.

'We never saw writing in Gaelic as a political statement,' Rory says. 'People tell us we've done so much for Gaelic, but we never ever set out to write in Gaelic in order to broaden the acceptance of the language.'

Calum is less certain. 'When you're writing songs you naturally don't want to be thinking of why you're doing it, but I really do feel immensely passionate about the language. We've consistently and deliberately avoided association with the Gaelic establishment because the only way in which we can function is by doing things our own way. Being part of that can just suck you in, and the end result would be a weaker one for both the band and the language.'

'We play music,' asserts Rory, 'we're not part of a campaign to promote Gaelic. But having said that we can never deny the huge debt we owe to the Gaelic media for their support.'

'But we know that has happened,' his brother interjects, 'and there's nobody happier than us that it has happened. Our Gaelic content must exist, because it is natural for it to exist. Anything else would be contrived and start becoming self-conscious. However, we can't help feeling that every Gaelic song we record has to count, and be special in some way. All I am and all that matters to me I have learned and experienced through the Gaelic language. To compare life's dynamic as communicated through Gaelic as opposed to English is linguistic chalk and cheese. As a language, Gaelic simply has much more flavour. Although my command of it is far from perfect.'

Although Calum is lyricist-in-chief, his brother also contributes to the verbal side of the band. 'What tends to happen is that while Calum will come up with a finished lyric, I will have a few lines,' says Rory. Both brothers write melodies, but each will work on the other's songs – hence the joint credits since 1987.

Both Macdonalds admit, however, that their commitment to writing in the language of their own culture has benefited from the renaissance which began in the mid-'70s, influencing them profoundly when they were both living for the first time in Glasgow. 'That was the start of Gaelic fighting back,' says Calum, 'especially within the student bodies. I was involved then with the Glasgow University Ossianic Society, and we did drama and music tours to the islands. Robert was involved with all that as well, as were a lot of students. They're now the ones who control the Gaelic media, by the way, people like Kenny MacQuarrie. There was a sort of groundswell of Gaelic activism.'

So the cultural movement to rehabilitate Gaelic was on the upswing, and Runrig were to some extent products of that. Have they benefited that movement as much as they have gained from it? Hamish Henderson, a self-taught but fluent Gaelic speaker, thinks so. 'Absolutely. It's a two-way process. Many people have become interested in Gaelic through Runrig. From the early days I've often played Runrig to people in this office [at the School of Scottish Studies] – mostly the Gaelic songs – and everyone sees that factor. It's definitely a two-way process and I've always seen it as one of the functions of the School to assist in this process and if possible to give access to new material for singers.' In fact, John Macinnes, also of the School of Scottish Studies, is one of Calum's mentors, involved in checking the Gaelic grammar on every album since *Highland Connection*. 'Runrig have certainly contributed in a huge way to the sung side of Scottish culture,' Hamish continues. 'Their popularity exceeds that of so many other groups – they've played a major role in it all.'

'You should remember,' points out Iain Macdonald, 'that the Gaelic stigma still applies in Scotland. There's still a viewpoint from some quarters that they're a good band despite being a bunch of teuchters singing in this odd language. It's not hip to speak Gaelic, and it's not very rock 'n' roll to be Gaelic – but it almost certainly soon will be!'

If it is, it will be due at least partly to the government's decision to invest some £9.5 million in Gaelic broadcasting. At the 1991 Celtic Film and Television Festival at Inverness – where Scottish Television won a major prize for *City of Lights* – sharply coiffured young Gaels were busy wheeling and dealing as if the Eden Court bar had suddenly become the Hollywood Hyatt House. Production companies are springing up throughout the Gaidhealtacht, and executives from Scotland's TV companies are falling over themselves to enrol in beginners' Gaelic classes. One who already has his O-level is, of course, Alistair Moffat. Just as he believes Gaelic programmes should have subtitles, he feels Gaelic is not just for Gaels.

'One of the things which has always attracted me to the music of Runrig is their way of seeing Scotland. Their view is of Scotland from the north.

What young people need is a sense of themselves. Runrig and Gaelic show how you can organise yourself differently. As far as the 98 per cent of Scots who have no Gaelic are concerned, they are describing something we can all see – *Alba* – but in Gaelic, and that's really important because it can't be more different from English. Gaelic makes you look at Scotland differently, and understand elements of its history better. How dare we Scots in Glasgow and Edinburgh do to the Gaels what the English have done to us? This disgraceful marginalisation, turning the whole place into hicksville? London is hell of a snobbish about Glasgow and Glasgow is hell of a snobbish about Stornoway. It's ridiculous.'

The idea that the wider interest in Gaelic represents a kind of nostalgia for those picturesque days of big hills, open moors and hairy legs, all to a soundtrack of *Siol Ghoraidh*, cuts no ice. 'If that were true then what Gaelic would be is some kind of musical-linguistic mouthwash, where you flushed it round your gums and then just spat out the same old things – you just did it for the quaintness of it. But it's not true.'

'I think it's right for us not to feel self-conscious about singing in Gaelic,' says the man who has to do most of the actual singing, Donnie Munro. 'We're all wary of being used as the flagship, as it were, of the Gaelic armada. We've tried not to make it self-conscious, by being primarily involved with music which happened by its natural existence to be Gaelic in origin; I think we owe a huge debt to Gaelic tradition.'

The band's three non-Gaelic speakers all appreciate the language's place in Runrig's existence. Malcolm has lived and breathed Gaelic culture nearly all his life. For Iain, the rhythms and musicality of the language are paramount.

'As a language, as a musical language, I think it's absolutely wonderful. You can interpret a Gaelic song because there's much more music behind it than an English song.' Peter, on the other hand, believes that the Gaelic contribution could be a little overstated. 'Gaelic as a culture is of immense importance to the idea of being Scottish and to the whole Scottish experience, but I'm not sure about the extent to which our home or international audiences particularly care about Gaelic. What they do appreciate is a music that knows where it is coming from – has substance and roots that can be identified and placed.'

So much of the history of the Gael is the history of land and how it was lost or stolen. It is a story of exile, banishment, leaving and yearning to return. The loss of the language's authority had at its root not only the religious fervour of early teachers of the Society for the Propagation of Christian Knowledge, but also the attempt to destroy it because of its political implications – as in Ireland, Gaelic had been the language of dissent and rebellion – and then came the moves to grind down the physical resources of its culture – the land, the crofting way of life – the Clearances. But the adolescent rejection of Gaelic which Donnie, Calum and Rory all speak of – and which will continue as long as parents and teachers are seen by children as the language's apologists – is merely the most obvious representation of a much bigger cultural attack. Alistair Moffat's speech to the Royal Television

With the Jocks in Germany: the *Searchlight* tour

Society puts it in typically abrasive style.

'A cultural hijack is what happened. At the height of the 19th-century Clearances, Lowland Scotland – often led by the Royal Family – began to frisk the Gaels for their distinctive outward characteristics: tartan, bagpipes, whisky, headgear and a great sackful of assorted cultural iconography. The less portable bits of Gaeldom, like the language, didn't travel south so easily. Cape Breton probably got more Gaelic than the central belt. Only the odd quaint and handy phrase like "*Slainte!*" as a chaser for *uisge beatha* went into Scots English. Tartan is actually a French word for partly-coloured clothes while "kilt" derives from "guilt". [Ironically, the Gaelic word for tartan is *tartain*.]

'For more than 150 years the Gaelic language has been in a terminal tailspin. As Border tweed mills churned out endless yards of tartan, at the other end of Scotland Gaelic shrank back into its island heartlands.'

Will the sudden linguistic passion of television executives and the government's cash investment be good for Gaelic, though? Calum agrees that there are signs that the ebbing tide of Gaelic culture and confidence is on the turn. 'I'm very excited and very worried. It's like for all these years there's been such a struggle, with everyone working away gradually, and then suddenly there's this massive injection of money.' Rory: 'There's even a risk of Gaelic becoming trendy – and we all know how long fashion trends last.'

Hence the preponderance of serious haircuts at the Celtic Film and TV Festival. 'If there's £9 million to make Gaelic television programmes, there are going to be some bad programmes,' says Calum, 'because there's simply not the infrastructure or the personnel capable of handling that expansion.'

Both Calum and Rory have serious worries about the pressure on television producers to invent culture – particularly youth culture – when none might exist in reality. Indeed, Rory is aware that some of the new generation of thrusting media Gaels reserve condescending sneers for Runrig as being the rock dinosaurs of Gaelic music. 'Good,' he says, now a youthful 42. 'I hope they go out and do something different. That would be really good. But to be honest, Gaeldom is dead at the moment musically, at least in a rock sense apart from Capercaillie who are trying to cross over, and of course Blair. There's absolutely nothing new coming up.' And mention of the BBC television programme *Brag* and its regular feature of young Gaelic bands brings concern from Calum. 'There's no such thing as *Brag*-type bands really. There's a budget and somebody is employed to go out and hunt for new Gaelic music which just doesn't exist, so a lot has to be invented or just cobbled together. I really sympathise with programme makers – their task is not going to get any easier. People are trying to invent all sorts of things which should be happening naturally. If there really is a vibrant Gaelic culture now emerging, then there should be radical, rebellious, energetic bands and young people desperate to express themselves.'

Without Runrig, would Gaelic have achieved what it has? Iain Macdonald doesn't think so. He describes the famous interview with Murdo MacFarlane, when the bard talked of walking down the street with a neighbour, speaking away, and, on saying goodbye, realising that 'in another generation the language won't exist, and this conversation will not be possible'.

'People have been saying things like that – and they're important things to say – for a very long time. They would still be voices in the wilderness if people like Runrig hadn't come along and made the impact on popular

Berlin: tearing down walls

culture, with non-Gaelic speakers, and that's the important thing that they did do. Those people would still be voices in the wilderness otherwise, and certainly there wouldn't be £9.5 million on the table now. I mean, it's far-fetched to say that the Scottish Secretary is influenced by Runrig! But I think you could trace a direct line from one to the other.'

One of the central catalysts for Runrig's own rediscovery of their roots in the early days was, of course, the *West Highland Free Press*, which rooted its brand of socialism very much in the history of repression by landlords and governments of the Gael.

'Looking back on it all,' says Rory, 'I think that the *West Highland Free Press* and Brian Wilson, who I was very friendly with at the time, were very influential. It definitely instilled a political awareness, the paper. A political awareness in young people in Skye which simply hadn't been there before. They took on the landlords, and they understood the reasons why they were doing it. It was an education.'

'And it took the *Free Press* quite a long time to be accepted,' Calum points out, 'because they were from outside the island.'

Always a keen supporter of the band, Brian – the only party politician ever to receive an official endorsement from Runrig (during an early parliamentary campaign in the Western Isles where, in Calum's words, 'the SNP had him on the run') – saw the paper and the band growing up together. 'During the paper's formative years its major importance was to raise the whole profile of land issues and I think that anyone in Skye who liked the paper would have become more aware of these. Everyone has the right to expand the awareness of injustice and it's a great thing that they translated that into a popular form.'

The man from Tama

Trying to pin down Runrig's political position as a band is difficult. Marlene, for example, is a staunch patriot with serious political ambitions. 'The political arena is definitely something I would like to enter,' she says. 'I would like to make the Scottish people aware of the nets they don't have to be tangled in. It's my lifelong ambition to help separate Scotland from England – but I don't and wouldn't use the band for those ends.' Similarly, Peter Wishart, inheritor of a radical family tradition which goes back to his grandfather's union activism, is no longer a member of the Labour Party. He remains unrepentantly socialist but has found that since joining the band his concern for the devolution issue has increased. 'I'm not saying I'm a nationalist, and I probably never will join the SNP, but Runrig's cultural involvement in Scottish mainstream life has made me see Scotland itself, how to shape the Scottish nation, as at the top of the political agenda.'

But no one is prepared to set down a Runrig political agenda. The notion of justice, as based in the whole question of land rights in the 1880s, is central, and in days gone by the band would cheerfully have admitted its Labour sympathies – indeed, in endorsing Brian Wilson, did so publicly. Participation in such events as Red Wedge and the TUC's Day for Scotland illustrate, these days, a non-specific socialism.

'Loosely socialist,' says Rory, 'and loosely nationalist too, and loosely green! It's very difficult. Really the only voice the band has is what every song says. We're really artists first, and we've been scunnered at people wanting to jump on us, dragging Runrig into some cause.'

'Loosely nationalist' Runrig may be, but the SNP have never been forgiven for using some of the band's music in a 1983 election broadcast without asking permission.

'That was really bad,' says Calum. 'A lot of people want you to represent their point of view, whether it be the SNP or the Free Church.'

Brian Wilson was extremely upset by the SNP's appropriation of his friends' music. 'It's inevitable that something with a clear Scottish identity which is popular will be claimed by the Nationalists. It's not my job to go around denying what they lay claim to on behalf of anybody, but it's obviously important that they're not allowed just to ambush people and images which are not theirs. It's because of the strength of the band's Scottish image that Runrig's feelings have to be repeated quite often, and that in itself must become tedious. It's not their job to have to go around denying things that other people pin on them.'

But Runrig will not affirm the Labour connection which Brian obviously still believes is current. Donnie is unwilling to be more than general: 'There is an identity at some level in that, if you asked us all, we would all affirm that we wanted to achieve something basic in the human condition that would be pretty much along the same lines. How you achieve that through a political system would probably be a point of great debate within the band. But I would say that I'm certainly left – slightly left of centre to varying degrees on different issues. In that respect I still wouldn't want to fly any convenient flag.' But it took the plethora of interviews following his elevation to rector at Edinburgh University to force Donnie into nailing his own

On tour: Donnie
waking up on the bus
alongside Mike Smith
from the Aberdeen office

personal colours to the mast, revealing what most already knew – that he
was 'a lifelong Labour supporter'. There were fascinating hints of a possible
future involvement in parliamentary politics – although the prospect of
Donald Munro MP remains a distant one.

Still, flags do sometimes fly during Runrig videos and on stage, and those
flags are red. Hamish Henderson takes a bluntly agitprop view: 'All art is
strictly brainwashing up to a point, but Runrig have a political stance which
I am in favour of and I would strongly defend their right to put over what
they do. It comes over well, and clearly, and so it should. If they didn't give
expression to what they feel, they wouldn't be doing their duty to themselves
or anyone else.'

Never on a Sunday. If Runrig ever had a gimmick, other than that they sing
in Gaelic, then surely it is their position as Britain's only Sabbatarian rock
band. Hogmanay concert with live TV coverage? Well, OK, but only if we
can go on after midnight . . . of course, the tabloids loved it.

It's been spelt out hundreds of times in the press, with Calum or Rory or
Donnie explaining quietly about the decision taken many years ago, 'partly
on religious grounds, partly out of respect for our background and the
relatives who still live there'. Keeping the Sabbath had many benefits, cynical
reporters were told. At the most basic level, the day of rest offered a chance
to do just that. And, of course, there were bizarre occurrences, like refusing
to start Sunday gigs in Catholic South Uist – where Presbyterian Sabbatarianism was without influence – until after midnight so that it was technically
Monday. And that was a decade before the stramash over the 1989 George
Square Hogmanay bash.

Having said that, the band have been known to travel on Sundays if it has been necessary, the Sabbath, after all, having been made for man, not man for the Sabbath. But while recording, for instance, they work – when possible – a five-day week, usually knocking off at about 6.00 p.m. and looking forward to the weekend just like any other workers. Family life has a special place in the Runrig scheme of things. It is central, *the* priority, which neither fame nor publicity is allowed to taint. The die-hard young female fans who camp outside Castlesound during recording sessions, sending the occasional red rose to their favourite band members, are dealt with firmly, and politely requested to go home.

What of the band's religious persuasion? This, after all, is a group which played at Greenbelt, the biggest evangelical Christian rock festival in Europe. But not without some heartsearching, it seems. 'I enjoyed it,' says Calum, 'but it was all a bit theologically zany around the fringes for my liking.' 'I didn't,' says his brother. 'It all seemed too . . . forced.' But then Calum will happily admit that for five years he has been a committed Christian: 'There was no dramatic Road to Damascus experience – it was just something my life confronted me with, and I had to respond. Although I would certainly align myself with that point of view.' Rory, however, will admit to having difficulty calling himself a Christian. 'I couldn't – not yet. I believe in God, and Christianity is definitely what I aspire to, but there's much more to it than that. It's one of those stumbling blocks for me personally.'

Rory: 'In many ways playing at Greenbelt was like playing with Red Wedge – we just felt so culturally detached, but really we were part in both cases of a group loosely unified under a banner.' Deacon Blue were there too, he remembers, although no big deal was made of it, and U2 had played the festival in the past.

Calum and Peter
breakfast in Norway

Both Macdonalds point out that their Free Presbyterian upbringing was nothing like as strict as might be imagined. Rory: 'There are very very few people in the FP church who actually attain church membership. Most are just adherents who never take Communion because they're made to feel unworthy.' Calum and Rory's parents were not church members, but nevertheless religious and committed, and the atmosphere in the household, as can be judged by the musical route their early lives took, was not restrictive. What they were left with, though, was a real respect for their parents' and grandparents' beliefs and culture, and a determination not to offend the people they hold dear.

Which was fine as long as the band comprised only people who were brought up in the Gaidhealtacht and understood the social background. When Iain Bayne joined Runrig, though, he thought they were daft.

'Would I play on a Sunday? I've spent half my life playing on a Sunday! When I joined the band I heard about this ruling and I thought it was absolutely crazy. I wondered how on earth they could choose the days when they could be say, here today, gone tomorrow, and I thought it was a really fickle and superficial thing. It's like a fear of the church rather than of any outstanding God. But over a period of time I began to realise that this was a sincere thing on the part of Calum and Rory and as you get older and wiser you begin to appreciate that when something's that important to somebody there's no point in arguing.' He had begun to change his tune when he saw the band survive onslaughts which would have crippled people with less moral and spiritual resolve. 'Funnily enough, at the end of it you could see the influence, because you knew that, against all the odds, where most bands would have been down the tubes, we were still rising. So that began to stir my own kind of sense of spirituality.'

But Iain would not call himself a Christian. 'I wouldn't want to see myself as any kind of crusader in any shape or form because I haven't given my life over to God. Christianity is a personal thing. It's really dangerous to get into the thing of Runrig being a Christian band, because you set yourself up to be shot down. I'd be a liar if I said that everytime I sit behind my drum kit I'm doing it for Christ. On the other hand, every night I do get behind my drums and I pray for inspiration, and I'm thankful to God for the talent I've been given.'

Peter too found the 'not on Sunday' rule hard to cope with. 'It's a bit radical to handle, but you have to respect the other members for their viewpoint.' With religious faith not on the Wishart menu, though, he still has no problem coping with the Christian element within Calum's lyrics. 'Overall there's a feeling, a spirit, an attitude which is probably recognisable as Christian. But really it's the music itself which is very potent, it means a lot to people and it has real feeling, regardless of the subject matter.'

'People look at things like lyrics,' says Donnie, 'and if there's a reference to God or something, on that basis they say the whole band is born again. Somebody actually told me the other week that I was a born-again Christian! People do get ideas about you.'

Donnie admits that he does not adhere to Sabbatarianism 'in a strict sense',

On the road: Billy Worton,
Marlene, Iain and former
monitor engineer Ian Newton
in Sweden

although he would now consider himself a Christian, whereas 'three years ago I wouldn't have said so. I actually like the idea of Sunday as I once knew it, although I have to say I rebelled against it when I was younger. I do appreciate it, though – that to some extent that quality still exists – and people's desire and right to have that sort of expression. If I were at home in Skye I would go to church in the way I've always done with my family, and that I would do here. But beyond that it's a very individual thing. It's your own particular faith and viewpoint.'

Marlene has always experienced difficulties with the Sunday question as the majority of European festivals are held over the weekend, and if Sunday's out, very often Friday and Saturday tend to be unobtainable. In the early days when she tried for guest spots with major touring bands, whole tours would be within her grasp until the Sunday issue was mentioned. 'I do not personally subscribe to that view,' she says, 'but totally respect those that do.'

Richard Cherns remembers 'many fascinating discussions in the van' about religion. 'Everybody had faith in how the music could move people and that there was something in it, which you can't really explain but which is amongst the most spiritually exhilarating writing that any rock band is putting across,' he says. However, he admits that 'Calum and Rory were probably horrified to a degree by some of my views and I'm sure there was a fair amount of clicking tongues.' The Christianity reflected in Calum's lyrics was never a problem, he claims, because 'a lot of the ways in which Calum embraces Christianity are completely in line with the ways I think . . . that matters should be addressed spiritually.

'I'm very pleased to have been born Jewish,' Richard concludes. 'But I still think that what Christianity has to say is, for the most part, fundamental to anybody's spiritual well-being.'

Perhaps one crucial thing to remember about Runrig is that, well, it's only rock 'n' roll. They cannot be expected to carry the torch constantly for not just one, but several 'big issues': Gaelic, politics and religion. As death and sex are also extensively dealt with in various songs, they effectively tackle all the great unmentionables, the great controversies.

In the end the songs have a point of view. But this is, without sounding too pretentious or upsetting Hamish Henderson, art. Not political propaganda; not evangelism; not a history lesson; not a lobby leaflet on Gaelic's behalf. Their songs have meaning and content – political, spiritual, sexual, historical, romantic and linguistic overtones, undertones and in-between-tones. But we are not talking about journalism here, writing hitched solidly to events and their description. We are not talking about persuasion or brainwashing. It's art, and art has the right to be evasive, mystical, strange, the right not to toe the party line – all of which, on occasion, applies to Runrig.

But better than that, as Zal Yanovsky of the late lamented Lovin' Spoonful once said about the music he performed: 'It's loud, and you can dance to it, and . . . it's loud.' Sometimes that's enough.

CHAPTER TWELVE

STICKS AND STONES

David Belcher once, in print, exhorted the population of Glasgow to burn my bicycle. Nobody took up the challenge, bicycles not being the most flammable of items, and eventually the then rock critic of the *Glasgow Herald* and myself reached a stage of cordially-armed neutrality. We agreed that REM, Alex Harvey and the Kent Soul re-issue LPs were fab, and disagreed about virtually everything else.

David doesn't like Runrig. It has to be said that a significant number of people feel the same way, for a variety of reasons: Runrig seem to attract either complete approval or outright dislike. There is no middle ground.

No one has expressed their dislike of Runrig quite like Mr Belcher has in the columns of the *Herald*. The response, every time a derogatory comment appeared, was always the same. Vast quantities of outraged correspondence descended on Albion Street in Glasgow, most along the lines of 'was-he-at-the-concert-at-all?', with various unprintable addendums. But then David doesn't really identify with the average Runrig fan.

'I first got to see them at Barrowland, I think it was in 1986, and I was struck by how musically old-fashioned I thought they were, and also how derivative. I felt it was a really pompous kind of plod-rock, harking back to the '70s and those dreadful sub-Genesis bands like Gentle Giant. It was twee and plodding, and in many ways I thought the audience was far too easily pleased. I recall being amazed at how many people were there wearing woolly jumpers and carrying rucksacks. I mean, it's not what you see at an average rock concert, although I dare say the world would be a better place if there were more audiences in woolly jumpers!' The band, however, point out that firstly they have never witnessed such apparel and secondly they find it inconceivable that anyone could possibly have the thermostat necessary to stand at a Runrig concert in a woolly jumper and haversack.

The woolly jumpers were something of a problem to David. 'I thought this reflected a general amateurishness in the whole event. Without wanting to sound elitist, I thought that Runrig's audience was basically an audience that had not been exposed to a lot of music. The whole thing had the atmosphere of a village hall show.' And the band's clothes were a problem too.

'Donnie was wearing a light-coloured satin jacket, which didn't fit the image of the rest of the band. Halfway through the show, rather than taking it off and throwing it across the stage in time-honoured rock 'n' roll tradition, he took it off, folded it up neatly and placed it beside the drum-riser. When the band were going off stage, he picked it up carefully and took it away. I

found this quite strange.'

He doesn't like the English lyrics either, 'a kind of nostalgic lament, saying things aren't what they used to be without offering any sort of alternative solution', but likes the Gaelic songs better, 'where I don't understand the lyrics – I think they sound more natural'. He has also detected an improvement in recent years, with the band sounding 'slightly less plod-rocky and slightly more countrified – I think Runrig should lean in that direction more heavily.'

Most bands, when they read this kind of thing, will try and shrug it off as the product of a hopelessly diseased mind. A few – in my own brief career as a rock critic, three bands, all from Glasgow – will attempt to wreak some form of physical revenge on the hapless writer. Runrig, provoked beyond the shrugging stage and not prone to violence – leaving aside a white-faced Peter Wishart, who reportedly stamped around hurling imprecations at the absent Mr Belcher and threatening revenge of the most terminal kind – decided to have a quiet word.

'It wasn't because of the opinions he had expressed – everyone has the right to their opinions,' says Donnie. 'But he had, we felt, misrepresented the band, and we thought we had the right to reply to that.'

'I was really surprised when Donnie phoned me up,' says David. If he had
known that Peter was urging Donnie in the background to 'tell that not-
very-nice person we're going to be extremely unpleasant to him in a not-
very-survivable way', he might have been even more concerned. 'It's very
unusual for a band with any degree of success to reply to a review. I think
part of their reason for phoning was a misinterpretation of what I'd written,
as they seemed to think I was accusing them of parochialism, which I wasn't.
I dug out the reviews again and, while I was mocking or taking the piss out
of certain elements of the show, there was also some constructive criticism
and positive points as well.'

'He was really nervous on the phone,' says Donnie. 'I think he thought we
were going to threaten him or something. Anyway we had a kind of discussion, and it was quite clear that he does not like what we do – he finds it
unpalatable. At one point he said, "Don't you think, though, that rock music
is really the territory of the rebellious teenager?" and I replied, "If that's
what it's all about, then I can't accept it, I can't accept that viewpoint." I
mean, it *is* about that, but it's not *just* about that. It's also about the rebellious
50-year-old who's always loved rock 'n' roll, or whatever. It's just a way of
expressing ideas and it does not have to be viewed as in any way the province

Open-air, Germany, 1990

of one tiny minority.'

'That attitude stems from people like *Melody Maker* and *NME*, that whole rock-as-teenage-rebellion thing,' says Calum. 'It's really a very conservative view, that rock music has to be street-wise and urban and overtly rebellious and hedonistic. It's utter nonsense. How can you embrace an art form in such a negative way? Maybe there is a softness about us, but we grew up in a different atmosphere, in a rural background, and we don't have that hardness. That doesn't mean we can't play rock music.' Rory agrees. 'That kind of adolescent rebellious music is great, and I love it. But everything in life can't be like that.'

Runrig are not about the crucial gesture which aligns them with rock tradition. If Donnie folds up his jacket on stage, it's because he values clothes which he has had to pay for. Waste – or being wasted, elegantly in the Keith Richard sense or otherwise – is anathema to a band which has had to struggle through times so hard anyone hooked on the rock 'n' roll live-fast-die-young myth would have quickly fled in horror and embraced chartered accountancy.

'Ultimately, I was just surprised that they could be bothered to get in touch,' says David. 'After all, it doesn't matter what I have to say about the band. They have a lot of fans, and the number of people going to Runrig concerts and buying Runrig records keeps growing, and hasn't shown any sign of decline since I gave them a bad review.'

But perhaps there is a simple problem of comprehension. David admits that 'I just don't like folk music, it's one of those blind spots I have.' He also has no interest in the Gaelic language and culture, and the notion of its history being important. Calum's 'history' songs in the end are not nostalgia but an attempt to universalise the lessons of the past. Hamish Henderson: '*Dance Called America* is an excellent example of a first-rate political song which can be applied universally. It's not just about one particular area or time in Scottish history. It has universal application and that's how it should be.'

One unlikely source agrees with David up to a point. Alistair Moffat, a man capable of raving about Runrig for hours at a time, finds the term 'plod-rock' sort of appealing. 'It's not state-of-the-art rock music – '70s plod-rock is probably about right – but I still think it's very high quality stuff. Not only that, it carries an immense amount of luggage with it, luggage which makes it different and interesting – and then there's the language as well. *An Ubhal As Airde* uses influences grabbed off every cultural shelf you can imagine, and it works. *Alba*, which is like a gigantic heartbeat, may be a very old-fashioned piece of music, but it's got a pulse, and if you add in all the Gaelic and the politics and bits of the Bible and stuff . . . it's poetry.'

Iain Macdonald believes that Runrig have managed to conquer the existentialism-as-an-excuse-for-hedonism that comes as part of modern rock's philosophical baggage. 'It's "I'm what I am and what I am is what's important and to hell with the previous generation", yet Runrig have managed to somehow get round that. *Siol Ghoraidh* conceives of the generation after generation thing, but how many bands do you know who would do a song like *The Old Boys*, which celebrates people who have lived through two World Wars, for God's sake, just as people, and make that appeal to a young audience?'

Is Runrig's music 'plod-rock'? Hamish Henderson takes a rather more high-flown view of it, making some seemingly unlikely comparisons. 'The Whistlebinkies have some similarities . . . Eddie MacGuire and his experiments . . . a functional classical composer taking traditional songs and reshaping them, although in a different musical style from Runrig. There's some similarity there.'

Indeed. What Runrig have done is take traditional music and interpret it using rock dynamics. To call them a Gaelic rock band is not just to refer to the language of the lyrics, but also to the huge musical tradition which informs their melodies. The band formed in the 1970s, but it's worth pointing out that it was also in the '70s that the first major experiments merging rock and folk began, with Fairport and Horslips. And the use of the widescreen rock dynamics pioneered by, say, Led Zeppelin – another band heavily influenced on occasion by traditional folk – enabled musicians to charge the subtlety of folk tunes with enormous visceral power. But not just power. Not just energy – which was all that punk could throw at folk music in the Pogues' amphetamine thrash – but musical light and shade.

Seventies rock is not plod-rock, not all of it. The worst of it – early Genesis, Yes, Greenslade, Gentle Giant – has no relevance to Runrig whatsoever. But yes, you can detect the enormous swoop, attack and feel for contrast . . . the *range* of Zeppelin in some of Runrig's work. A bad thing? Only for people who don't rate Led Zeppelin, most of them deaf from birth.

Billy Sloan identifies the overall sound of Runrig as important, and does not label them in terms of past rock forms. 'I don't think their appeal is particularly the music or words, more the overall noise they make. I find that with some of the Gaelic songs, I don't know the titles and I don't have a clue what they're about, but I just love the sound of them. In some ways I think it is comparable to what you get on some of David Byrne's Latin-American stuff that is sung in native tongues, or the kind of thing Peter Gabriel has done with Youssou N'Dour. The sound is more important than its component parts.'

Peter Robinson of Chrysalis takes a sober view of the music's commerciality. 'It doesn't fit into any obvious category, and that can be both positive and negative. I think they have a mainly adult audience, but they're not as mainstream as the likes of Chris Rea, Chris De Burgh or Dire Straits, partly because of the themes of the songs, partly because of the Gaelic. They are also probably not seen as having the necessary edge to be accepted along with more contemporary rock acts.'

No 'edge' on *The Cutter*? Some would beg to differ. Stephen Pope of the *Independent* – an Englishman – was blown away by the concerts he saw in 1988 in Inverness – 'we came for two and ended up staying for all four'. For him it's not just the music, 'it's what the music stands for – it's

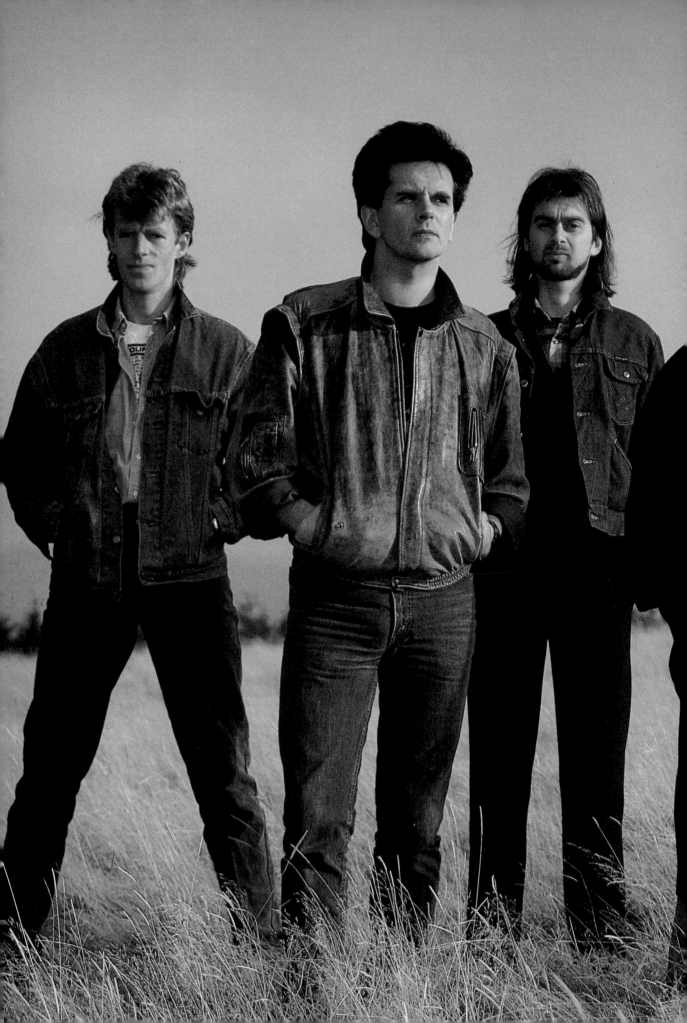

that authenticity with a capital 'A'. And that's also its Achilles' heel. Look at the music which goes down well in the south. It's brash, it's sexy, it's metallic – like Prince, or Madonna or any dance-orientated pop stuff.

'All that is very post-modern, very sophisticated, and Runrig are at the opposite end of the scale. People to whom I've pushed Runrig stuff have thought it was embarrassingly unsophisticated, but they're people who wouldn't give it the time of day anyway. I've also taken others, like my dad, who now loves Runrig. It's an identification with what the music is about. It's about the Scottishness, the Celticness, the regional position, the localness, identification with home. The homeland thing is very very important and you can identify with the need for the homeland even if you're not a Scot. I live in London, but, God knows why . . . I feel as though I don't really have a home, and something about Runrig touches that in me – and I'm certainly not a Highlander.'

For a Scot, that effect can be even more shattering, as Bob Flynn found out. 'The cynic was knocked out of me,' he says, 'when I heard them live. It was awesome and at times painful. I put them on the same plain as U2 and as far as capturing the feeling of Scottish culture, I put them above Simple Minds. I know that both bands have nodded approval at points.' Bob too finds the Gaelic songs impenetrable but overwhelming. 'You and I both know that Runrig could sing about nothing and still carry an audience with them. In a sense, that's what the Gaelic material is like for someone who doesn't understand it at all, like me. But I have to say that there is something particularly moving in some of the Gaelic numbers, even if you don't know what they mean.'

Others in the rock biz have been long-term public supporters, like Radio Scotland's Tom Ferrie. 'It's fabulous to see the band doing so well,' he says. 'They've remained the same throughout everything, and I'm very pleased for them.' Others are less likely. Tam Coyle, one of the key figures in the Glasgow punk and indie scene over the past decade and a man whose musical tastes run from the obscure to the bizarre, cheerfully admits to being a committed Runrig fan.

People who grew up with, and eventually away from, the band have few bad words to say. According to Campbell Gunn, they are 'unbeatable', with no band in Scotland capable of touching them live. 'They have developed into the best live band there is. Their sound is tremendous but I still think their real strength lies in their own music. The stuff they are writing is wonderful.' Jim Wilkie, cynical about the early Runrig's chances of success, now recognises their importance.

'They've tapped a deep-rooted Scottish cultural nerve, and Gaelic is the principal element of that,' he says. 'Lowlanders and Highlanders alike can feel their past through it and become in touch with our Celtic past. They represent that, but they're also contemporary. Musically, it's been a very long haul for them. It took them a long time to find their style. But their idea has been a good idea and a big idea. They stayed with it and the phenomenon has grown with it. I think Scotland is a better place as a result.

'Where I once saw the vocals of Donnie and Rory as "too rounded", I now think they've added something to the Scottish canon. Rory himself says he didn't try to copy black singing because he couldn't do it. But coming from a background in black music I think there's a lot of common ground with Gaelic music, particularly vocally. Scottish music has been dominated by two distinct trends. One is a disproportionate interest in black music, as evidenced by Dundee soul music and Glasgow chart bands like Wet Wet Wet. There's a long tradition of that, and there's also a tradition of Scottish music crossing over into pop, sometimes in a kitsch way, but often in a better way. Runrig represent the better way.'

Jim also pays tribute to the musicianship of the band, particularly that of Malcolm, whom he describes as 'having good ears'. Chris identifies the songs and Donnie's voice as being the most crucial elements of the Runrig sound. 'The style of music is actually defined by Calum and Rory's writing. Runrig are a Scottish band, whereas groups such as Deacon Blue and the like are not. They're bands *from* Scotland.'

As were the Corries. It seems a daft comparison, but it keeps coming up. 'They probably wouldn't thank me for it,' says Jim, 'but I do see parallels with the Corries in that they appeal to young kids, old people and everyone in between. That is something to do with the quality of Donnie's voice, firmly in the Scottish tradition, and good live performance. Donnie has also developed very well as the front man. In order to develop further, instead of looking forwards to modern commerciality, I think they should continue to draw on looking backwards because that is what has propelled them this far. There is still tremendous artistic scope there.'

Peter is aghast at the idea of Corriedom. 'It's probably a more respectful thing to say about a band now than five years ago, given the Corries' rising credibility, but no, I don't think so. The Corries represent the quick, safe image of Scotland, very much like the cabaret thing, where you can turn up anywhere and play. When you go to a Runrig concert folk are expecting much more than that. It's a spectacle, but more, it's a feeling of spirit which is amongst the band. That can only be achieved in the special environment of a Runrig gig with the full production available. Also, what the Corries wrote, it was too simple. We're not about making a straightforward point on issues. What Calum and Rory have is a gift for the sense, the spirit and the feeling of the music, and we communicate it. It's nothing like as definable as the Corries.'

'On a musical level, the comparison just doesn't happen at all,' says an amused Donnie Munro, 'although maybe we have both become institutions. You know, it's funny you should mention that, because the year I was at Moray House – the same year I was dodging all my lectures and skiving off to make *Play Gaelic* – I did a short film-making course with a guy called Townshend. He was a lecturer at that time, and I can remember one day in conversation, he was talking to me about the fact that I was spending a hell of a lot of time away from my courses, and he said: "You know, I had a couple of lads here, not all that long ago, and they were doing exactly the same things as you." And it turned out to be two guys called Ronnie Brown and Roy Williamson, who had been doing the Art post-graduate course at

Moray House. The Corries, in fact. It's quite funny . . .'

Perhaps the greatest failure in the way so-called rock journalists have dealt with Runrig lies in the nature of the genre – assuming the semi-literate scribbling of we incoherent fans justifies such a high flown appellation. Because in the end that's what rock hacks are – fans with typewriters, laden with prejudices, inconsistencies, insecurities and bias. Sometimes we are bent on revenge, motivated not by any objective search for truth but by the desire to impress or destroy for our own private reasons. Sometimes we're just chipping away at the word face for cash. Mostly we are more interested in the qualities of our own writing than in the objects of our attentions.

Runrig are hated, or rather dismissed, by people whose rock aesthetic is severely limited, not to say stunted. That an entire critical overview on an art form can be based on the notion that drugs, decadence and some spurious concept of youthful rebelliousness are key values is patently ludicrous. Limit-

Searchlight and *Once in a Lifetime* go gold. Peter Robinson of Chrysalis with the band

ing analysis of Runrig simply to their musical style misses the point of the band, their importance. No one would write about the Rolling Stones only in terms of how Afro-American open guitar-tunings coalesce with a fake Cockney attempt to sound like Muddy Waters. There is a great deal more to the importance of the Stones than that.

I'm not saying that Runrig are beyond criticism. Simply that the wrong kind of critical guns have sometimes been trained on them, by people who have no knowledge of the band's background, influences or culture, and whose narrow interpretation of what makes good rock music makes their writing largely irrelevant to their readers.

A now-famous pop star once turned to me in a bar and said, 'I despise your profession.' Most pop stars do, although they would never say so to a rock hack's face. Most musicians simply want praise, because they're essentially kids who entertain in search of ego-massaging acclamation. Criticism they can do without. Rock critics, unfortunately, are often kids too: only many of us get our kicks from lashing out, kicking over the other guy's sandcastle. One – and yes, it's an old cliché – we could never build ourselves.

Runrig are one of the few bands who actively court intelligent criticism, and who take it seriously. In certain organs of the Highland press, where their sociological and cultural importance is recognised, and where writing can be free of an impotent urban desire to imitate Hunter S. Thompson, Tom Wolfe, or that duo's *New Musical Express*-reared imitators, they have received that kind of attention. Nationally, the critical response has often been sneering, ill-informed and occasionally laughable in its attempts to justify ignorant bias as in some way an essential quality of good writing.

Runrig have borne it all with dignity. They deserve better.

CHAPTER THIRTEEN

THE BIG MACHINE

Runrig's cover version of that great, apocalyptic Dylan song, *The Times They Are a-Changing* remains a treasured memory to those who attended the 1988 concerts, one captured partially on the *News from Heaven* B-side version.

> Come gather round people, wherever you roam
> And admit that the waters around you have grown

(© *Bob Dylan, M. Witmark and Sons, 1963*)

But what of Runrig's future? How far can they go, this band who have progressed from village ceilidhs to giant festivals such as Midtfyn; from being Skye local heroes doing Thin Lizzy songs to having their own songs covered by duff local bands from Melrose to Mallaig? They've changed with the times to some extent – but will the times to come change them out of all recognition?

Chris Harley and Calum Malcolm with head-cleaning machine

'They were a big fish in a small pond,' says their producer Chris Harley. 'The next two years will be critical, because it's time for the band to cross over. Now they're coming up with world songs, as opposed to songs which are restricted to Scotland. Donnie is the voice of the band, and he carries the songs – it's a question of whether he can sing to a world audience, and whether he wants to.'

Chris's views are those of a producer who sees enormous potential in the band which he would love to draw out in the studio – although he stresses that his opinions are not necessarily the band's. 'If they are content to stay at this stage, then they will, and they won't have to change anything to do that.' But he feels that *The Big Wheel* has the songs and the overall feel to take the band forwards . . . what? 'Well,' he continues, 'if they have ambitions to play at, say, the Hollywood Bowl or Shea Stadium, then they'll have to enlarge the scope of the songs. That doesn't have to mean compromise. It really means the actual sound has to expand.'

Runrig could be a big-time stadium band in America, Chris believes, but the lyrics might not connect with the average American heartland audience, reared on Bon Jovi, Bruce Springsteen, Guns and Roses and all the rest. 'The big trouble is that an American rock band can sing about any aspect of American life or culture, and it's hip. They can sing about their cars, the freeway – anything. To take a band from Scotland to the States and have them sing about islands, heaths and mountains – it doesn't have quite the same cachet.' And would the Gaelic have to disappear too? 'It wouldn't

This page and opposite: Midtfyn Festival, Denmark

have to go, but it would have to be applied where it counted. Deep down I think Rory and Calum feel that what started in Uist has the potential to reach the States, the Far East or anywhere. I'll be surprised if they don't go for it.'

Will they, though? Runrig have managed to retain their Gaelic identity and their roots in most people's eyes while moving into a wider, all-Scotland, indeed, all-Britain arena. Would Scotland still hold them as dear if they expanded their range and content to take on the rest of the world? Indeed, can they not conquer these new territories without changing?

Alistair Moffat has no time for the moaners who think Runrig have already sold out. 'It's not fair to do a Billy Connolly to them. Connolly went to London and everybody said oh, he's betrayed his roots, he's sold out, and now he's moved to Los Angeles and we don't want to know him anymore – he speaks to the Queen, for God's sake! That's all balls. Connolly's still as funny as he ever was and that's all that counts. Runrig are still as good musically as they ever were, and that's all that counts. I happen to think that a lot of that power comes right out of where they come from, and I believe they will leave that behind at their peril. The psalm tradition and all that – there's more to be quarried out yet. It would be an awful

shame if they lost that connection. I feel it is a risk, because what I heard on *Searchlight* only just hung on by its fingernails to being Scottish. What's that wonderful phrase? "Be pungently parochial to be absolutely universal." I believe that's true. I mean if all they ever did was to sing in Gaelic or about Scotland, then there's still a chance they could do something massive – the whole explosion in world music has shown that. Everything's loosening up, becoming less formulaic.'

'Runrig definitely have a stadium sound,' says Bob Flynn, 'they've proved that at Murrayfield and abroad. But they need to do something along the lines of what U2 did. They didn't really develop their sound fully until Brian Eno got hold of them and worked on *The Unforgettable Fire*, and then, of course, *The Joshua Tree*. Runrig need to do the same with their own recordings.' Bob, however, feels that the Scottishness of the band would be the key to American success. 'Why haven't Chrysalis pushed them in America? That should be the natural area for Runrig, not just with the Scottish dimension but the size and strength of their sound would be loved in the States if it were given the right push. America is the big one for them, and the record company should have them out there.'

Well, the record company don't have the same confidence in Runrig's

American prospects that some people – including one of the USA's main distributors of traditional folk records – do. 'In America,' says Peter Robinson, 'their chances suffer because of the lack of an identifiable category. In the States you really need to be able to place a band into a particular radio format, and it is impossible to do that with Runrig. I think the band's Scottishness can be a bit of a disadvantage, but I'm sure that the English can be won over if they get a chance to see the band live. At the moment they still aren't getting enough airplay or TV exposure to be able to play enough of the bigger venues to create a really big following for their live shows south of the border. Things are definitely going the right way – we just need the right single.'

Chrysalis see their priorities as Germany – a bigger record market than the UK – and Scandinavia. 'We are also going to see what we can do in Canada,' says Pete, 'but even so, our priority must be increasing their profile in the UK to supplement their Scottish following. For Runrig, bizarre as it may seem, England, Wales and Northern Ireland have to be viewed in the same way that we view international territories.'

'Runrig might make it in England eventually,' thinks Billy Sloan of the *Daily Record*, 'but it really depends on how they are perceived. A lot of acts who are very clearly depicted as Scots suffer in England because of that. A lot of people in England hate the Proclaimers and Jesse Rae for little more than the fact that they are Scottish and make a big deal of it. Runrig have certainly built up a huge following in Scotland over quite a long period of time, but I think they will have to be patient with regards to England. They will eventually be successful there, but that success may be further off than they think.'

Stephen Pope, whose interest in Runrig goes back to teenage holidays in Plockton in the mid-'70s when Runrig played the local village hall, was astonished at the response to his *Independent* pieces about the band ('I probably got more mail from readers asking about Runrig than I got about anything else I ever wrote about . . . and people stayed in touch') but still feels the break into England may be some distance away.

'There definitely should be a bigger audience in the south, and it's getting there but it's taken a long time. They could be a bigger minority. They're never going to break through because they keep doing the wrong things. They're against the tide. That kind of rock is dead in the water in the market we have at the moment. I can't imagine them ever being a big chart band with singles. They might get it through an album getting into the upper reaches, but I just don't think it's possible for them to sustain weeks and weeks up there. I can't imagine them coming up with the change in direction that would make all that possible, and I don't advise it either.

'I would advise them to stay the big fish in a small pond . . . or grow bigger still in that same small pond . . . enlarging their audience and not letting go of the Celtic aspect because that's what's specific and special about the band. It's not that they've had fantastic musical originality, although there is something about it that's still different. It's the fact that the whole thing is unique . . . almost odd. They work in a way no one else does. There's something similar about the likes of U2 but there really isn't anything exactly like Runrig. It's warm, and it's sentimental in a positive way. That's what I like about them.'

Back inside the band's own organisation, there's a quiet confidence that anything's possible, if the members of Runrig want it badly enough. But ambition in this band will always come second to a sense of artistic integrity – and family life.

'There's as much development to do as we want to do,' says Marlene. 'As far as I'm concerned, the band can go as far as they want to go now. They could be doing stadiums throughout America for the rest of their lives if that's what they want. I know it isn't. We're much more comfortably off now, but you can't sit down and wallow in the comfort of it, you do have to keep on going on and up, as we've always done.

'I see the next step as getting Germany developed to the same extent as Denmark and Scotland. Canada I see as a huge market, and that's the next one after Germany. We could go on and on – the music is getting better and better all the time and the lads are getting better at their craft. We're all getting more experienced.'

'They can be as big as they want to be,' agrees Iain MacDonald. 'I'd find it hard to argue with the philosophy they do have, which basically says we have lives outside of Runrig – for Donnie and Calum and Rory in particular – and we'll stick to those lives and make them work, and as well as that we'll be in Runrig. I'm not sure which would be the greater achievement, being in your own terms a fully realised human being, or being the biggest rock band ever to come out of Scotland – or certainly out of Skye! I'm not sure which is more desirable. Even now, after all this time on the road, they could still become a huge international band if they wanted to. I'm not sure they do.'

Peter does, although he's happy to compromise. 'I think the band will become a lot bigger. A potential will be achieved and Runrig will survive for many years to come.' Touring in the USA and Canada might be a burden they have to bear, he reckons – but all in good time. 'Personally, I'm a lot more relaxed now about how I see the future of the band. When I first joined, it was push, push, push all the time – do this, go there. But now things are starting to look up. Doors are opening for us without us having to rush to get anywhere.'

Iain Bayne believes the band is still only halfway there. 'I think we've realised only about 50 per cent of the band's potential to go on and actually do what we're capable of doing, and I think it's up to us to decide if we want to be as big a band as U2, for instance. It's only up to us to decide and without taking any short cuts or making any compromises. I mean, I'd never be happy if we ended before we'd begun. You see, the music belongs to the people, if you like. We can get across to a whole cross-section – it doesn't matter what nationality they are, it doesn't matter what age – and I think people identify with it really strongly, both with what's being said politically and with what's being said musically. Given the right break and the right series of events at the right time, I don't think there's any reason why we can't go all the way, and I certainly wouldn't rest easy myself until we at least tried to get the feeling of succeeding.'

But not everyone feels like that. Runrig decisions are taken democratically, at band meetings which can last for hours and often feature spectacular disagreements. One infamous occasion saw a discussion on the thorny question of the sponsorship of a tour by a drinks company – an offer which Runrig accepted in the midst of condemnation of such sponsorship by Ricky Ross of Deacon Blue and Pat Kane of Hue and Cry, both of whose bands had appeared at drink-sponsored events in the past. The minutes of the discussion show demands for a Runrig-sponsored 'campaign for sensible drinking', and total opposition to sponsorship of any kind from other quarters. An energetic debate then closed 'amongst general disorder'. So there would definitely have to be a democratic majority in favour of any plan to conquer the Americas by, say, donning chest wigs and dyeing the entire band's hair platinum.

At the moment that seems unlikely. Malcolm Jones, musically perhaps something of a purist – although his diffidence might fool the casual conversationalist – hopes only that the band 'sticks by its guns musically and plays and sings successfully', while his personal ambition is just to remain a professional musician. 'If that's not to be then I'll always play music. I'll never . . . well, it's just something that I want to do.' Committed to Scottish country-dance music, Malcolm's time off from Runrig is often spent with friends either jamming or playing in impromptu bands at such unlikely functions as weddings. And in relaxing moments during a tour, he's as likely to be found in a corner practising his accordion as anywhere else. Malcolm is first and foremost a musician, happy to endorse, he says, 'anything the band or any individual in the band takes as a moral standpoint.'

Down in the band's engine-room there is a certain sublime unwillingness to look into the future. 'I haven't got a clue,' says Rory. 'We've never done that,' says Calum, 'we've never planned the years ahead. We write songs, they reflect our lives. We change, they change; and for the foreseeable future that's what we'll probably continue to do.'

And how about the notion, much put about, that Runrig can go as far as they are willing to go? 'We could,' replies Rory. 'We could go much further, but it would take a very long time. We've always gone very gradually; it's always been the nature of the band that we never exploded anywhere. We've just moved gradually along at that pace because that's the pace we move at anyway . . .'

'. . . with a reluctance if it did suddenly explode, almost,' his brother says. 'I think we'd have the tendency to say, "Oh well, maybe next year". Because we have spent so long grafting away, trying to get this thing in which we all believed so passionately, up and running. Now that that great burden has been removed, I know the band is more relaxed and happier within itself. A lot of people say that the best art is produced out of adversity and I know that that's true up to a point, but it is something I can't entirely go along with. I find our present situation much more conducive to the writing of songs and making music. People ask, "What's your ultimate ambition? When will you say you've been successful? When will you know you've made it?" I mean . . . how irrelevant. Music is music; you write and perform, you let people hear it and that's all there is to it. I remember my late father way back in the early days saying he'd really liked one of the songs I'd written. To me that was success. Maybe conquering America is an irrelevance. Maybe having expressed yourself is enough; success is an extremely relative thing.'

Marlene, in many ways, is Runrig's buffer between the 'big machine' and the members' art and private lives. She herself has ambitions outside the band, apart from in the field of politics. 'There are many things I'd like to do,' she says. 'I'd like to start a clinic for drug and alcohol abuse, for instance. But my main priority will be as it has always been – my family life with my two sons, who are so supportive in all that I do.' But in her dealings with all the pressures of the record business and all the demands of the band, she still feels very like a nurse. 'I have always felt my role within Runrig was one of understanding the needs of all the people involved, especially the band and the crew and their respective families. When you're dealing with the big machine it is a very difficult and complex job, trying to create a working environment which is acceptable to everyone.'

'The nursing background is invaluable. To me it is the most disciplined background that you could come from. It's a very, very hard training – or it was when I did it! It doesn't suffer fools, and it doesn't make life easy for you, so whatever you get hit with further on in your life, you take it much more square-on than you would if you had been pandered to in some nice little job. Because nursing is a hard one when you're meeting so many people, seeing so many different sights, surrounded by paranoia . . . but then,' she grins, 'your artistic people are like that anyway, and you're surrounded in the music business by all these different types of people.' And, she claims, it keeps you young: 'I'm 46, and you know, I don't feel it.'

As for Donnie, he brushes aside questions about the future of the band. 'I've never had a projected idea of the band at any time in the past. The only thing I judge the band on is what we're achieving at the time or what we're capable of doing – what sort of potency there is, and how you can communicate that to people.' His own personal ambitions have moved on since becoming rector of Edinburgh University, and it is likely he will become more and more visible in the political arena, as did Muriel Gray before him.

Five members of the band are married, four have children and all know the importance of a settled, separate home life. Given that priority, it seems unlikely that the lure of virtually constant touring in America could possibly tear them away for the necessary amount of time. Indeed, as Graham Pullen of Solo says, 'I can't see them putting up with the American attitude to things. You have to spend a year of your life out there to crack it and you have to want it desperately, and there are no guarantees. They'd hate it,

I'd never advise them to do it.' But who can tell? As for the worries expressed about pressure to produce commercial music, to move away from the subjects rooted deep in the Gaidhealtacht, in the generations past, in the way of life of today . . . It's quite clear that although such pressures exist, Calum and Rory's artistic ambition far outweighs everything. Runrig are their own fiercest critics, of their own motives as much as anything else. They can be trusted to remain true to their own vision, just as they always have been.

In the end, there will always be home. Ask Calum and Rory Macdonald what originally brought about their own rediscovery of their culture, and their answers are very simple. Calum: 'Pop culture caught you for a few years as an adolescent, brilliant and stimulating as it was; it took you out of where you were. And then you came home.' And for Rory, it all began in the returning. 'I always remember when I first came back, that first long summer after my first year at college, and there was Skye, and I was just bowled over with it. I saw it in a completely different way.'

Many years ago, Donnie discovered he was descended from Donald Munro, a famous blind Skye fiddler of the 19th century, An Dall Munrotha. Coming under the influence of the evangelical preachers who were then touring the islands, Donald was converted, got the *cuiream*, and smashed his fiddle into smithereens. He became a holy man, a travelling preacher whose music had been lost.

On hearing this story for the first time, Donnie immediately went out and bought a fiddle. He can't play, but the fiddle remains as a potent symbol of the connection back down the generations.

'I've considered moving back to Skye,' he says. 'I consider it all the time because there's always something lurking at the back of your mind that is for you, that's right for you. There was a point when I may have gone. I was asked to go for a job in the local school, and I had a good chance of getting it, I was on the verge . . . I would have had a career out of it and all the rest, but I suddenly decided that although I wanted to go and live on Skye at that point, the motive wasn't the right one. It wasn't the right reason to be going home.

'It was quite a difficult decision because I knew I wanted to live there, and it was the perfect opportunity because for many people like me who have been educated out of the islands, there are very few chances to go back.

'In the long term, there is no place in this land that I'd rather be. It's as important as that, really, and I don't mean important just because of relatives or friends. That's an important part, but it's more important than that. It's the only place I know where there's a total sort of . . . *honesty* that allows you . . .' Donnie laughs, embarrassed, but he knows by now that he's in too deep to pull back. 'I think I'd better clarify that, because it sounds a wee bit airy-fairy, doesn't it? It's just that there is a kind of thing which relates to the music we're involved in. I've always had a very strong sense of the past, you know, just a historical thing of the people who have gone before me, and the things that have formed me, that I grew up in. I feel very much a part of that whole kind of thing and when I'm in Skye I'm more aware of it than anywhere else because I can see the signs around about me. I can see the signs of what people of my grandfather's generation did for my development and for my benefit, and when you respond to a land, to a physical place which has that sort of immense power, it gives you a sort of yardstick. And society's attitude towards you might change, depending on how successful you appear to be. But it just doesn't matter. If you have that yardstick you can always start again.' He smiles.

'Nothing you do will ever make you greater than you were before you started doing it.'

> Failte gu mo thir
> Eilean geal an iar
> An t-aite a chi gach tuigse is firinn
> Glaiste 'na mo chridhe
>
> Failte gu mo chainnt
> Is i dh'ionnsaich mi 'nam phaisde
> Canan uasal mor na Gaidheal
> Mar bhratach dhomh gach la

> (© C. & R. Macdonald, Chrysalis Music, 1989)

CHAPTER FOURTEEN

MIDSUMMER

The rain was spattering the gravel from the platform at Rutherglen Station, hammering on the waiting-room roof, dismantling complex hairstyles as their owners ran for cover: portents of the expected quagmire.

Runrig and rain have been close companions down the years, and on the morning of Saturday, 22 June 1991 that relationship seemed set to be sealed with a day's downpour. After all, it was midsummer and this was Scotland. The bonnie, bonnie banks of Loch Lomond, a setting made in song for the biggest Runrig gig of them all . . . but what about drainage? How much mud would 40,000-odd people churn up? And would they sling it at anyone?

The sound of jaws dropping had echoed throughout the land when the Loch Lomond concert was first announced. Could the band sell sufficient tickets, particularly with no support acts announced? They could, and more so. In one fell swoop, riding the crest generated by *The Big Wheel*'s release, Runrig proved themselves the biggest live attraction in Scotland.

It had rained all week. Thursday saw panic calls to Moray Firth Radio in Inverness: was it true that the Balloch Castle site had been deemed unusable because of ground conditions? Had a pitch inspection revealed the surface as unplayable? The ticket distributors Regular Music denied it, and the source of the rumour was traced to announcements on BBC Radio One about the cancellation of another open-air midsummer concert at the Milton Keynes Bowl in England. Sighs of relief were breathed. As it turned out, the rumour may have had its origin elsewhere, and was almost prescient.

I got off the train at Argyle Street, although on any other day I could have gone straight to Balloch from Rutherglen. In the city centre, sunshine was steaming the streets, and buskers were unwrapping battery-powered amplifiers. At Queen Street Station, the Balloch-bound were easy to spot. They were the ones with bags, flasks, umbrellas and Runrig T-shirts from all eras. On the low-level platform, the all-age crowd thickened, and a sense of anticipation quickened. Once again, I marvelled at Runrig's ability to attract people to a live concert who normally never go to gigs. As well as thousands upon thousands of inveterate concertophiles. Upstairs, although we didn't know it, the sun was readying itself for a steady, day-long reign.

Twenty-four hours beforehand, it had all been very different. I had driven out to Balloch, parked at the castle and caught my first sight of the massive stage through rain and mist, black and slightly sinister between the trees at the bottom of the slope. Roughly where, I realised, I had attended a rain-sodden student barbecue during my first week at university some 18 years previously.

Backstage, controlled mayhem was the order of the day. In the Regular Music production office – one among dozens of portable sheds – phones and fax machines bleeped and burped perpetually, while demands for laminated all-area passes increased by the moment. Senior policemen turned up to discuss safety and security, but there was a definite hint of something immensely problematic in the damp Loch Lomond air. And avoided, as it turned out.

Barry Wright of Regular, a pony-tailed bear of a man whose working relationship with Runrig goes back almost a decade, was calm and casual as ever, fielding freeloaders and fire safety officers with the same politeness. 'There have been surprisingly few technical hassles,' he began. 'In fact, it's been one of the most relaxed outdoor concerts I've ever been involved in. It's been a delight, it's really been so easy. . .' But Barry's an essentially honest chap, and gradually the full horror emerged. There had been a hassle over the trees, he admitted, from environmentalists. 'I feel that it's a story which has gone round the block in Chinese whispers and by the time it came back we'd destroyed an entire forest. In fact, only one tree, 35-foot high, was taken down and apart from that it was only one scrub sycamore and a few rhodedendrons. . .'

But those removals – carried out, it should be said, by the Dumbarton District Council Parks Department who own and operate Balloch Park – had sparked panic in the breasts of local officials. Dumbarton District had provided the park free of charge, on condition it was fully reinstated afterwards. Suddenly, the vision of a defoliated Balloch must have swum before various eyes and the trouble began, just two days before the concert.

When I spoke to Barry that Friday, most of the concert administration team and Runrig's management had been up all the previous night, trying to work out how the concert was to be saved. The council's legal department wanted the sum of £100,000 lodged as a deposit against the repair of any damage, and on Friday, backed that up with an interim interdict, legally blocking the event unless it was paid. Agreement was reached, the money was hastily scrabbled together and more sighs of relief were breathed. . .

Marlene wouldn't say anything about the exhausting hassles, but Barry did. 'We are contracted by the council to reinstate the park as it was, and we've volunteered to plant extra trees. We have managed to come to an agreement so that not only do we have £5 million of insurance but also the £100,000 on deposit to satisfy them. It's very unusual, we've never had to do it before, but we're happy to do it if helps them feel secure. . .'

So the rumours had been on the right lines. The concert had been on the brink of cancellation. . . or had it? Andrew Nisbet, chief executive of Dumbarton District Council, explicitly denied that, and the idea was whole-heartedly pooh-poohed once everything had been sorted out. But there were a lot of relieved faces around on Friday, even if, as Barry said, it had all been a case of the council's legal department making 'a simple agreement as complicated as possible'.

Anyway, such glitches out of the way, Barry was happy to talk of triumphs on a mega scale. Sewage was one major success. 'We've put in enough toilets for the city of Stirling, and we've had to create a sewage system. What was here was a Victorian cess tank, and we had to dig out three feet of solid shit, congealed at the bottom, with a pick and shovel, then completely rebuild and reroute it.'

But nothing had been too much trouble, according to Barry, for 'the fastest selling-out open-air crowd in Scottish history – faster than Simple Minds, faster than the Rolling Stones, faster than U2, faster than Rod Stewart, faster than Genesis.' If 60,000 tickets had been available, they would all have sold. 'It's extraordinary for an outdoor show to put up sell-out stickers three weeks before, and without any support acts being advertised. It's great to have Hothouse Flowers – but they weren't necessary. The tickets were sold entirely on Runrig.'

At £17.50 each, that was a stunning achievement. The advance sales were advertised as 50,000 but the actual number, according to Regular's Pete Irvine, was 'somewhere between 39,999 and 50,000'. It was not only a sign of the enormous size of Runrig's Scottish audience, but a tribute to their commitment. The band's sheer importance to the lives of people in Scotland could not be ignored.

On the train to Balloch there wasn't room to swing a mouse. I stood cheek by byte with two computer buffs ('Can you get full graphics using that language?') some nurses, some women and girls from Arran and a short-haired heavy metal fan wearing an Anthrax T-shirt. As we stopped at stations ever nearer to our destination, the sun grew brighter and brighter and more and more people squeezed on. 'It's like a party at our house,' said somebody. The atmosphere matched the upwardly-mobile weather outside.

Out at Balloch station, where the platform had been especially lengthened, and into the queue for special late-night return tickets. Then the walk.

There were banners, singing, nationalist fervour with a small 'n' and occasionally in giant-sized capital letters. We were a football crowd on our way to see Scotland play a match we knew we'd already won. To be a nation again, party politics and analysis aside, we were marching to the core of Runrig's best-known, best-loved song, the bonnie banks, the romantic heart of the heartland. . . Only that, in reality, would have been Skye, and there probably wouldn't have been nervous London beer-bellies flogging dodgy pirate T-shirts for four quid apiece. 'Look at Donnie's face – it's all blue,' said one girl. 'And this smells funny.' These were the nasty and cheap shirts, easily avoided by fans of taste and discrimination.

Indeed, Marlene spent a frustrating part of the big day at Balloch wrathfully engaged in tracking down the pirate T-shirt sellers, and was not having as much success as she would have liked. Barry Wright was philosophical as usual. 'I think the stories going round about merchandise being confiscated

Over:
Lochside
Main picture:
Right at the front
Inset:
Sound checking and
Donnie and the crowd in
an intimate moment

and then handed back are wrong,' he says. While tales of an organised team of English pirates arriving for the previous night's Pixies gig at Glasgow and for Loch Lomond abounded.

'Marlene's not been sleeping for two nights just thinking about her T-shirts,' joked Calum. Adding insult to injury – and tens of thousands of pounds in lost income – was the fact that the pirate T-shirts were generally thought to be better than the official ones – and cheaper.

'They're selling four-colour T-shirts for less than our two-colour ones,' said someone gloomily, and Regular's Pete Irvine admitted they were 'the best bootlegs I've seen all year'. But were the shirts from England? The pirate garments carried the Gaelic legend 'Saor Alba', Free Scotland, an overt – and well-known – nationalist motto which would never be officially sanctioned by Runrig. Who were the guilty men and women behind the scam? We shall probably never know.

Meanwhile, no carry-outs were to be taken inside the arena, separated from the rest of the park by a high metal fence and security men. Much, therefore, was imbibed outside, with Balloch's pubs resounding to chants and nationalist songs. The revelation in various newspapers since his elevation to rector of Edinburgh University that Donnie had been a Labour supporter all his life had obviously passed unnoticed, or been forgiven.

The crowds swelled at the various entrances to the huge sweep of grass down from Balloch Castle to the lochside. Being inside was an odd experience. At 1.45 p.m., the sellers of hamburgers, stuffed croissants and whole-food were prepared, along with the collectors of anti-nuclear-dumping signatures, while unidentified carriers of laminated passes wandered around and Wolfstone finished sound-checking. It was weird. Helicopters whirled overhead, as Chrysalis Television prepared their airborne cameras for filming the event. If *City of Lights* was Runrig's *Under a Blood Red Sky* – selling more copies than U2 did of their ground-breaking video when it was initially released – the Loch Lomond cassette seemed set to be their *Rattle and Hum*, consolidating a vastly increased audience.

At 2.15 p.m. the gates were opened. There were complaints about the security searches and the general slowness in getting in, but by the time Wolfstone kicked off a confident and impressive set, the Inverness band had a significant several thousand in front of them.

The main attraction, their families, the management, the Regular staff and the ever-increasing collection of administrative personnel involved with Runrig were staying across the loch at the Cameron House Hotel and Country Club. A shuttle ferry ran throughout the day, and Runrig came ashore in time to hear Wolfstone. 'It's a great day,' said Rory, dressed all in black and in a pair of '60s retro shades, looking like he'd just stepped from one of the early Skyevers photographs. 'We came down here last night to do the sound-check, had a look at the stage, and I said to Donnie, "I wonder who the hell's playing here, then?" ' Calum couldn't take it in either. 'It's a bit like being at your own wedding and you don't feel the centre of attention at all.' All agreed it was only overwhelming when you sat down and thought about it.

Donnie, also immaculate in black, wearing Lennon sunglasses and with his jacket sleeves, as ever, rolled up à la Kevin Keegan, was in understandably good humour. Rector of Edinburgh University and a director of C3 Caledonia, the television company which failed in its bid to take over the Grampian franchise for the North of Scotland, his prominence in Scottish affairs had escalated since last we'd met. At speed, he defended the decision to join the C3 Caledonia board ('Far better, surely, to be involved in something like that than to stand on the sidelines and criticise'), and shook his head in disbelief at a bizarre, brutal critique of his rectorial speech by *Press and Journal* Highland columnist Colin Campbell, headlined 'Simplistic Views of a Rich Rector' ('as a very wealthy man assailing the rights and privileges of other wealthy men, Mr Munro is in a vulnerable position, and he must know that'). 'I have a caravan in Skye, which I inherited, and that's the limit of my Highland landownership,' said Donnie. Even Colin Campbell admitted that the rectorial speech had been 'emotive and powerful' and, backstage at Loch Lomond, the thought returned that Donnie might be on his way, eventually, to a political career. After all, hadn't he told the *Free Press* that 'politics would be quite interesting, and a challenge'? But Midsummer's Day, backstage at a gig, was no time to discuss such possibilities, for the hilarious sights and sounds that only the glistening world of rock 'n' roll can bring were gradually beginning to take over.

There was a compound for the support bands, entered through an archway made from two gold-sprayed papier-mâché deer, containing portable sheds labelled with each band's name – their dressing-rooms – and a miniature garden, complete with trellissed ivy, fountains, fake marble statues and caged canaries. Such symbolism. Food was fed and drink flowed. Donnie found the whole thing rather funny. 'It's all something Regular arranged, but it's nice for the support bands. Have you seen Hothouse Flowers' dressing-room? – it's like something from the Roman Empire!'

Runrig had their own little compound, stark by comparison but not quiet, as various Runrig children and babies arrived during the day. And the press had their own play area too, but, cunningly – and very unusually – they had to pay for their own food and drink. This caused some disgruntlement, and there were minor problems with long-term supporters of Runrig suddenly finding their usual access forbidden by unfamiliar people sporting unassailable authority. Photo passes were for some reason issued to non-professionals wishing snapshots, and one or two newspaper photographers, already smarting at being searched by security men, became exasperated later when they tried to capture Karen from Capercaillie's cheekbones or Liam from Hothouse Flowers' feet. It began to come home just how enormous Runrig had become, especially as the real sunlamp-and-razorcut liggers began to arrive from Glasgow and all points south, people who two years previously would have sneered at the uncool nature of all things Runriggian.

Some still did. 'I'm only here for The Big Dish and Hothouse Flowers,' said one hipster, 'and to get drunk.' Elsewhere, bandwagons were being jumped on with a vengeance. Yes, I did overhear the following. Really.

'It's such a spiritual atmosphere – I always knew Runrig would do it. I've always rated them – really, you could see it coming years ago.'

Out on the hillside, the people who had been there all along, through bad times and though good, always believing, always paying to get in, quietly generated a genuinely spiritual, very moving atmosphere that even the liggers could dimly sense. And badly wanted to be part of. Many faces from Runrig's past emerged too, there simply to celebrate or to work or both. There was Campbell Gunn of the *Sunday Post* en famille and having a great time. Bob Flynn, now of the *Guardian*, taking a blown-out interview with resigned good humour. Douglas MacKinnon, one of the people who originally urged me to see Runrig and now one of Scotland's most up-and-coming film makers, with Runrig promos to his credit to boot. The genial Stewart Cruickshank of Radio Scotland, Lorraine Mann of Scotland Against Nuclear Dumping, Torcuil Crichton of the *Free Press*, Robbie the Pict and others. Uneasy at the feast was David Belcher of the *Herald*, patently Not Having a Good Time.

Meanwhile, Ireland's The Fat Lady Sings arrived, four hours late, to play a blistering set. They had been held up by traffic, and the stories emerging of horror holdups, cars parked on hard shoulders, disastrous delays and the like made me thankful I'd let the train strain me.

Capercaillie came and quietly conquered, hypnotic and soothing in the increasing heat. Up on the hillside families picnicked, some with great sophistication. All bottles may have been banned but not barbecues, and one or two groups organised complex sausage-sizzles using hibachi grills. Children seemed astonishingly well behaved, and at the fringes there was space to stretch and relax. And I remembered that first sight of Runrig, in Queen's Park six years before. The two or three hundred people then had multiplied, and not just by having children. The support bands went down well, but the crowd were there for one band, and one alone.

There was a truly bizarre press conference of almost *Spinal Tap*-ish hilarity. At first the questions aimed at the entire Runrig line-up were straightforward. The band were delighted at the incredible reaction to the concert, Peter said. There were questions about Gaelic and the song *Loch Lomond* (asked at least three times). There were questions nobody could hear, let alone understand. And there were questions about trees and toilets, one of which met with the tongue-in-cheek reply from Donnie, 'We are not directly involved with the digging up of toilets'. It was a moment to treasure. Again, this was Runrig on a hitherto unknown scale. A press conference? Such a clamour for interviews it was simply impossible to do them all? Microphones, television cameras, English newspapers? And then you remembered that *The Big Wheel* had gone straight into the national UK charts at number four, and as midsummer dawned it was still there.

I went down to the lochside, briefly escaping the increasingly jumpy atmosphere backstage. No Woodstock this. The notices firmly forbidding bathing were backed up by perspiring security men in yellow oilskins. Far to the north of Loch Lomond, the beginnings of the Highlands could be seen, the source and partly the subject of *The Big Wheel*. It was the album the band had hoped for, and more. Despite the usual scathing piss-take in *NME* – clever enough to fool several people, including, to hilarious effect, Brian Burnett of Radio Clyde whilst on air – and a curiously muted, but four-star, review in the prestigious *Q* ('Simplicity and conviction are powerful allies, and Runrig have both on their side'), the initial critical reception was on the whole excellent. And this time there was simply no getting away from a band who went straight into the UK top ten without a single being released. Signing sessions in Aberdeen, Glasgow, Edinburgh and Inverness were mobbed. The level of attention gained by the album was on a different scale from anything seen before.

Simply – it's a killer of a record, and a brave one. A deliberate step back from the giant-sized anthemic approach of *Siol Ghoraidh* or *Alba*, the sound has been cut back to the bone and clarified; Malcolm's guitar in particular sounds almost vocal in its effects – pure, sweet, fierce and growling. There are distinctly European influences and – as Murdo from Lewis pointed out – 'something that sounds a bit like the Stone Roses'. Irrespective of such reference points, this is a grown-up album, and one which requires some committed listening. It repays the effort handsomely.

I'd already bumped into the ever-friendly Chris Harley at Loch Lomond, and praised his production work on *The Big Wheel* to the sunny skies. He shrugged. 'It could have been even better – that's always the way, though. We could have had it just right.' The clarity of sound, he said, was 'largely down to Calum Malcolm's ears'.

Headlights opens the LP with a wonderfully convincing picture of those long summers in Skye, carried in fragments of memory, glittering images and phrases. To anyone who's ever lived on an island, those night journeys home from village-hall dances are perfectly encapsulated here. It sets the tone for the album. Memory, personal memory, is the key, but not in a wallowing-in-nostalgia sense. The much discussed link with Neil Gunn's *Highland River* is obvious in the way that the past intertwines with the present and the local with the universal. The road goes ever on. Here we are at the start of adult fumblings with sex, music, creativity, the land, life. 'The long road home' jumps out as the central phrase in one of the great Macdonald lyrics.

Musically, it all sounds so integrated. There are echoes of the traditional chant, but the wholly contemporary drum and keyboard patterns complement them perfectly. *Healer in your Heart* is melodically more familiar, medium-paced Runrig territory, but the lyric is an amazing chunk of Christian mysticism, melded with that tremendous sense of ancestry and rootedness which pervades Gaelic culture – the genealogies which, Rory says, mean you can feel part of those who have passed away from you forever.

I love *Abhainn an t-Sluaigh* for its combination of almost *Play Gaelic* simplicity and a rhythm track which does, indeed, sound like something the Stone Roses might have attempted. Lyrically, the road has led to London, a place of despair and decay. The longing for escape is overwhelming, 'the need to be far from the crowded river'. Sung by Rory, it's one of

We built this city on
rock 'n' roll

Runrig's best gentle songs; like much of *The Big Wheel*, it creeps up on you.

Always the Winner is not, as one London journalist imagined, a song about the Gulf War. It's a song dedicated to the late David Gibson, the young leukemia sufferer the band befriended and whose cause they supported, a moving tribute to what winning really means. Beautifully played and sung, it's what they term radio friendly.

This Beautiful Pain moves effortlessly between past and present, with another lyric going far beyond the simplicities of yore to a territory where a song about human love is also about love of place and time and territory, about religion and source. Some will find such writing overwrought or baroque, but, coupled with the music, I think it makes the output of every other Scottish pop writer seem one-dimensional, drab and petty. The reference points here would have to be Sorley Maclean and Iain Crichton-Smith rather than Bob Dylan or Paul McCartney.

The sound of departing trucks opens *An Cuibhle Mor*, as the road motif becomes overt. 'This is the big wheel which never stands still. . . turning our youth to old age.' This album is about ageing, about moving out into the wider world while holding fast to your roots, and to the spirit of youth, and the song communicates that sense of the present being not just 'the only time we have' but also the summation of all that has gone before and will be. The anticipation of being young is never lost, nor ever need be.

There is thrill in expectation, being starry-eyed and laughing and waiting for the world. But in the end the big wheel turns 'towards the place you call your own'. Sounding very European, very dance-orientated, the track meshes Donnie's vocals with a totally irresistible bass line, drums, guitars and keyboards into something quite different from the rest of the Runrig canon. The Cold Cut remix should be something else.

Any male over the age of 30 must love *Hearthammer* as it perfectly captures those great moments of youth associated with music and football. The early formative Macdonald influences are spelt out – the Byrds, Neil Young, Jethro Tull, the Beatles – and then there's football, although Rory's orgasmic moan when Donnie praises 'the Di Stefano twist' always makes me laugh. The memories never grow old, but neither does the wonder at new thrills, new stimuli. 'I'm still here with the eyes of a child.' A great pop song.

Better, in fact, than *Edge of the World*, intended as a single – coupled with live tracks from the Loch Lomond show – which lacks its natural exuberance. The lyric, too, lacks the resonance and poise of others on the LP, although the central symbol of the St Kildan going 'over the cliff on a winter's day' is powerfully contrasted with the paraphernalia of modern life. But what the hell does 'adrenalin infrastructure' mean?

The Munro tonsils hit a new peak performance with *I'll Keep Coming Home*, the words again picking up that recurring theme: 'Wherever the highway unwinds, I'll keep coming home.'

Home to a family, to a belief, to a God, to a past, a heritage, and always to a place. A place of birth and rebirth, of holy ground steeped in the

Rehearsing for filming the concert

Families in tow

blood of generations. *Flower of the West* sums it all up using the place names of Uist in a stunning lyric which will doubtless feature on school syllabuses in years to come. It's the nearest the album comes to the great celebratory anthems of yore, and it's destined to be a live classic. You can see the Dunlin, the breakers; hear the collies barking. And the map used on the inner sleeve of the album perfectly sums up the song's exploration and celebration of place, family and the past. It was found by Calum and Rory's father in a captured German tank during a World War Two tank battle. On one side was a normal German map, but printed on the other, much to tank commander Macdonald's astonishment, was not only a map of North Uist, but a detailed map of the area in which he was brought up. Quite why a German tank commander should have been carrying a map of North Uist about Europe is something of a mystery.

Back at Loch Lomond, the midges seem to have declared a truce for the day. Down by the loch, I am backstage, and it's odd approaching the hin' end of the concert. The Big Dish are on stage, Steven Lindsay's voice as poignant as ever; close to the front they're very loud, although up the hill it's not overwhelming. *Swimmer*, from their criminally ignored debut album, closes their set.

I struggle through the ever-increasing throng to the stage again, and bump into the debonair Graham Pullen, one half, with John Giddings, of Solo, Runrig's super-heavyweight agency.

Graham has his golf clubs back at the hotel, ready to take advantage of this visit to the home of the game. But he's here for Runrig, to work and to celebrate.

As befits an agent, Graham is prepared for the worst. But his golfing umbrella is useful only as a pointer. 'There's some of our helicopters up there,' he smiles, waving the unnecessary object at the sky. Solo are involved with Chrysalis in the filming of the great day, and Graham is proud of his part in what is the peak of Runrig's career.

But he's a fan, too. 'I love this band. You know, I turned up at Glasgow airport for some reason once, and Donnie was there to meet me. He had driven to pick me up. There was no need for that – but I would do the same now if they came to London.'

What he's waiting for, he says, is that moment when *Flower of the West*, unheard live by the vast crowd, becomes one of the classic Runrig anthems. 'That's going to happen tonight, and I can't wait to hear that audience singing it.'

There's only Runrig to go now, and the level of tension has increased; the park is as full as it's going to get. Viewed from the front in the fading sunlight, it's an astonishing, thrilling sight.

Donnie is absolutely gobsmacked as he arrives off the boat from the hotel. 'There must have been. . . hundreds of boats came with us across the loch,' he says breathlessly. 'They were all full of people with banners, singing and shouting. . . it was an amazing sight – unbelievable.' Earlier

he had looked around at the crowds, the staging, the helicopters, and murmured, 'You know, you can begin to understand how people let this kind of thing go to their heads – if it's happening to them all the time. It's like living in a goldfish bowl.' Better get used to it, I said, and Donnie grinned: 'We'll just have to make sure ours is tinted.'

So I recall that comment and joke that he shouldn't let the armada go to his head. It's the wrong thing to say. From here on in to show time it should be confidence-boosting build-ups, not mildly funny put downs. After all, it's Donnie who actually has to speak to the 50,000 people out there. 'It's always at times like this,' says Donnie, 'that Robert still keeps us in check and memories of his classic "I think we're kidding ourselves on here, lads" delivery helps keep things in their proper perspective.' Calum has been to hospital to have a suspect wrist checked, but as an injury scare this is not in the Denis Law class, and all is well. The pre-show dressing-room session is understandably private. Calm overrules the tension. After all, this is not the biggest crowd Runrig have played to. There have been bigger audiences at foreign festivals. But this is Scotland, Loch Lomond, a home game with victory assured. All that remains is to play to form. It's an emotional moment, and some tears are shed.

The late David Gibson with the band at the blood transfusion service

Out at the mixing desk, Billy Worton is preparing for the biggest job of his career. The band have nothing but admiration for their trusted sound engineer. 'He stuck with us through the really bad times, and does a superb job,' says Calum. 'We owe Billy a great deal. This is his day as much as anyone's.' Marlene herself pays tribute to the man 'who more than anyone else has forged the live Runrig sound'.

A lengthy musical introduction, and on they go, the six members of the band which began with Calum and Blair and Rory 18 years before in Glasgow. Balloch Park erupts, and as *Headlights* sweeps over the hillside, Runrig's greatest moment has arrived and some more tears are shed out on the hill as the shadows lengthen.

New songs assuming muscular on-stage personalities. Donnie asking the crowd if we knew what a magnificent sight we made. A child on a father's shoulders. Trampling on sandwiches and picnics amongst the shifting throng. Dancing at the sides. Senseless – but speedily recovering – bodies plucked from the crush at the front. An inevitable, titanic *Dance Called America*. A few rough moments from the band, perhaps overcome by emotion or seeming technical problems. Chris Harley's ridiculous jacket, apparently worn for a bet, and his complete lack of concern as he jauntily watches the show minutes before having to join the band on stage. Climbing up the hill to watch *Loch Lomond*. Fireworks. The whole Scottish land-scape seemingly captured as a backdrop. The wonder and triumph of it all.

And afterwards, one of the best stories of the day. On the special platform for the disabled, the wheelchair-bound watched the band. Then – a miracle. Slowly from his wheelchair rose one fan, apparently cured. As he nonchalantly walked away, others waited for the Runrig effect to work on them too. But the perfectly hale and hearty man with the stolen wheelchair

Snappers snapped

Speed bonny boat: the
ferry which carried the
band to and from the
Balloch Park site

had simply found a good way of getting in for nothing. . .

'It's been a wonderful day,' said Calum, but it was more than that. It was the day Runrig's importance in Scottish terms was made flesh. The day they proved they could attract a bigger audience than anyone else, had a better-behaved audience than anyone else (only eight arrests, all outside the park and all for minor problems), could put their music across in the biggest context. It was the end of a long, hard, 18-year road, and the beginning of life in an albeit tinted goldfish bowl. Runrig had proved their songs, their musicianship, their management, themselves. They were the biggest band in Scotland, without question. And now for the rest of the world. . .

Or some of it anyway. At the inevitable party after the show, they were all just the same. Not changed, magically, into incandescent figures of distant mystery. Iain and Peter and Malcolm chatted with family and friends. Calum, Rory and Donnie eventually wanted to get back to the hotel. There were babysitters to check on. The biggest day in their lives was over. Time for the ordinary things to assume their importance, for a sense of proportion to come back into play. For family and friendship and love and the land to dwarf once again that glittering stage. For the smile and the spoken word to silence the roar of 200,000 watts in amplification. Time for the miles of scaffolding to be taken down, the litter cleared, turf and new young trees planted for the sake of the generations to come.

Time for everyone to be going home.

The crew and band at Broadford

AFTERWORD

Back to the beach

The big top comes to Benbecula

And waking up the next morning, unexpectedly sunburned, wondering. Wondering how anyone could possibly top that; glad not to be clearing up the litter.

'It was an incredible experience,' says Donnie, 'looking out at that number of people, and knowing they were our home audience, our own fans. We've played to bigger crowds, at festivals abroad, but that was the biggest concert for us by far.'

Within two days, Runrig were in Orkney, playing to the hardly-setting sun of the 'simmer dim' at the St Magnus Festival, and then off to Denmark for another festival appearance. Less than a week after Loch Lomond, an Edinburgh press conference saw them back in Scotland, and it was announced that Van Morrison would play one concert on the Edinburgh Castle Esplanade, in the arena used for the Military Tattoo. Runrig would play the only other show.

The tickets for Runrig's castle concert sold out in three hours, all 7,500 of them. The promoters battled to organise a second show, and were successful. Another 7,500 tickets duly sold.

'It's frankly astonishing to be playing at such a place,' said Calum before the gigs. 'Not only is it at the centre of Scotland's history and culture, Edinburgh Castle is such an important image of Scotland worldwide.'

But before Edinburgh came the road back: back in time, back to the source, to the root of it all. The run-up to Edinburgh would take Runrig on a trip to the lost summers of the '70s, the island and Highland stamping grounds where their inspiration was born.

'It was time to go back, to take the whole band, the whole show, to the places we have loved, the places which bore us and in many ways, made us,' says Rory. 'We will always go back. This was a chance to pay a debt to the people there who have supported us for so long, and to be a part again of that very real and strong community.'

'It was wonderful,' says Donnie now. 'It was great to see old faces. It was wonderful but hard. The logistics of putting on the full Runrig show in some of Scotland's remotest corners were almost beyond belief.

But as a homecoming, it was more than a success, the perennial problem of truck-meets-bog, bog wins not withstanding. It was a reunion, a meshing of music with its inspiration, a place and a people, the Gaidhealtacht, the Gaelic-speaking community and the overwhelmingly powerful landscape they inhabit . . . and the Castle concerts were the inspired result.

In Edinburgh, the Highland connection was re-inforced by the presence of legendary Gaelic poet Sorley Maclean at one of the two shows, reading in both Gaelic and English from his poem *The Cuillins*. Now recognised worldwide as perhaps Britain's greatest living poet, his presence brought to the event a sense of history, of Runrig's inheritance, the great body of Gaelic culture which is only now being generally recognised in Scotland itself. 'It was a truly humbling experience, having Sorley with us,' says Calum.

When Runrig took the stage, history shifted. The perspective from which Edinburgh Castle is usually seen, as a garrison of British troops, changed. Runrig's music – the music of loss, the music of rebellion, of the dignity of men and women who live for and by the land which they cannot possess, of a new audience who long for a cultural identity ripped from them by generations of neglect – swept over the ramparts to victory.

The ferry

As I write, the greenness of the Black Isle is fading in the fall, and 1991 is beginning to end. Runrig's first chart single success has materialised with *Hearthammer* entering the top 40 at number 25 and even a brief video appearance on *Top of the Pops*. Now they are on their way to Europe, at a time when small countries are asserting their identities throughout the continent. Runrig, from Scotland, will take their music and the history and life and loves and struggles of their own land to a host of venues where neither English nor Gaelic are the native tongues.

Yet they will communicate, they will unite with the audiences as they do at home, because there is an internationalism to their music which breaks down barriers and borders. Because it is so rooted in a small island, a small country, paradoxically it is accepted and understood throughout the world. The long awaited breakthrough in England has now arrived with a November sellout tour of major venues.

Then the winter will draw Runrig back to Scotland, and eventually back to the north, to finish their biggest year. To go home.

TOM MORTON
Cromarty, October 1991

Sorley Maclean meets
rock 'n' roll: the poet
about to sound-check

DISCOGRAPHY

1978
PLAY GAELIC LP and cassette. Originally released on Neptune Records (a Lismor subsidiary) NA105. Now deleted. Re-released as *Runrig Play Gaelic – The First Legendary Recordings*, LP, cassette and CD, in 1990 on Lismor Records LICS 5182. LP version now deleted – still available on CD and tape.

Side One: *Duisg Mo Run*; *Sguaban Arbhair*; *Tillidh Mi*; *Criogal Cridhe*; *Nach Neonach Neisd A Tha E*; *Sunndach*

Side Two: *Air An Traigh*; *De Ni Mi/Puirt*; *An Ros*; *Ceol An Dannsa*; *Chi Mi'n Geamhradh*; *Cum 'Ur N'Aire*

Tracks from *Play Gaelic* also appear along with material from various other artists on the Lismor compilations *Highland Magic* (LILP 5103) and *Popular Songs Sung in Gaelic* (LILP 5117). Both are still available.

THE HIGHLAND CONNECTION LP and cassette, Ridge Records RR001. Released on CD 1989. Still available in all formats. Also released in Ireland in 1981 on the Claddag label.

Side One: *Gamhna Gealla*; *Mairi*; *What Time?*; *Fichead Bliadhna*; *Na Luing Air Seoladh*; *Loch Lomond*

Side Two: *Na H-Uain A's t-Earrach*; *Foghar Nan Eilean '78*; *The Twenty-Five Pounder*; *Going Home*; *Morning Tide*; *Cearcal A Chuain*

1981
RECOVERY LP and cassette, Ridge Records RR002. Released on CD 1989. Still available in all formats.

Side One: *An Toll Dubh*; *Rubh Nan Cudaigean*; *'Ic Iain 'Ic Sheumais*; *Recovery*; *Instrumental*

Side Two: *'S Tu Mo Leannan/Nightfall on Marsco*; *Breaking the Chains*; *Fuaim A Bhlair*; *Tir An Airm*; *The Old Boys*; *Dust*

1982
LOCH LOMOND, seven-inch single, Ridge Records RRS003.

B-side: *Tuireadh Iain Ruaidh*. Deleted. Also released in New Zealand in 1982 on the Epic label.

1984
DANCE CALLED AMERICA seven- and 12-inch single, Simple Records Ltd (12)SIM4. Deleted.
B-side: *Na H-Uain A's t-Earrach*; *Ribhinn O*

SKYE seven- and 12-inch single, Simple Records Ltd.
B-side: *Hey Mandu*. Deleted.

(*Skye*, *Na H-Uain A's t-Earrach* and *Lifeline* are all available in their Simple guises on the Alba Records album *A Feast of Scottish Folk Music, Volume One* (ALBA 001) LP and cassette, distributed by Celtic Music in Yorkshire and also featuring tracks by Dick Gaughan, Barbara Dickson and others.)

Former member Blair Douglas released his first solo album in 1984, on his own Red Burn label:

CELTOLOGY LP and cassette, Red Burn Records, 1984. Still available from Macmeanmna, Portree, Skye.

Side One: *Failte (Do'n Ghaidhealtacht)*; *Eisd (Ris an Oigridh)*; *Mhairead*; *Err In/Peace/Roisin (Dubh)*; *Donald Willie and his Dog*; *Range Games*

Side Two: *Eilean Uibhist Mo run*: (a) *Eilean Ubhist Mo run* (b) *Welcome to Bon Accord* (c) *Iain R. Douglas*; *The Dark Island*; *Step Dancing*: (a) *Alex Maceachearn's Strathspey* (b) *Beverley in Barra*; *Gu Tir*: (a) *Alan Macpherson of Mosspark* (b) *Crossing the Minch* (c) *The Brolum*

1985
HEARTLAND LP and cassette, Ridge Records RR005. Also released in Germany. Released on CD 1989. Released in France in 1986 on the Off The Track label.

Side One: *O Cho Meallt*; *This Darkest Winter*; *Lifeline*; *Air A Chuan*; *Dance Called America*; *The Everlasting Gun*

Side Two: *Skye*; *Cnoc Na Feille*; *The Wire*; *An Ataireachd Ard*; *The Ferry*; *Tuireadh Iain Ruaidh*

1986
THE WORK SONG seven-inch single, Ridge Records RRS006.
B-side: *This Time of Year*. Still available.

1987
ALBA seven-inch single, Ridge Records RRS007.
B-side: *Worker for the Wind*. Deleted.

THE CUTTER AND THE CLAN LP, cassette and CD, Ridge Records RR008. (Now deleted in its Ridge Records form: see below).

Side One: *Alba*; *The Cutter*; *Hearts of Olden Glory*; *Pride of the Summer*; *Worker for the Wind*

Side Two: *Rocket to the Moon*; *The Only Rose*; *Protect and Survive*; *Our Earth Was Once Green*; *An Ubhal As Airde*

1988
PROTECT AND SURVIVE seven-, 12-inch and CD single, Chrysalis CHS (12)3284.
B-side (seven-inch): *Hearts of Olden Glory* (live)
12-inch and CD include seven-inch mix of *Protect and Survive* plus the live *Hearts of Olden Glory* and the live *Protect and Survive*. Deleted.

THE CUTTER AND THE CLAN re-launched on Chrysalis, CHR 1669. Still available in all formats.

ONCE IN A LIFETIME LP, cassette and CD, Chrysalis CHR 1695. Still available.

Side One: *Dance Called America*; *Protect and Survive*; *Chi Mi 'n Geamhradh*; *Rocket to the Moon*; *Going Home*

Side Two: *Cnoc Na Feille*; *'S Tu Mo Leannan/Nightall on Marsco*; *Skye*; *Loch Lomond*

1989
NEWS FROM HEAVEN seven-, 12-inch, CD single and limited edition picture disc, Chrysalis CHS 3404
B-side: *Chi Mi 'n Tir* (seven inch); *Chi Mi 'n Tir* and *The Times They Are a-Changing* (12-inch, CD and pic disc). Deleted.

SEARCHLIGHT LP, cassette and CD, Chrysalis CHR 1713. Still available.

Side One: *News from Heaven*; *Every River*; *City of Lights*; *Eirinn*; *Tir A 'Mhurain*; *World Appeal*

Side Two: *Tear Down These Walls*; *Only the Brave*; *Siol Ghoraidh*; *That Final Mile*; *Smalltown*; *Precious Years*

EVERY RIVER seven-, 12-inch and CD single, Chrysalis CH3451.

Seven-inch B-side: *This Time of Year*
12-inch and CD: *This Time of Year* and *Our Earth Was Once Green*. Deleted.

(*Hearts of Olden Glory* from *The Cutter and the Clan* also appears on the double Stylus Records compilation *New Roots* (SMR 972) along with tracks by Tanita Tikaram, Gregson and Collister and many others. Still available in all formats.)

1990
CAPTURE THE HEART EP, 12-inch, CD and limited edition 10-inch, Chrysalis CHS 3594.
Stepping Down the Glory Road; *Satellite Flood*; *Harvest Moon*; *The Apple Came Down*. Deleted.

CITY OF LIGHTS video. Chrysalis/Channel Five CFV11542.
Air A Chuan; *City of Lights*; *Dance Called America*; *Cnoc Na Feille*; *Siol Ghoraidh*; *Precious Years*; *The Wire* (intro); *Instrumental*; *Rocket to the Moon*; *An Ubhal As Airde*; *The Cutter*; *Harvest Moon*; *Stepping Down the Glory Road*; *Alba*; *Hearts of Olden Glory*; *News from Heaven*; *Skye*; *Only the Brave*; *Loch Lomond*; *Ataireachd Ard* (outro). Still available.

Also released in 1990 was the second solo album by Blair Douglas, *Beneath the Beret*, cassette and CD only, Macmeanmna SKYE 02. It was produced by Chris Harley. Blair wrote the songs and plays accordion and keyboards, but the vocals are by Michael Marra, Jim Wilkie, Arthur Cormack (who Blair regularly accompanies in concert and with the ensemble Macmeanmna) and Kim Beacon.

Side One: *Braigh Uige (Braes of Uig)*; *Iain Ghlinn Cuaich*; *Solus m'Aigh*; *Kate Martin's Waltz*; *Celtic Jive*; *Blair's Got a Wah-Wah Pedal (and he's gonna use it)*

Side Two: *Ghost of Glasgow*; *Growing Up*; *Mardi Gras Music*; *Glove Game (Benny Lynch)*; *Irish Eyes*; *King is King*

1991
THE BIG WHEEL LP, cassette and CD, Chrysalis CHR 1858.

Side One: *Headlights*; *Healer in your Heart*; *Abhain an t-Sluaigh/The Crowded River*; *Always the Winner*; *This Beautiful Pain*

Side Two: *An Cuibhle Mor/The Big Wheel*; *Edge of the World*; *Hearthammer*; *I'll Keep Coming Home*; *Flower of the West*

HEARTHAMMER EP, seven- and 12-inch, CD and cassette, Chrysalis CHS 3754. 12-inch and CD include booklet with names of Loch Lomond live backing singers.

Side One: *Hearthammer* and *Pride of the Summer* (live)

Side Two: *Loch Lomond* (live) and *Solus Na Madain*

Released on October 28 1991

FLOWER OF THE WEST EP, seven- and 12-inch, CD and cassette, Chrysalis CHS 3805.
Seven-inch B-side: *Chi Mi 'n Geamhradh*
12-inch (in a special boxed edition) and CD: *Flower of the West*; *Ravenscraig*; *Chi Mi 'n Geamhradh*; *Harvest Moon* (live)